CHRISTIAN EDUCATION

ITS MANDATE AND MISSION

 **BOB JONES UNIVERSITY PRESS**
Greenville, South Carolina 29614

Library of Congress Cataloging-in-Publication Data

Christian education : its mandate and mission / [edited by Ronald A. Horton]
    p. cm.
    ISBN 0-89084-639-1
      1. Christian education.   I. Horton, Ronald Arthur, 1936- .
    BV1471.2.C4985   1992
    377'.8—dc20   92-22625
                                                      CIP

NOTE:
The fact that materials produced by other publishers are referred to in this volume does not constitute an endorsement by Bob Jones University Press of the content or theological position of materials produced by such publishers. The position of Bob Jones University Press, and the University itself, is well known. Any references and ancillary materials are listed as an aid to the student or the teacher and in an attempt to maintain the accepted academic standards of the publishing industry.

Christian Education: Its Mandate and Mission

Edited by Ronald A. Horton, Ph.D.
Chairman of the Division of English Language and Literature,
Bob Jones University

Prepared on behalf of the faculty and adminstration of Bob Jones University at the direction of Dr. Bob Jones III, president, by the philosophy committee.

20   19   18   17   16   15   14   13   12   11   10   9   8   7   6

Contents

Preface

The present volume brings together a set of statements issued as booklets over the course of a decade (1978-88) by the Bob Jones University Press. Some awareness of the circumstances that brought them into existence will illuminate the purposes they are meant to serve.

The occasion of the series was the decision of University executives to furnish the Christian school movement with materials for all subject areas on every grade level, kindergarten through high school. It soon became obvious that such an effort would require clear philosophical direction from the outset if it were to proceed in a systematic, Biblically accurate way. The need was compounded by a state of confusion then existing in Christian education about what educational methods are Biblically permissible, what impermissible, what obligatory, and so forth, and about the relation of Christian education to modern and traditional education.

Clearing up this confusion seemed especially urgent because of the threat of governmental litigation. Some Christian school administrators and pastors had been required to prove in court that their commitment to Christian education had the status of a religious conviction: that Christian education was not only desirable but Biblically mandated. To prove that mandate required, in turn, the demonstration that Christian education is distinct from and incompatible with modern secular education. The legal defense of Christian education required, then, the ability to articulate clearly the uniqueness of its mandate and mission and to prove these from Scripture. This proof some defendants, to their embarrassment, were unable to deliver.

Their inability, furthermore, seemed indicative of an even deeper problem. It appeared that the educational enterprise some Christian schools were engaged in conducting was Christian in name only. Their goals were secular, albeit unconciously, if they existed at all. There seemed, therefore, an opportunity, indeed a responsibility, to offer guidance of a basic sort to a fledgling movement believed to be crucial to the survival of Biblical Christianity in coming generations.

In order that the undertaking be not merely self-vindicating, a permanent committee was chosen from several disciplines and charged with the responsibility of determining precisely what Scripture has to say about education and applying the resulting principles rigorously to the teaching of subjects that form the standard curriculum. Among the members of the permanent committee there existed from the first a sincere willingness to do what was necessary to bring customary practice into line with Scripture—to apply the Biblical measure without flinching—but also a concern to free educational functions from constraints that are falsely ascribed to Scripture. After the general statements were completed, committees of university faculty met with the permanent committee to apply the concepts and principles to their specific disciplines (see chapters 5-15 below). The resulting subject-area statements appeared at the rate of about one per year from 1979 to 1988.

The first statement, *The Philosophy of Christian Education,* is the shortest of the series but required the longest time (three years) to produce. It supplies the definition and root concepts of Christian education which the other statements elaborate and apply. The next three, *Christian Teaching and Learning, Christian Educational Methods,* and *Objectionable Elements: The Biblical Approach,* (appearing in this book as Chapter 4, "Christian Educational Censorship") develop a methodology from premises established in the first statement. The final group of eleven apply the content of the preceding statements to the subject matters of the secondary curriculum, showing how the teaching of these subject matters can serve the goal of Christian education. The first statement of the final set is given precedence in that the study of Bible is the center from which all other studies must radiate. The study of Bible cannot be peripheral and detached in a curriculum worthy to be called Christian.

It follows that the contents of this volume are not essays but position papers: systematic, concise accounts, whose ideas and language have undergone thorough critique. It also follows that the last eleven are philosophies not of their subject areas primarily but of the teaching of those subject areas. Their arrangement reflects the divisions of the secondary curriculum rather than just categories of knowledge. For example, speech is grouped with music and art as a fine-arts elective, since the speech course in high school is usually optional and focuses on performance skills. The arrangement, in this instance, is somewhat misleading, for speech logically borders English as the oral counterpart of written communication. Though the discussion of speech in Chapter 10 includes both speech as performance and speech as general oral communication, its location in the list was determined by its formal status in the curriculum.

The statements in part III are intended to be both theoretical and practical. They not only define a standard for their subject areas but also show how it can be reached. The direction within each of them as well as throughout the volume as a whole is from definition of objectives and standards to practical application in teaching and learning. The core argument is that these objectives and standards are both essential to Christian education and distinctive within education. To lose them from either external constraints or carelessness is to deprive Christian education of its identity and very soul.

Finally, a word of clarification is in order. The account of Christian education offered in the following chapters does not presume to be a theologically exhaustive discussion, or even for all Christian groups a definitive treatment, of every issue it raises. Its approach is deliberately minimalist. Also, it does not assume that the ideal it sets forth must be fully realized by those who profess it in order for it to have the force of religious conviction. The very nature of spiritual standards precludes their absolute fulfillment in the present world. It does claim to be representative of Protestant fundamentalist belief and, especially, to be *distinctive*. Its premises and aims are mutually antagonistic with those of modern secularist governmental education.

Introduction

Education in the Christian school is radically different from education in secular schools since it springs from radically different premises. Secular education begins with the assumption that man is born good and remains good if his environment is favorable to his natural development. The function of education, therefore, is to remove the obstacles to the free and full expression of his natural impulses and thereby to make possible the self-determination of his personality. While doing so, it prepares the child for the social realities of life. The purpose of education is to help the child realize his potentialities so that he may contribute most fully to the progress of society. The role of the teacher is to help the child explore and expand his world. He is a facilitator, not a director, of the child's education. That is, he provides the environment and the materials for the learning process but does not impose his own beliefs, viewpoints, or attitudes upon the child.

There are, of course, profound contradictions within this set of presuppositions. The secular teacher is not so passive or the secular learning environment so value-free as this position suggests. Both teacher and environment are agents of social conditioning. The goal of self-determination conflicts with social adjustment and usefulness. Excluding educational hindrances from the learning environment makes it artificial rather than natural. Furthermore, there seem to be, after all, some absolutes: someone has to decide what are educational hindrances and what are not, what is social progress and what is not, and even what is natural. Self-determination, naturalness, and ethical neutrality are in reality a facade. The secularist knows very well what he wants to achieve, believes it to be above question, and pursues it with vigor. Nevertheless, from these assumptions, or pretenses, comes the enterprise of modern secular education.

The premises of Christian education, on the other hand, are sincerely held and self-consistent, for they are convictions based on the facts and principles of Scripture. Rooted in the infallible, supernaturally revealed truth of God, these principles cohere, for they exhibit the unity of Scriptural revelation.

The Bible not only is the source of infallible premises for Christian education but also provides its educational model. The Old Testament records God's teaching of man in person and through human instruments and physical circumstances. The Gospels show the instruction of the disciples by Christ, the Master Teacher. The Epistles are inspired examples of educational content and strategy. Finally, there is the pedagogical model of the Bible as a whole. Its goal, to conform redeemed man to the image of God in Christ, is that of all Christian education. Its means are the most suitable and effective for attaining this goal. Genuine Christian education follows closely the model of Scripture, for as an infallible agency of Christian growth it exemplifies perfectly its own principles. From the statements and examples of Scripture, therefore, come the premises and the model of Christian education, and from these premises and this model Christian education takes its distinctive shape.

P A R T

PREMISES

No movement can remain on course without periodic reference to its first principles. Paul told the Corinthians, "Examine yourselves, whether ye be in the faith; prove your own selves" (II Cor. 13:5). Similarly Christian educators do well to review frequently their educational undertaking in the light of their educational theory.

Educational theory is least reliable when it derives from logical categories inferred from experience, even from Christian experience. It is most reliable when it is deduced directly from Scripture itself. The following account draws directly from Scripture a philosophical basis for the existence of the Christian school and for the conduct of its mission.

The Christian
Philosophy of Education 1

What is a Christian education? Although the term *Christian education* does not occur in the Bible, the Bible speaks of the moral and spiritual instruction of believers in general and of children in particular. It places a high value upon knowledge, both of God and of His works. It describes the moral and spiritual fruits of this knowledge and defines its ultimate purpose.

The present Christian school movement can be understood only as a part—certainly in these times a very significant and necessary part—of the total endeavor of Christian education. A full understanding of this movement requires an examination of the basis upon which its educational theory and practices rest: its "philosophy of education." Accordingly there follows, first, a presentation of the basic beliefs of Christian education and, second, an application of these beliefs to the specific mission of the Christian school.

Christian Education

Definitions

Biblical Christianity—The God of the Bible is not a god of man's own making or choosing. The eternal Creator of all things existed before man and exists independently of man. God, however, has revealed Himself to man, speaking through His Word (the inerrant, divinely inspired and preserved sixty-six books of the Old and New Testaments) and His works. His self-revelation is the substance of Christian belief. What we call *Biblical Christianity* is a system of certain basic truths that God has revealed. Among these truths, the following are fundamental to Christian education.

1. God created man in His own image. Of all created beings, only man is spoken of in the Scriptures as being created in God's image. "And God said, Let us make man in our image, after our likeness. . . . So God created man in his own image, in the image of God created he him; male and female created he them" (Gen. 1:26-27). This creation of man was instantaneous—by a direct act and not by an evolutionary process. Possessing the divine image, man reflects God not only in his moral, intellectual, and emotional capacities but also in his aesthetic sensibility, social inclinations, and other qualities of his personality. To acknowledge this correspondency is not to claim a degree of deity for man but to recognize that man, the creature, uniquely bears the stamp of his Creator.

2. The image of God in man was marred when man fell through disobedience to his Creator. God created man for fellowship with Him. This fellowship was not to be forced but voluntary. Man, however, prompted by Satan, chose to rebel against God (Gen. 3). His rebellion, which we call "the fall of man," brought all mankind and all creation under the dominion of sin.

All human beings, consequently, are born essentially evil, not essentially good, having inherited the evil nature of the first man, Adam (Ps. 51:5; Rom. 5:12). All stand condemned before God because of their sin and are in need of a Saviour (Rom. 3:23; 6:23). Though the image of God in man was not entirely destroyed by the fall (see Gen. 9:6; James 3:9), it was severely marred. The mind of the natural man, for example, is capable of intellectual but not of spiritual perception. He "receiveth not the things of the Spirit of God: for they are foolishness unto him: neither can he know them, because they are spiritually discerned" (I Cor. 2:14). On matters of the greatest importance to man, his mind is not to be trusted, for it has been impaired by sin.

3. God has provided for the restoration of His image in man through the person and work of Jesus Christ. This restoration is not accomplished by the fanning of a supposed inborn "spark of divinity" in the individual, as religious liberalism has traditionally maintained, but by the giving of a new nature. "If any man

be in Christ, he is a new creature [i.e., creation]: old things are passed away; behold, all things are become new'' (II Cor. 5:17).

Jesus Christ, the virgin-born Son of God, is the designer, Creator, and preserver of all things and is to have preeminence in all things (Col. 1:16-19). He is the answer to those persistent questions: Where did I come from? Why am I here? Where am I going? Speaking of Jesus Christ, the Bible declares ''For of him [where I came from], and through him [why I am here], and to him [where I am going], are all things: to whom be glory for ever. Amen'' (Rom. 11:36).

In Jesus Christ, God became man (I Tim. 3:16), and, as the unique God-Man, Jesus Christ is completely God and completely man. Though no man has seen God at any time (John 1:18), man possesses in Jesus Christ the ultimate and complete revelation of God (John 1:1; Heb. 1:2). Jesus Christ, God's only begotten Son, came into the world to redeem mankind by His substitutionary death on the cross (I Pet. 2:24; Luke 19:10; Rom. 3:24-26). His bodily resurrection proved Him the Son of God (Rom. 1:4) with power to save all who come to God by Him (Heb. 7:25). When He ascended, He gave gifts to the Church ''for the perfecting of the saints'' in the image of God (Eph. 4:7-12).

The Church—The Church is that group of individuals who have been regenerated by the Holy Spirit through faith in Jesus Christ as Saviour and who have openly confessed this faith (Rom. 10:9-10). The Church thus is not a building or even a denomination. It is the Body of Christ, composed of every true believer on the Lord Jesus Christ from Pentecost to the rapture (Eph. 5:25-30; Heb. 12:22-23). Although true believers are commanded by Scripture to assemble themselves together in local churches (Heb. 10:25), to be part of the true Church is not merely to be religious or to belong to a religious group. It is to possess the life of God in the soul. The believer is made a partaker of the divine nature (II Pet. 1:4).

Education—From the moment a child is born, certain forces are at work influencing his development. As his inherited powers and tendencies surface and interact with his environment and his will, he takes on the characteristics of his adulthood. Human growth, however, does not end with physical maturity. Some faculties of the personality are capable of expansion and refinement into old age. Education, whether of child or adult, is the directing of this total ongoing process of development toward specific objectives.

Purpose

The purpose of Christian education is the directing of the process of human development toward God's objective for man: godliness of character and action. It bends its efforts to the end "that the man of God may be perfect, throughly furnished unto all good works" (II Tim. 3:17).

This goal of godliness presupposes the experience of regeneration. As education in general begins with physical birth, Christian education proper begins with spiritual rebirth, when the life of God is communicated to the soul. To say that Christian education proper begins with the new birth is not, however, to say that it is pointless before regeneration. The student can be provided with necessary awarenesses of God and responses to His Word so that when the Holy Spirit brings conviction of sin he will readily and with full understanding accept Christ as his Saviour. Timothy from childhood knew "the holy Scriptures, which are able to make thee wise unto salvation through faith which is in Christ Jesus" (II Tim. 3:15). To make children and even unregenerated adults "wise unto salvation" is no less a legitimate function of Christian education today.

Growth in godliness proceeds step by step from regeneration toward full maturity "in the knowledge of our Lord Jesus Christ" (II Pet. 1:5-8). This growth, like regeneration, is made possible by divine grace (Titus 2:11-13). It results from the emulation of Christ, who, as "the express image" of "the Majesty on high" (Heb. 1:3), is the visible manifestation of the divine nature that God has ordained for man's imitation. As regenerated man continues to occupy his mind with the truth of God revealed in Christ, he is "changed into the same image from glory to glory, even as by the Spirit of the Lord" (II Cor. 3:18). His full conformity to the image of God in Christ—his Christ-likeness—is the goal of Christian education (Rom. 8:29). This goal is pursued with the recognition that its complete realization awaits the full view of Christ in the life to come, when "we shall be like him; for we shall see him as he is" (I John 3:2).

Recipient

The focus of the educational process is, of course, the student, a unique individual created for a specific purpose in God's plan. He must be properly qualified and motivated if he is to perform his cooperative role. Without a regenerated, willing student, Christian education cannot carry out its purpose. Regeneration does not eliminate the old nature—what the Apostle Paul called the "old man" or the "flesh"—and carnal attitudes and inclinations can hinder spiritual growth. It is the student's responsibility to bring with him a pure heart and a willing mind. With these and the proper instruction, his success is assured, for "the pure in heart," Christ promised, "shall see God," and the diligent search for knowledge, as for silver and hid treasures, will be rewarded (Matt. 5:8; Prov. 2:3-5).

Responsibility

In the Scriptures God has commanded two institutions to educate: the home and the church. As an extension of either or both of these institutions, the Christian school has a Biblical mandate to educate.

The home—The Bible makes clear that education is to begin in the home (Gen. 18:19; Deut. 6:7; Prov. 22:6; Eph. 6:4; II Tim. 1:5; 3:15). It makes parents responsible for their children and charges them with an educational task.

The church—The New Testament indicates that the responsibilities of the church include edification as well as evangelism (Matt. 28:19-20; Acts 2:42; II Tim. 2:2). The Scriptural representation of the church as a body—an organism that grows and matures—implies a teaching function for this institution. Also, the recognition of the gift of teaching by the New Testament (Rom. 12:4-7; I Cor. 12:28) assumes the necessity of teaching in the local churches.

The Christian school—Christians have a Biblical mandate to educate in their homes and in their churches. In order to reinforce the educational ministries of these institutions or to protect their ministries from secular interference, Christian parents or church members, acting either individually or in concert, may elect to form a Christian school. In doing so, they are acting from religious conviction. To deny them their choice of means in carrying out the Biblical mandate of Christian education is to deny them the exercise of their religious convictions.

It follows that the education of children is the prerogative not of the state but of the parents or church members. Furthermore, it is evident that allowing the state to dictate the standards and procedures of Christian education jeopardizes the ability of parents and of church members to carry out their responsibility to God for the education of their children. The subjection of the Christian school to the control of the state or of any other secular agency is, in effect, the subjection of the Christian homes and churches to secular domination. It is rightly regarded as vicious, for secular control (even that which may appear benign) is incompatible with the aims of a spiritual ministry.

The Christian School

The work of the Christian school is an extension of the Christian educational ministries of the Christian home and the church. Its purpose, therefore, is the development of the student in the image of God. This purpose determines both the content and the means of instruction.

Content

King David exhorted his son, "And thou, Solomon my son, know thou the God of thy father, and serve him with a perfect heart and with a willing mind" (I Chron. 28:9). How perfectly David must have understood that the education of the child of God must include both the knowledge of God and the preparation for exercising that knowledge in service. Accordingly, in Christian education students are taught to *know* God and to *imitate* Him in His character and in His works.

The knowledge of God—The whole body of Christian educational theory rests upon the recognition that all truth is of God. He is the God of truth (Ps. 31:5); His Son is the Lord of truth (John 14:6); His Spirit is the Spirit of truth (John 14:16-17). All truth, whether discerned or undiscerned by man, comes forth from a single source and, therefore, is one harmonious whole. Consequently, God's written self-revelation is the starting point of all rational inquiry and the guide to all interpretation of reality. No concept can be true that conflicts with the statements of the

Scriptures. Conversely, no untruth is a legitimate support of divine revelation or has any place in the ministry of spiritual truth. A reverence for the God of truth compels a conscientious regard for accuracy in all areas of factual investigation and reporting.

Since it is the purpose of Christian education to develop redeemed man in the image of God, Christian educators must point students to the original of this image, God Himself. Students come to know God by studying His revelation of Himself in His Word and in His works. Of these, the more fully revealing of God is His Word; and, therefore, the Bible is the center of the Christian school curriculum. The Bible is not only the most important subject matter but also the source of the principles determining the other subject matters and the way in which they are taught. The presentation of Biblical truth is thus not confined to a single segment of the curriculum—the study of the Bible—but diffused throughout the teaching of all subjects. The teacher's knowledge of the Scriptures controls his selection and interpretation of materials and determines his whole perspective on his subject matter. The Scriptures possess this privileged status in the curriculum, for they are the primary means of conveying the knowledge of God.

This knowledge of God implies more than just knowledge *about* God. Certainly an acquaintance with the facts about God in the written revelation is important. But the knowledge of God that is unique to Christian education is a *personal* knowledge that begins with repentance of sin and faith in Jesus Christ as Saviour and develops through obedience to and communion with God. To know God is to be born into the family of God and to live in fellowship with Him (I John 5:20; Phil. 3:10). It follows that without a student body composed mainly of students possessing this personal knowledge of God, no school can legitimately be regarded as a Christian educational institution.

Though the Word of God is the main source of the knowledge of God, both factual and personal, and therefore deserves precedence, the works of God are also an important part of the Christian school curriculum. The creation reveals the Creator, and that which reveals God is a proper study for man. Indeed, the Scriptures themselves invite man to consider God's earthly handiwork and hold him responsible for recognizing in it the work of God (Job 38-39; Rom. 1:18-20).

Especially is God revealed in His rational creation, man, who having been created in the image of God is the highest of God's works on earth. It is for this reason that the Christian school gives emphasis to the "humanities": the study of man's language, his literature, his artistic achievements, the record of his history, the logic of his mathematical reasoning, and other forms of his personal and cultural expression. But the natural sciences are not disregarded. The glories of the vast universe and the myriad wonders of man's earthly habitation testify that their Creator is a God of order, of beauty, and of power (Ps. 19:1; Rom. 1:20). The perfect suitability of man's physical environment to his needs and the fact that God committed the earth to man to subdue and enjoy (Gen. 1-2) witness to the goodness of God in His love for and delight in His human creation. Though the study of nature has often displaced the study of nature's God, even to the point of man's worshiping the creation rather than the Creator (Rom. 1:25), nevertheless God Himself pronounced the material universe "good" and established its laws and processes as means of accomplishing His will for man (Gen. 1:31). The Christian school curriculum includes astronomy, physics, chemistry, biology, mathematics, and related subjects because they provide a knowledge of God's nature and His work in this world. In the curriculum of the Christian school, the voice of creation joins with that of the written revelation in praise of the glory and goodness of God.

The imitation of God—In endeavoring to fulfill the purpose of Christian education—the development of Christ-likeness in redeemed man—the Christian school teaches, as a consequence of the knowledge of God, the imitation of God. Students learn of God so that they may imitate Him. They are to become "followers of God" (Eph. 5:1).

In following God they imitate both His nature and His works. The imitation of God's nature results in holiness of character. God commands His people to imitate His holiness: "Be ye holy; for I am holy" (I Pet. 1:16). The fruit of the Spirit (Gal. 5:22-23) is the expression of the holiness of God in the believer's character. The imitation of God's works results in service. Service is the consequence of following the one who said of Himself, "For even the Son of man came not to be ministered unto [that is, to be served], but to minister [to serve], and to give his life a ransom for many" (Mark 10:45).

The imitation of God's works by the Christian student necessitates a continual emphasis upon the goal of service and a provision in the curriculum for instruction in skills and disciplines that equip students for service. Academic subjects—whether in the humanities or in the natural sciences, whether general or strictly vocational—are studied not as ends in themselves but as means of improving the student as a servant of God. Such instruction includes not only mental but also physical culture: training in the proper care of the vehicle with which God has provided man to serve Him. The student learns that bodies must not be abused or neglected but developed and disciplined for the service of God and presented to Him for His use and His glory (Rom. 12:1-2; I Cor. 6:20).

The imitation of God's works by the student requires provision in the curriculum for the development of all the powers with which he has been endowed by his Creator and the direction of these refined powers into channels of godly action. The Christian school encourages the development of the student's creativity, for man has been given the ability to create in imitation of God. Christian creativity, unlike that of the unbelieving world, attempts to reflect God's ways as completely as possible. The Christian school is concerned with the improvement of the student's tastes. If the student is to imitate God in His judgment, to obey the injunction to "approve things that are excellent" (Phil. 1:10), he must possess the aesthetic as well as the moral perceptions and inclinations to prefer the best in all areas of his experience. To imitate God in His actions as well as in His attributes is to develop abilities into skills and to exercise them as instruments of God's will.

Means

The Christian school is concerned that the manner, no less than the matter, of its teaching be consistent with the purpose of Christian education: conforming the student to the image of God in Christ. This purpose requires imitating God in the means of teaching as well as in the content taught. Therefore, the educational procedures and vehicles of Christian education in the Christian school must follow Biblical example and norms.

Methodology—A method is, of course, a means to an end, not an end in itself. Methods are chosen for their power and efficiency in accomplishing designated goals. In the Christian school they are chosen also for their reflection of the example of God, with the assurance that God's methods are the most effective in carrying out His will. Of course, Christian methodology rejects any method contrary to the principles of Scripture.

The Christian educator finds Biblical warrant for the use of a wide diversity of educational methods. In His teaching, Christ, the Master Teacher, used an amazing variety of methods and materials. In the Old Testament from Genesis onward, God taught man through a diversity of means. In the Garden of Eden, He used a tree to teach Adam. Since the Flood He has used a rainbow to teach the world that He will not again destroy the earth by water. The entire tabernacle was a prophetic object lesson, setting forth the person and work of His Son, Jesus Christ.

Biblical methods, as a rule, require some effort on the part of the student, though the effort need not be tedious. They provide for the "discovering" of truth (actually the revealing of truth by a God eager to reward diligent study), as well as for the reinforcing of learning, by man's search (Prov. 2:4-6). The parables, for example, required a searching on the part of the disciples before their truths were fully revealed. That which is learned at the cost of effort is not soon forgotten, and God delights in blessing those who are zealous for the knowledge of Him.

The instruments—The means of achieving godliness—the purpose of Christian education—is the imitation of God. The imitation of God by the student depends upon and conforms to the imitation of God by the teacher. The teacher in the Christian school stands in much the same relation to his students that Paul stood in with regard to his Corinthian converts when he wrote, "Be ye followers of me" (I Cor. 4:16). The Spirit-filled Christian teacher stands in the place of God, representing God to the student. What the student knows of God is often what he sees in his teacher. "Ye became followers of us, and of the Lord," Paul reminded the Thessalonians (I Thess. 1:6). It is for this reason that the Christian school must pay careful attention to the character and conduct of its teachers. No school that is careless concerning the Christ-likeness of its teachers can hope to fulfill the purpose of Christian education.

Of course, a Christian school should be concerned about the professional as well as the spiritual preparation of its teachers.

Knowledge of the student and mastery of the subject to be taught as well as of the methodology of its presentation are necessary for effective teaching. Jesus Christ knew His students (John 2:25) and His subject matter and was competent in every conceivable legitimate technique of imaginative, resourceful teaching. He, therefore, taught with a commanding assurance and vigor that amazed the multitudes (Matt. 7:29). No amount of carefully prepared educational materials, however important they may be as tools, can compensate for the lack of a carefully prepared teacher: one who has followed the spiritual and professional example of his Master.

The position of the teacher is one of authority and service, and the two are intertwined. In Scriptural leadership, he who leads must also serve (Matt. 20:25-28). In fact, he rules in order to serve. Christ, our Lord and Master, not only served mankind supremely in His death but also continues to serve His people. He can serve most fully those who accept His rule. Similarly the Christian teacher exercises authority over the student in order to serve the student in his quest for Christ-likeness. The teacher's ability to serve the student depends to a great extent upon the student's acceptance of his rule.

Likewise the Christian school administrator exercises authority over both the teacher and the student in order to serve the teacher in his service of the student. The chief responsibility of the administrator is to provide the most favorable environment possible for the communication of Christ to the student. The teacher can function as a ''teacher come from God'' only as the administration serves his needs and, through him, the needs of the student. Conversely the administration can serve the teacher and the student in the process of Christian education only as they submit to its rule. As a godly administration undergirds the ministry of a godly teacher to a responsive student, the goal of godliness in the student's character and action is increasingly realized.

P A R T

METHODOLOGY

The purpose of Christian education may be simply stated: to develop redeemed man in the image of God restored in Christ and revealed in the Scriptures. The means of Christian education are less obvious. Chapters 2-4 describe these means, expanding the concise discussion on pages 9-11 of Chapter 1.

Christian Teaching and Learning

2

The Bible both ordains and controls the Christian educational undertaking. It establishes its theoretical grounds, as we have seen, and determines its participants, process, and setting.

Participants

The participants in the Christian educational process are regenerated persons with a zeal to see God's will performed in and through themselves. In the learning process both student and teacher are colaborers with God.

Student

Christian education views the student as an individual created by God with a unique personality and for a specific purpose. Whether his unique personality becomes Christ-like and whether his specific purpose is fulfilled depends upon his regeneration and his teachability, for he is endowed with a will and is not just a creature of his environment. He must be saved in order to have a capacity for Christian education; he must be submissive to the agencies of Christian education (the Scriptures, the leadership of a godly teacher, a Biblically centered curriculum) in order to progress toward Christ-likeness, the goal of Christian education. Both salvation and submission are necessary to his success in the will of God.

The redeemed student therefore needs a zeal to learn prompted by humility and eagerness to gain true wisdom. His humility appears in a low estimate of his present achievement and faith in the person God has provided to instruct him. He does not set himself up as a judge of what is and is not valuable in his educational experience and adjust his sense of responsibility accordingly. He trusts his teacher's greater wisdom and experience to determine the knowledge and skills that are relevant to his future service of God. His eagerness arises from a sense of stewardship causing him to "buy up" his learning opportunities as means of growing in Christ and gaining resources for Christian service. His role is not to lead but to follow, not to demand but to obey. His submission is, however, not passive but responsive; for he understands the importance of his growth in Christ, and he desires to please both his teacher and the one who has provided his educational opportunity.

Teacher

The role of the teacher is essential in Christian education. The student needs a visible pattern of the goal toward which he is striving and a human instrument to assist him toward that goal. The goal consists of moral and spiritual as well as intellectual characteristics and of personal graces and refinement—qualities that can be communicated only by a person. The teacher therefore must be a person of spiritual, emotional, and social maturity. He must be steeped in Biblical wisdom and have a Biblical zeal to impart it. His moral character and conduct must be above reproach, for he exemplifies to the student the nature and work of God. He needs the gift of clear explanation and the virtues of patience and love. He needs a sense of excitement stemming from an awareness of the significance of his function. These are necessary if he is to show a spirit of sacrificial, loving concern and of joyful earnestness in performing his ministry of teaching. His students must recognize that he cares deeply about their success and that he enjoys helping them. Often the first and deepest impression a student receives of a teacher, and the most crucial to his success, is whether he is his friend. But personal maturity, godliness, and natural gifts are not enough to produce excellence in teaching. The Christian teacher also needs thorough professional preparation, for he must have a command of his subject and its techniques of presentation and must understand the needs and capacities of his students. To the well-prepared, diligent teacher, time will bring an increasing enrichment and refinement of knowledge, resources, and skills.

These qualities are necessary if the teacher is to perform his role as a director of the student's growth. In his role he guides, motivates, and, as necessary, corrects. This directing is both general, with respect to the students' common goal of Christ-likeness, and specific, with regard to the students' individual vocational ministries. The teacher is not only an academic overseer but also a spiritual adviser who prayerfully and gently steers the student according to his aptitudes and propensities in the direction of God's will for his life. As a director the teacher is a figure of authority but also a gracious helper. He is intolerant of insolence and laziness but altogether tolerant of weakness and inexperience. He embodies the wisdom "from above" that is "first pure, then peaceable, gentle, and easy to be intreated, full of mercy and good fruits" (James 3:17). So Christ taught the disciples; so Paul, the infant churches. No amount of educational apparatus, however Biblically justifiable and important it may be, can compensate for the lack of a properly prepared teacher whose ministry follows the example of Scripture.

This example appears most vividly in the ministry of the Son of God. Jesus Christ, the Master Teacher, was rightly identified as "a teacher come from God" (John 3:2) and is the supreme pattern of godly teaching. The Gospels show Him continually engaged in teaching (e.g., Matt. 4:23; 5:2; 7:29; 9:35; 11:1; Mark 4:1) and refer to what He said as His teaching ("doctrine" means *teaching*). He was frequently addressed as Master, which means "teacher," and five times spoke of Himself as a teacher. His followers were called disciples, or "learners." Before His ascension He gave them a commission that included teaching as an integral part of their function in the present age and promised that He would be with them as they performed this function (Matt. 28:18-20). Christian teachers find in the ministry of the Son of God a model of their role and teaching performance. They also find in Him a sustaining presence as they carry out the momentous responsibility enjoined upon them by the Great Commission.

Process

Human beings grow according to known principles of development. Education in the general sense is the directing of this growth toward specific objectives. Modern secular-humanistic education directs human growth toward human objectives: self-realization and service to society. Christian education is the directing of the growth of redeemed man toward God's objectives for man: godliness of character and conduct. Of course, with the acquisition of godliness come true self-realization and genuine service to mankind as the believer is conformed to the image of God in Christ (Rom. 8:29) and represents Christ to the world (II Cor. 5:20). The process of education consists of the reciprocal actions of teaching and learning. Christian teaching and learning consist of the revealing of truth by God through His human instrument, the teacher, and the student's receiving of that truth and acting upon it.

Extent

That which Christian education communicates to the student is the knowledge and imitation of God. The knowledge of God implies more than just facts. Therefore Christian teaching must aim not only at the transmission of factual content but also, and especially, at belief. This belief presupposes the student's personal relationship with the One who said "I am . . . the truth" (John 14:6) and centers on the Scriptures. The knowledge of God includes knowledge of what pleases and displeases Him and a conviction that His will is best. It includes a knowledge of His works and a belief that He is the author and sustainer of creation. The belief at which Christian education aims is not just in facts; it is in principles. Christian belief is grounded on certain historical and theological facts. Christian education likewise must be concerned with facts: specific truths about specific things. But facts alone are insufficient to unify the student's thinking and affect his life according to the purpose of Christian education. He must be brought to believe in general truths of life that can mold his character and control his behavior in the will of God. Christian education, in short, integrates Biblical faith and learning.

The belief in principles implanted by Christian education leads to the imitation of God by the Christian student. The imitation of God's nature results in godly character; the imitation of God's works results in Christian service. Thus knowledge precedes but is fulfilled by imitation; godly character precedes but is fulfilled by the service of God. Christ "ordained twelve, that they should be with him, and that he might send them forth to preach'' (Mark 3:14). They were first to learn of Him and then to imitate Him in His life and ministry. In genuine Christian education, facts lead on to principles, and principles, having become convictions, are lived out in the realm of duty. A Biblical education, like the Bible itself, endeavors ''that the man of God may be perfect, throughly furnished unto all good works'' (II Tim. 3:17).

Even secular education recognizes the importance of going beyond the mere acquisition of facts to the application of principles in behavior. Most educators see at least five specific levels of the learning process. Through lecturing and other forms of direct teacher-to-student communication, as well as through assignments, research, and special projects, the student comes into contact with factual content. He reaches the *exposure* level of learning. After the student has been made aware of a body of content in a subject area, he must do something mentally with the information; it must become part of the stored material in his mind. In other words, he must be brought to the *activation* level. On this level the teacher makes use of drills, recitations, explanations, illustrations, identifications, and other devices of reinforcement to allow the student an opportunity to absorb the content to which he has been exposed. The third level, *comprehension,* is more difficult, for it consists of relating the acquired information to other areas of knowledge and experience. For the Christian, comprehension consists of seeing the connection of the factual material with revealed truth and forming patterns of thought based on these observed connections. Interaction between teacher and student is an important means of developing this understanding. Though the child's comprehension level is limited by his maturity (I Cor. 13:11; Heb. 5:12-14), the teacher constantly tries to develop his comprehension by giving him new avenues of approach to information. No teacher can take for granted that a student understands what has been covered in class simply because he can repeat a memorized answer on a test or in a class recitation. The student reaches the *conviction* level of learning when, after deliberate considerations, he is able to say, ''I believe this for myself.'' The highest level of learning, *application,* is reached when the student puts into practice the truth that has been communicated, permitting it to change his life.

Christian students, on this level, become "doers of the word, and not hearers only" (James 1:22).

Much Christian education takes place on the levels of exposure and activation, but Christian education must include also the higher levels of comprehension, conviction, and application if Christian attitudes and values are to be implanted in the student and expressed in his life. Something like this hierarchy of learning appears in God's command that the law be read publicly to all the inhabitants of Israel every seven years "that they may *hear,* and that they may *learn,* and *fear* the Lord your God, and observe to *do* all the words of this law" (Deut. 31:12). Four words summarize God's view of education: *hear, learn, fear,* and *do.* God's people were not just to "hear" the words of the law (to have the information poured into their ears); they were to "learn" it. Their learning was to produce the proper attitude toward God; they were to "fear" Him, to hold Him in reverential awe. Ultimately all their learning was to the end that they might actually "do" the law. Only when an Israelite performed all the requirements of the law, day after day, could it be said he truly had learned it.

Scope

Secular education in recent years has tended to emphasize emotional, social, and physical development at the expense of the intellectual. The Christian educator recognizes that the activity of education is primarily intellectual. Belief in principles is initially intellectual, for principles are general truths that must be first received intellectually before becoming deep emotional convictions. Academic skills essential to educational and professional achievement are primarily intellectual. Nevertheless, Christian education is concerned with the total process of the student's development in the will of God. The image of God in Christ is more than just intellectual; it includes the entire personality. Jesus, as a youth, "increased in wisdom and stature, and in favour with God and man" (Luke 2:52). The student needs more than just intellectual training if he is to be "perfect, throughly furnished unto all good works" (II Tim. 3:17; II Pet. 1:5-7).

Differentiation

Since Christian education regards each student as an individual with a unique personality and a specific calling, it provides as much as possible for individual differences. Individual differences of ability and maturity may require subgroups within a class. Certainly they require varying degrees of supportive attention. Jesus often taught his disciples as a group, but He also separated them—on one occasion a subgroup of seventy (Luke 10:1-14); on many occasions, of twelve; at certain times, of three (Matt. 17:1-13; 26:36-46). The Christian teacher is sensitive to differences in maturity and ability among students in similar age groups and certainly among the different age groups themselves, and he adjusts the demands of the curriculum accordingly. Though there are enough broad similarities between individuals of the same age group to warrant standardization, there are enough individual and class differences to necessitate flexibility and differentiation at certain points. Christian education seeks to educate each student to the extent of his particular capacities and prepare him as fully as possible for his particular area of service.

Christian educators must be especially sensitive to the differing capacities of separate age levels. To give ''strong meat'' to students who are not ready for it, in any subject area, violates both educational and Scriptural principles (Heb. 5:14). It is true that highly motivated Christian teachers and students working together in a disciplined learning environment may expect to achieve more than their counterparts in secular education. But it is also true that student ability levels cannot be violated without serious consequences. The amount and difficulty of study must agree with the capacity of the average student within the student group. To push students to perform above what is normal for their age creates either frustration or a false precocity that may dazzle the uninformed observer but produces superficial, lopsided learning, rarely exceeding the exposure and activation levels. The child's study of a particular subject must be adapted to his degree of mental growth and experience and follow the sequence of steps prerequisite to its advanced stages. Moreover, excessive homework demands can be harmful. They may create a habit of superficiality that will follow the student through life. They may also hinder family influences on student growth. The school cannot be in competition with the institution first ordained of God for the work of Christian education. The wise teacher knows the limits of his students, both individual and collective, and provides them with the instruction best suited to their capacities.

Motivation

The teacher shares with the student the responsibility of motivation. The teacher may not entirely blame the student for insufficient interest, nor may the student excuse his lack of interest on the basis that he was not properly motivated by the teacher. The Christian teacher recognizes that the attitudes and expectations the student brings to the learning situation affect how much he will learn. How he feels about the class, the lesson to be taught, the teacher, and his purpose for being in the class is very much the business of the teacher, for students learn best when they are interested in what is to be learned and sense that their needs will be met. Effective motivation is usually positive as well as negative. God motivates the believer by incentives of pleasure and pain, of encouragement and warning. Accordingly, the Christian teacher keeps before the student the value of what he is learning and the disadvantage of not learning it. He points up the relevancy of the subject matter to the student's present and future needs, linking it with the aims of Christian education. As the student matures, he will become less dependent on external motivation and more responsive to internal. The teacher can never entirely discard such external prods as competition, tests, grades, prizes, and special recognition but should be able to rely increasingly upon the student's developing inner sense of responsibility. The teacher will take advantage of the inborn desire to succeed by helping the student set reasonable but challenging goals and inciting his will to reach them (Phil. 3:13-14). He will capitalize on the natural human desire to learn by whetting the student's curiosity and thus enhancing his pleasure in seeking and finding truth. Especially he will appeal to the student's sense of Christian responsibility and stewardship in urging him to take advantage of his learning opportunities and persevere in his divinely ordained course (II Tim. 2:2, 15). He inspires the discouraged student to develop a positive faith attitude—a realization of the mighty power of God working in his life (Eph. 3:20; I Thess. 5:24). He warns the unconcerned student that, though it is not necessarily a sin to fail, it is a sin to do less than one's best. The student thus understands that he must strive for the approval not only of his teacher but also of God (II Tim. 2:15).

Evaluation

Periodically in the learning process the teacher must evaluate the student's work. This evaluation is normally expressed as a grade. Though grades can be valuable student incentives, their purpose is not reward or punishment. Their purpose is to inform the teacher, the student, and those responsible for him of the student's degree of achievement and progress so that he can receive the kind of attention he needs to succeed in his educational experience. A grade therefore is a description, as objective as possible, of a student's performance. Since it affects educational procedures respecting its recipient, it must be as accurate as possible. Artificially inflated grades are not only dishonest but also, in the long run, harmful to the student. Since students regard a grade as a symbol of their success and since it affects plans and future opportunities, it must be fair. That is, it must be based on an equality of learning opportunities for the group being evaluated and on standards applied evenly throughout the group. Evaluation must also, however, be conducted in a spirit of reasonableness and sympathetic support. A test may be postponed or even retaken if extenuating circumstances prevent its accurate revelation of a student's achievement in relation to the group. Grading scales, like assignment schedules, are tools, not inviolable moral absolutes that cannot be adjusted without dire consequences. Special consideration, whether of the individual or of the group, is justifiable on the basis of the aim of evaluation: accurate measurement of student achievement according to consistently applied objective standards.

James 3:17 states the characteristics of Christian educational evaluation. "The wisdom that is from above is first pure, then peaceable." It is first truthful and accurate and then considerate of personal feelings. It is "gentle, and easy to be entreated, full of mercy and good fruits." Christian teaching provides ample remedial support for students with limited ability or experience before assessing their achievement. The Christian teacher not only is accessible to his class but also seeks out the students who are having difficulty and gives them special attention. It is, however, "without partiality and without hypocrisy." A grade must represent the same degree of achievement by one student as by another and may not be arbitrarily adjusted for personal or institutional reasons (e.g., making a student eligible for athletics). If a grade is sentimentally raised or vindictively lowered, it violates its purpose of measurement and the Biblical principle of fairness. It must be true, and it must be just (Prov. 11:1).

Grades can be overstressed and often are. They can become ends rather than means to an end. They can symbolize personal worth rather than indicate particular achievement in a specific area of a student's development. The Christian teacher will use them properly according to their purpose and discourage obsession with grades on the part of some students and negligent disregard on the part of others. He will help the students to regard grades as useful points of reference for their goal setting and, especially, as tools by means of which God shapes and directs them in His will.

Setting

Christian education does not, like secular education, regard environment as the main determinant of educational success. Some of the most valuable learning for the Christian comes from very adverse environments. The Christian student must determine to progress in Christ-likeness regardless of the advantages or disadvantages of his environment. Nevertheless, it is the responsibility of the Christian administrator and teacher to provide an educational environment as favorable as possible to the student's growth in Christ. The setting of Christian as well as secular education is therefore thoroughly artificial. It is carefully prepared and controlled in keeping with its educational purpose—to conform regenerated students to the image of God in Christ—and is modeled on the Scriptures. Consequently it is both structured and protective.

Structured

Though systematic procedure can become an end in itself rather than a means to an end, the Christian class must have order to function in the will of God. Order implies a figure of authority, the teacher, and submission to his authority by the student. The student must recognize that all authority emanates from God and must make up his mind to be obedient to divine authority in all areas of his life (I Tim. 6:1-2). If this obedience is first learned and practiced in the home (Eph. 6:1-3), it will be easier to accept in the classroom and in other situations. Teachers must train students to recognize and respect the boundary lines of acceptable behavior in any situation, must closely supervise student conduct with regard to the limits established for the class, and must take remedial action when these limits are not observed. Order thus implies fixed standards and procedures, and these imply rules backed by disciplinary pressure. Though such pressure can be excessive, it is related to motivation; a reasonable amount is necessary to prompt achievement and to teach students to succeed in the difficult situations of life. It is the student's responsibility therefore to conform to the policies and procedures established by the teacher, and it is the teacher's responsibility to make them instrumental to the student's growth in Christ.

The discipline in the classroom must be purposeful. Rules must be enforced firmly and consistently so as to maintain an orderly learning environment and to impress upon students the certainty of moral consequences. Standards must be consistently upheld in order to ensure fairness and accuracy in grading and to teach that there is no shortcut to genuine achievement. Observing standards and enforcing rules also help the student establish habits such as punctuality and attention to detail that are important to his growth in Christ and future Christian service. Most success is achieved within limitations, and the student needs to learn to submit to the prescribed procedures and norms of the class in order to cope with circumstantial hindrances in his service for Christ.

Discipline should be preventative as well as punitive. Undesirable student responses can often be anticipated and circumvented before they cause problems for the student and for the rest of the class. The alert, well-prepared, experienced teacher should rarely be caught by surprise. Individual conferences with potentially disruptive students reduce the likelihood of having to deal with defiant attitudes in class. When insolence or deliberate violation of prescribed behavior does occur, the teacher must react quickly and firmly to prevent deterioration of order in the class. Various remedial measures and punishments are available to fit offenses of various types and degrees. Suspension or expulsion may be used in extreme cases, for attendance at a Christian school is a privilege and not a right. In correction, as in evaluation, the teacher or administrator can be no respecter of persons (James 2:1-9).

Externally imposed discipline is no enemy to self-discipline, as some believe. It is instead a means of developing self-discipline. When a person has learned to adjust his behavior to standards and rules conceived by others, he is more able to govern his behavior by the standards and rules he determines to be necessary for his personal success. Of course, most of the standards and rules of the Christian classroom are based on moral and spiritual principles, and the student, having adopted them, will benefit from them throughout life. But the resultant attitude of humility and submissive responsiveness will help him to work easily and productively under authority and to be resourceful and persevering in the difficulties of life.

External control thus precedes internal control, and internal control is essential to normal growth. It is a truism of aesthetic achievement that discipline releases, not represses, creative genius. It is no less true that discipline, imposed in a wisely controlled learning environment, produces individuals rather than stereotypes. Though extreme regimentation that takes no account of individual differences can be stifling, some kind of prescriptive framework is usually necessary to human development and productivity. This truth of life expresses a deep spiritual principle. It is only as a person subjects himself to the will of God that he becomes free to realize his possibilities. Discipline is especially necessary to spiritual growth and achievement, for without it one cannot focus his affections on things above (Col. 3:2) and his thoughts on whatsoever is pleasing to God (Phil. 4:8) or concentrate his efforts on a task long enough to accomplish anything substantial for God.

Providing a structured learning experience for the student requires that the teacher be well disciplined himself. He must have definite goals for the students and establish policies and procedures for reaching these goals. He must translate these goals into daily objectives supported by careful lesson plans. In systematizing the student's learning experience he should not commit himself to his plans so absolutely as to prevent adjustments to extenuating circumstances or to ignore unique teachable moments when they occur. Good teachers, like good preachers, remain flexible within their organizational scheme and sometimes depart from it altogether. There is, however, a vast difference between purposeful digression from a plan and the meandering that bespeaks the lack of a plan. A teacher who does not set a personal example of disciplined conduct—who conducts his class randomly and without forethought and who is not punctual in returning student work—can hardly lead his students to a disciplined habit of life. His own behavior undercuts the effect of the structured learning environment on student growth in Christ.

Protective

Christian education, like secular education, excludes the elements that hinder the fulfillment of its purpose. The Christian learning environment can no more tolerate alien elements than can the secular learning environment. Just as secular education censors according to its educational aims—excluding, for example, materials that affirm traditional family roles—so Christian education censors according to its aims, excluding all that would hinder the student's growth in godliness.

Secular educationists, quite inconsistently, condemn Christian schools for conducting education in a hothouse environment. The hothouse comparison is, however, an excellent analogy for the Christian educational setting. Students, like young plants, are placed in a secluded, artificially controlled environment for a certain phase of their growth. They will not stay there forever. But their present artificial surroundings will enable them to be more successful—more productive and disease-resistant—when they are transplanted into the world. Hothouse plants are universally preferred by gardeners for their greater beauty, strength, and fruitfulness. The analogy is, moreover, an ancient one. It appears in the word *seminary,* which literally denotes a seedbed for young plants. Christian educators see the wisdom of this Biblical, and ancient, concept and provide a protective atmosphere for the cultivation of youth in the knowledge and imitation of God.

The fact that the setting of Christian education separates the student from hindrances to his growth in Christ does not, however, mean that it excludes all reflections of his sinful environment. The Biblical teacher, like the Bible itself, is a guide to the student's present and future environment—physical, cultural, moral, and religious. In fact, he uses the Bible to interpret the elements of this environment for the student and to train him to shun the evil and embrace the good. The student learns to "prove all things" and "hold fast that which is good" (I Thess. 5:21). The image of God in redeemed man—Christ-likeness—includes moral understanding, and moral understanding requires an awareness not only of good but also of evil and "the end thereof" (Prov. 14:12). Those who are spiritually "of full age" are "those who by reason of use have their senses exercised to discern both good and evil" (Heb. 5:14).

In communicating to the student moral understanding, the Christian teacher follows the general method of the Scriptures: precept and example. His examples, like those of the Scriptures, are both positive and negative. The writers of the Old Testament historical books, Proverbs, the Gospels, and the New Testament epistles state with precision and emphasis the commandments of God and reinforce them with abundant examples both of right behavior and of behavior we must shun. The Israelite parent was charged with instructing his children in the commandments of God and in his nation's past, a past replete with negative as well as positive examples of Israel's obedience (Deut. 4:1-9; 9:7). To exclude either the positive or the negative example from the Christian educational experience is to depart from the pedagogical model of Scripture.

For this reason, the Christian teacher explains evolution to the students—as a theory and not a fact—showing its error and its moral and spiritual consequences. He condemns the contemporary attack on the home (by, for example, advocates of the "rights" movements, unisex lifestyle, and sexual permissiveness), showing its terrible consequences on the individual and society. At times and in ways suitable to the maturity of the student he warns him not to allow Satan to get control of any of his divinely bestowed gifts or faculties—his sexual nature, his intellectual curiosity, his aesthetic judgment and preferences. All the while he holds up to the student the beauty and wholesomeness of the good.

A Christian education patterned on the Scriptures thus includes commendation of good and condemnation of evil. It is a carefully directed sifting experience in which the student learns to recognize and react in a Christian way to elements, both good and evil, that form his cultural environment. Though he must never consider himself completely immune to the evils against which he has been fortified (I Cor. 10:12), he cannot be easily deceived by them and has been trained to respond to them in a godly way. Christian education undertakes to prepare those who are not of the world to live safely and productively in the world, thus fulfilling Christ's prayer to the Father (John 17:15).

Christian
Educational Methods

An educational methodology implies methods, but the two are not the same. Educational methods are instructional techniques and processes used to facilitate learning. A methodology is "a body of methods, rules, and postulates employed by a discipline" (*Webster's New Collegiate Dictionary,* 8th edition). As "a body of methods" with its rationale and controlling principles, a methodology expresses a philosophical point of view. The methodology of secular education expresses a humanistic view of man and his needs. The methodology of Christian education expresses a Biblical view of the human condition. Its methods are instrumental to the purpose of Christian education: to develop redeemed man in the image of God. The postulates of Christian educational methodology are concisely stated in Chapter 1 and Chapter 2. The present discussion therefore focuses on Christian educational methods.

First, we must clarify what we mean by a method. A method should be distinguished from a material, which is the physical vehicle of a method, and from a teaching strategy, which is a combination of methods designed for a specific instructional purpose. Virtually all instructional techniques and processes commonly in use are varieties of a few basic methods. These methods are exemplified in the Scriptures. Some of them, like discussion and question-and-answer, have been avoided by Christian educators because they have been harnessed to the purposes of secular-humanistic education. They have appeared as parts of teaching strategies that have been found destructive of Christian character and

Methodology

("a body of methods, rules, and postulates employed by a discipline")

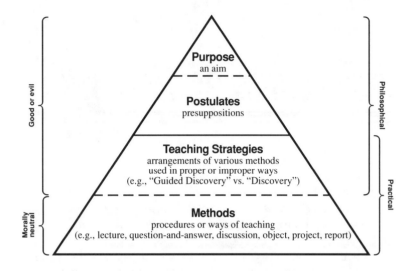

belief, and therefore the methods themselves have been rejected. We must be careful that in condemning a false educational philosophy or harmful teaching strategy we do not deprive ourselves of educational methods with timeless value that can increase the resources of Christian education.

If the perverse applications of these basic methods and the harmful strategies that employ them are considered methods themselves, then we must distinguish between good and bad methods. If, on the other hand, applications and strategies are considered more accurately not as methods but as perverse uses of legitimate methods, we may regard actual methods as neutral and apply judgment to the modes in which they appear and to the strategies and methodologies of which they are a part (see diagram). In either case we are exercising Biblical discrimination. In the latter case, however, we are less likely to go astray.

Criteria of Selection

Christian education, in selecting its means, looks to the Bible for a pattern of teaching that is spiritually and pedagogically sound. From the Bible it derives both its principles and its pedagogical model.

Spiritual soundness

Since Christian education aims at Biblical belief, its means must be conducive to belief in Biblical certainties. The use of open-ended questions, or even of open-ended discussion that fails to resolve the issues raised, conflicts with the purpose of establishing Biblical belief. It encourages the notion that mature persons work out their own solutions to life's problems and do not expect to arrive at final answers to most serious questions. The effect is to undermine faith in the Bible as a sufficient guide to the problems of human existence. Therefore, these perverse applications of the question-and-answer and discussion methods should be avoided. Biblical teaching gives answers and solutions and implants convictions. It does more than just activate minds.

To encourage Biblical beliefs, the means of Christian education must give clear direction to the student. They do not leave the student "free" to find his own way, implying thereby that there is no right way. The so-called discovery method—actually a strategy combining various methods—has a legitimate role. This approach, used by Christ in the parables, capitalizes on a student's God-given curiosity by providing for his personal recognition of truth. The world, however, has devised its own version of this teaching strategy, causing the student to pursue a relatively uncharted course—a personal adventure—through an ill-defined set of experiences in order to arrive at his own version of the way things are or ought to be. It presupposes the subjectivity of human perception and the ultimate unknowability of the human environment. The "discoveries" of the disciples were not merely private perceptions but the responses of prepared minds to the revelation of truth by God. The suspense preceding their full recognition of this truth aided their retention of it. Learning that follows the example of Christ's disciples is teacher-directed and structured so as to result in Biblical convictions.

Since Christian education aims beyond establishing belief to inspiring a life of fruitful service, Christian educational means are conducive to the development of a trained Christian servant. From some educational sources comes the notion that learning should be fun. There is, of course, no virtue in making learning as painful and tedious as possible. Learning should never become the dreary business that some traditional education has been in the past. There is an inborn pleasure in learning, and a good teacher knows how to spur his students to their best efforts by praise and by appealing to their sense of accomplishment, as well as by a judicious use of pleasurable devices of motivation. Still, substantial learning normally requires effort, sometimes of a taxing and painful sort. It is so ordained of God. Sustained effort can have a disciplining effect on a student's character and can help a student realize that solid achievement generally requires hard work. A method should not be chosen simply because it requires intense effort; there is enough difficulty inherent in genuine learning without increasing the student's burden unnecessarily. But a method should not, on the other hand, be avoided because it taxes the student. It may be the most efficient and comprehensive means of conveying a certain body of truth. If so, the purposeful expenditure of effort can help prepare the student to accomplish difficult tasks for Christ.

The goal of Christian service can be hindered but also well served by another teaching strategy favored by worldly educators: learning by doing. Secular education emphasizes ''useful'' knowledge—knowledge that makes a child useful to society—and conceives of education as a process of social adjustment. As a result, the learning experience tends to become one of exploration and experimentation in which the child is conditioned to proper behavior and attitudes by trial and error and is said to succeed in an area of study when he has worked through to his own solutions of the problems it raises. As an expression of relativistic, pragmatic educational philosophy and as a vehicle of modern social engineering, learning-by-doing, like the "discovery method," is a destructive tool for undermining belief in certainties and encouraging rebellious self-assertion. In restricting learning to that which the child can act out in a present situation, it errs also in not taking into account that knowledge can be stored up for future use and that learning can be justified by its future as well as its present relevancy. A potentially legitimate teaching strategy, specially designed to serve an evil purpose, is an extension of an evil methodology and an expression of an evil philosophy of education. However, the methods it employs existed long before they were taken up and exploited by secular-humanistic education. Christ taught His disciples not only by His words and by His own example but also by having them put into practice what they had heard and seen. On more than one occasion He sent them out, two by two, on preaching missions. The experience was for their learning, not only for the good they could do. Their learning experience was not, however, unstructured or self-directed. They were told what to take with them, what to do, and how to conduct themselves in the event of apparent failure. When they returned, they reported to their teacher and received further instruction on the basis of their experience (Matt. 10:1-42; Luke 10:1-20). Christian educational institutions recognize the value of having students participate in preaching and witnessing activities. These activities have great educational value when the students are carefully prepared and directed and when their experience is thoughtfully analyzed in the light of Biblical purpose and principles. Learning by doing is essential to preparing the Christian student to serve God most effectively in later life. The alternative is learning by unguided experience—a slow, painful, and costly process, resulting in much waste of time and resources and in heavy casualties.

It should be clear that the spiritual soundness of a method depends on how it is used and on the degree to which it is emphasized rather than on its inherent qualities. Just as different methods have different educational properties, they lend themselves to different kinds of misuse. One would not wish to discard the lecture method because it is used so effectively in brainwashing. Christian education therefore distinguishes between the legitimate form and use of a method and its misuse by secular-humanistic education. The criterion of spiritual soundness rightly makes the Christian educator wary of imitating the means of secular education. It also requires that he consider whether the evil of an educational method or strategy is due to its nature or to its misuse as an expression of an evil educational philosophy and that he not arbitrarily reject a means that has potential for developing Christian students in the image of God.

Pedagogical soundness

Though spiritual soundness is the most important criterion for evaluating educational means, it is not in itself sufficient. A method or combination of methods must be judged also by its ability to produce the desired learning—whether this learning is of a set of facts, a skill, a habit, an attitude, or a quality of personality or spiritual character. The best methods for a particular type of learning are those that have the greatest power, efficiency, and appropriateness and that, together, show a proper concern for variety.

Power—Various methods are suitable to various types and levels of learning. Those methods should be preferred that induce the necessary degree of mastery and motivate most strongly. Some methods, such as the visual object, excel in arousing interest and serving as a springboard for discussion, which in turn may be the prelude to an extended, systematic explanation in the style of a lecture. The lecture in itself can hardly engage and focus the students' minds with the same power as can the object or even the discussion. The discussion cannot develop the points with the same precision and thoroughness as can the lecture, and the object alone is not likely to answer the questions it raises. Each method excels in its own realm. In working together they enhance the power of one another, and their impact in concert is greater than it would be were they employed separately. Methods should be chosen for their power in performing specific functions in a particular pedagogical strategy.

Efficiency—The consideration of the efficiency of a method or a set of methods must qualify the consideration of its power. Time is an important commodity in the classroom. One cannot devote many days to field trips to learn how cloth is made or how squirrels prepare for winter (though direct observation, when carefully structured, has undeniable value). Some methods waste time when mishandled. Homework assignments should not take more time than the necessary degree of learning requires. Poorly conceived and directed projects can waste hours of student, and parental, time. The teacher must consider economy not only of the student's time but also of his effort. Unrelieved lecturing is economical of class time but not of student effort. Although a degree of effort is normally essential to the mastery of any subject, there is no merit to taxing students unnecessarily, especially when weak students under the best of circumstances may have to struggle to learn the material.

Economy of time and effort of the teacher and of the institution is a secondary but necessary consideration. Sometimes a method that enables the students to learn with the greatest ease and rapidity is difficult, time-consuming, and costly to implement.

The teacher and the administrator must be good stewards of their personal and institutional time and resources if they are to serve the student most effectively. In short, the principle of efficiency dictates that methods be no more demanding of the student, teacher, and institution than their value warrants and that they be used strategically and to a suitable degree.

Appropriateness—A method may have acceptable power and efficiency and yet be poor in appropriateness to a certain subject. It may simplify a subject to the point that a student has difficulties with it at a more advanced stage of study. It may cheapen a subject so that the student has difficulty taking it seriously thereafter. Some songs written for young persons are frivolous in their representations of Christ, heaven, sin, and Satan. Lilting music with flippant words is a poor means of conveying truths of great seriousness. Christian pictorial illustration must be handled with judiciousness and spiritual sensitivity if it is to reinforce spiritual content. Of course, some simplification is necessary in almost all teaching, and gaiety helps to enliven a dull subject. A method must, however, be instrumental to the specific type of learning it is supporting, and its effect must not conflict with the general functions of Christian education.

Variety—A master teacher, like a master musician, commands a wide range of approaches and techniques. He draws on a rich accumulation of methods and materials in designing his teaching strategies, just as an organist varies the stop settings on his instrument according to the requirements of the music he is performing. All teachers need a variety of methods in order to respond properly to differences in subjects, situations, and student abilities. Christ did not limit Himself to one or two methods of teaching. He knew the uniqueness of each person's circumstances and characteristics (John 2:24-25) and chose His methods of teaching on the basis of His purpose for the particular person or group of persons at the particular time. Even when He healed, He did not repeat His methods; the need of the recipient, not the universality of the method, was of primary importance. The Lord healed one blind man simply by speaking to him (Mark 10:46-52). He healed another partially (so that he could see men as trees walking) before healing him completely (Mark 8:22-26). On another occasion He used mud made with saliva to restore a man's sight (John 9:1-7). Christian teachers emulate the Master Teacher in developing a variety of methods suitable to a diversity of individual needs and circumstances and to differences in types of content. A variety of methods is especially important for teaching subjects that are difficult to grasp and students who have limited ability or maturity.

Financial limitations may restrict the use of some methods of proven value. If an institution cannot afford costly electronic equipment, it can still engage in the activity of Christian education. It should not, however, make a virtue out of its necessity and rationalize that audiovisual methods in general and the electronic media in particular are somehow subversive to genuine Biblical learning. God is not honored when our principles follow our practice and our practice is the result of what we perceive to be the necessities of our situation. It is true that some education and communications theory tends to emphasize the electronic media above the printed word and to regard the transmission of the message through audiovisual means as more important than the message itself. The sense experience indeed becomes the message. Christian educators of course reject this educational methodology and communications philosophy. But the audiovisual method itself is very old. In the Bible God's teaching of man appealed to the whole gamut of the senses. Ezekiel, in his vision, was told, "Son of man, behold with thine eyes, and hear with thine ears, and set thine heart upon all that I shall shew thee" (Ezek. 40:4). One of Christ's disciples, many years after the ascension of his Master, expressed the power of the auditory, visual, and tactile methods in His teaching: "That which was from the beginning, which we have heard, which we have seen with our eyes, which we have looked upon, and our hands have handled, of the Word of life; . . . that which we have seen and heard declare we unto you" (I John 1:1-3). Multiple methods have a cumulative clinching effect. Any method or set of methods used exclusively and constantly tends to become educationally sterile. Teachers should, as much as possible, combine diverse methods for maximum comprehension, retention, and application of truth by the students.

Some Common Methods

Some Christian educators hold that the only Biblical methods are lecture, drill, recitation, memorization, and repetition, since these may be readily found in the Bible. However, the Bible contains examples of more types of methods than these or others commonly cited. In the ministry of Christ Himself we may find methods analogous to those generally in use today in both Christian and secular education. We are not bound to imitate the exact strategies that Christ used so effectively, for the exact circumstances that elicited them may no longer exist. From the outdoor setting of Christ's parable of the fig tree we need not infer that Christian teaching should frequently be conducted out-of-doors in an agricultural setting, though the fact that the Lord thus taught makes it impossible to rule out such a setting. We do, however, infer from it the value of the visual object in teaching and of the use of materials that are familiar and near at hand.

In their totality Christ's methods exhibit great variety, and His approaches utilizing these methods exhibit great flexibility. From the great diversity of His methods we do not, however, deduce that all uses of such methods are acceptable. Jesus touched many of those He dealt with in His ministry (Matt. 8:3, 15; 9:29; 17:7; 20:34). Teachers who work with physically afflicted or mentally retarded children know that these respond to physical expressions of affection—that a hand on the shoulder or pat on the back can communicate love and concern in a way that words alone cannot do. In Christ's teaching there is, however, no semblance of justification for the sensual physical contact practiced in modern sensitivity training. Though Jesus permitted an outcast woman to touch Him—and was criticized for allowing it—He did not touch her or any other woman in a morally compromising way (Luke 7:36-39). Christian educators follow the example of Christ in distinguishing the legitimate from the nonlegitimate uses of the methods available to them.

Lecture

The lecture, which is an oral presentation of ideas by a single speaker, was employed extensively by the Lord. He lectured everywhere: in city and country, in synagogues and in the temple, on mountains and by the lake. One of His lectures fills two chapters in Matthew (24 and 25). His Sermon on the Mount takes three chapters in the same Gospel (5-7). The longest recorded lecture by Christ is His farewell to His disciples on the way to the cross (John 14-17). All of these lectures are practical, inspirational discourses which caused the people to say of His teaching, "Never man spake like this man" (John 7:46).

Like all methods, the lecture has both strengths and weaknesses. For a large group that needs specific information, it is an ideal means for communicating that content precisely and fully. It can be formal or informal as the need requires and lends itself to combination with other methods. It need not be abstract and dull. The skilled lecturer can adapt his presentation to the needs, interests, and background of his audience. But the lecture can produce boredom if not used well; and, used alone, it tends to stifle student responsiveness since it requires students to listen more than to interact. The lecturer must rely upon visual impressions of his audience to determine whether he is communicating effectively. An exclusive use of the lecture method is not conducive to the learning of skills, attitudes, and qualities of personality important to Christian service.

Question and answer

The Lord was a master of the question-and-answer method. Though effective in leading a learner, by steps, to the truth, the question-and-answer method is especially valuable for drill and review to demonstrate to the teacher whether further information or explanation is necessary. Since this method involves the student more completely in the class experience than does the lecture, it forces him to be more active mentally. The skilled teacher can use questions to gain the attention of the class and to determine whether students are comprehending what they are being taught.

One of our first glimpses of Christ in the Gospels shows Him asking questions of the learned men at the temple (Luke 2:46). The Gospels record more than one hundred questions asked by Christ in the course of His ministry. He used questions to gain the attention of His hearers and prepare them for what He had to say (Matt. 16:13-15). He used questions to secure information from those who heard Him (Mark 10:36) and to prod His hearers to think through issues (Mark 3:1-5). He used questions to clarify or illustrate points (Mark 2:23-28), to advance arguments (Matt. 21:25), and to apply what He had taught (Luke 10:36). His questions were always purposeful and practical, never pointless or leading men to wrong conclusions or doubt.

The question-and-answer method has been misused by secular education. The student rather than the teacher becomes the judge of validity. Questions are open-ended and issues are left unresolved. They are used to elicit skepticism concerning moral values and traditional ideals and institutions. The method is employed as a means of cutting the student adrift from his moral and spiritual moorings and developing in him a spirit of skeptical open-mindedness. Its misuse is an expression of an educational philosophy and an extension of an educational methodology that acknowledge no absolute truth and provide no stable frame of reference for human thought and behavior. In Christ's teaching, this method was a means of conveying truth and continually led the student back to the Old Testament Scriptures as an infallible source of that truth. The student was not his own authority and was not left without satisfying answers once his interest was aroused.

Discussion

The Lord often combined both the lecture and question-and-answer methods with discussion. His use of this method did not conform in all points to modern educational practice, but the principles are there, especially in His conversations with such persons as the woman at the well (John 4:1-30), Nicodemus (John 3:1-21), and the rich young ruler (Mark 10:17-22). The Samaritan woman, for example, is guided step-by-step through the reciprocation of ideas toward the ultimate goal of comprehending the truth.

Legitimate discussion directs student interaction toward a predetermined goal. It encourages the student to think through the issues with which he is presented and helps to keep him actively engaged in the learning process. It should not be confused with haphazard talking that displays no plan and serves no purpose. Abused in this way, discussion is a prime tool of secular education, which ascribes inherent value to self-expression, whatever the worth of the ideas expressed. God's contempt for such discussion is conveyed in the tone of Luke's remark describing the assembly on Mars' Hill (Acts 17:21). But purposefully directed discussion is one of the best methods to enable students to advance toward the Christian educational goal of full comprehension and firm conviction.

Storytelling

The Lord commonly used storytelling, often in conjunction with one or more of the previously discussed methods, to illustrate abstract truths for His listeners. He used stories to establish the teaching situation (Matt. 13:1-9), to illuminate content previously taught (Luke 10:25-37), or to provide the core of the lesson (Luke 15). Stories thus have a legitimate place in the Christian teacher's stock of methods. They generate interest in the lesson, shed light on abstract truth, and aid retention of the points they illustrate.

Objects

Christ frequently used objects that engaged the various senses. On one occasion He used a coin to remind His detractors that they had a responsibility both to the government and to God (Matt. 22:15-22). At another time He placed a child in the midst of His hearers to teach them a lesson in humility (Matt. 18:1-10). Experience has shown that students learn more, learn faster, and retain what is learned longer when more senses than one are engaged by the teaching process.

Demonstrations, projects, and reports

Other methods employed by the Lord include demonstrations, projects, and reports. When Jesus told John's disciples to return to the doubting prophet and show him again the miracles that He was doing (Matt. 11:2-19), He was teaching through a report of demonstrations what could hardly have been taught to the prophet in any other way. One of the most impressive demonstrations of Jesus was His own act of humility when He took the towel and basin and washed the disciples' feet (John 13:1-5). To cause His disciples to learn by practice, Jesus sent them out two by two on a preaching project (Matt. 10:1-42), as we have already seen. Later when He sent out the seventy, He received them back for a report of their experiences (Luke 10:1-20), which became the basis for further instruction. Thus, the disciples learned by observation, by practice, and by the Master Teacher's review of their performance. These methods were purposefully directed and regulated so as to produce substantial learning, not employed, in the manner of some secular education, so as to give the student the impression that his own perceptions are the touchstone of truth.

Educational methods and materials may be classified according to the concreteness of the learning experience they produce. We may distinguish three levels of concreteness, each requiring a different degree of student involvement. The first and basic level is direct learning through firsthand sensory experience. When the Lord paused in a discourse to point out an instance of a specific truth that He was teaching (''Behold the fowls of the air,'' Matt. 6:26), He was recognizing the value of the first and most concrete level of learning. The second level provides vicarious learning experiences through realistic representations of reality. An object artificially selected from its environment or altered in some way as a representation of reality exemplifies this level. When the Lord ''called a little child unto Him, and set him in the midst'' of His disciples in order to represent Christian humility, He removed him from his normal activity and environment to use him as a teaching object. Jeremiah and Ezekiel frequently used objects as signs to Israel. Ezekiel on one occasion simulated the siege of Jerusalem with a piece of tile and an iron pan (Ezek. 4:1-3). The third and least concrete level communicates to the student through language or other abstract symbols. Learning through the spoken or written word is on this level since the sounds and letters employed are abstract devices used to indicate thoughts and ideas.

Christ's teaching was constantly moving back and forth between these levels. The Master Teacher used methods from them all, rarely in isolation. In Biblical history God taught His people by methods and materials from all levels: by sending fire to consume a sacrifice (level one); by their living in booths during the feast of tabernacles (level two); by the messages of the prophets and by the written law (level three).

Teaching that is most effective and that follows most closely the divine pattern recorded in the Scriptures draws its methods and materials from all three levels. It takes advantage of modern technology just as Jesus took advantage of Peter's boat (Luke 5:1-3). The electronic age has enhanced the teacher's resources for both the concrete and abstract representation of reality, and electronic teaching devices need no more be spurned by the Christian teacher than the electronic communications media need be rejected by the Christian preacher. The utilization of a wide array of instructional resources by the teacher results in richer learning and greater retention by the student and in fuller support of his development in the image of Christ.

Christian Educational Censorship

Educational censorship remains one of the most controversial issues in public life, linked as it is to political censorship and freedom of the press. The issue is sometimes posed as if it were only religious conservatives who insist on moral controls and apply arbitrary standards in excluding uncongenial elements. Nothing could be further from the truth. Secularist educators, no less than Christian, censor according to their educational aims.

These aims are moral and religious in nature as much as intellectual. To exclude racism, sexism, and all religious coloration from secular teaching and materials is as serious a goal and as holy a cause in the progressive agenda as to develop the child in the image of God is in the Christian educational program. Mark Twain's *Huckleberry Finn* is censored in some school districts today for its alleged racism whereas it was censored in conservative schools a century ago for its religious cynicism. The reason is obvious. The shape of the curriculum will affect the shape of society in a nation with universal compulsory education.

Censorship, therefore, whether in Christian or secular schools, is inescapable. Every thoughtful teacher makes choices according to criteria devised to implement specific course objectives, which in turn reflect general educational goals. More and more in public schools, these choices are being made for him. The general goals of public education reflect a liberal social agenda that has moral content antagonistic to Christian belief and traditional values. Recent textbook controversies make clear the determination of the liberal educational establishment not to relax its grip on the content of public education. The issue is not whether to censor but what.

The issue of what to censor not only separates Christian educators from secular but also divides Christian educators themselves. Though united in purpose, they may differ in what they deem appropriate methods and materials for accomplishing their purpose. Is the traditional curriculum in literature compatible with or a betrayal of Christian educational goals and standards? Can Christian students be rendered ''culturally literate'' without compromising the spiritual objectives of Christian education? These are questions that conscientious Christian teachers and administrators wrestle with. Not only must they justify their decisions to themselves; they must be able to defend them to inquiring parents, pastors, and lay leaders of the church and, perhaps eventually, to civil authorities.

Beleaguered by doubts and conflicting advice, the Christian teacher or administrator turns to Scripture for standards he can confidently apply and uphold. The Bible itself is the most important textbook in the Christian educational curriculum. It not only contains the most important information for the student but also provides a pattern for the instruction. Other textbooks are Christian to the extent they reflect and conform to this spiritual and pedagogical model. Classroom teaching is Christian to the extent that it emulates the objectives, approaches, and methods of the Scriptures.

The Bible speaks of itself when it says, ''Every word of God is pure'' (Prov. 30:5) and ''Thy word is very pure'' (Ps. 119:140). Every part of Scripture is free of that which is in conflict with or extraneous to its purpose. The Christian teacher, led by the same Spirit that inspired God's Holy Word, will scrutinize prayerfully his methods and materials to ensure that they likewise are free of that which hinders and diverts from his purpose: the conforming of his students to the image of God in Christ. He will censor for the sake of his students and, in the case of the materials he uses, ascertain whether the necessary censoring has been done by the authors or may otherwise be done by himself.

Censorable elements

In order to do his job of censoring in a Biblical way, the teacher will need to be aware of the common categories of censorable elements.

1. Profanity (blasphemy whether in statements or epithets; all sacrilege)
2. Scatological realism (specific references to excrement or to the excremental functions)
3. Erotic realism (specific references to physical love between the sexes)
4. Sexual perversion (the portrayal of any sexual relationship or activity—such as adultery, fornication, homosexuality, or incest—other than that which is sanctified by God in marriage)
5. Lurid violence
6. Occultism (Satanism, witchcraft, necromancy, astrology, fortunetelling, and the like; a representation of the supernatural powers that oppose God in a way that fascinates the reader or implies the existence of a supernatural order other than the Biblical one)
7. Erroneous religious or philosophical assumptions (un-Biblical root ideas or attitudes expressed overtly or covertly, explicitly or implicitly, in theme, tone, or atmosphere; these appear, for example, when a writer invents a fictional world in which no divine presence is felt or in which no moral order is perceptible.)

It is not difficult to spot the censorable elements of categories 1-6 and to miss the often subtler and more dangerous elements of category 7. The practical atheism and antiestablishmentarian attitude of Mark Twain's character Huck Finn, the pantheistic mysticism of Wordsworth and Thoreau, the naturalistic thesis of Stephen Crane's ''The Open Boat,'' and the melancholy pessimism of A. E. Housman's lyric poems would appear safe enough in terms of criteria based on only the first six categories. Unfortunately, it is the un-Biblical premises of a work that are taken least seriously in discussions of censorable elements and in the formulation of policy concerning them. This category, like the others, requires serious attention.

Positions on censorable elements

Those who discuss classroom censorship tend to adopt either of two diametrically opposed positions. Each position, by its deficiencies, fortifies the other. A third position results from the first two. All require examination in the light of the Biblical standard.

The **permissivist** view is common among evangelical intellectuals. It is what one might expect to find in an article in *Christianity Today* or in booklets published by Intervarsity Press. Those who hold this view allow at least a degree of the censorable on either of two bases: (1) the existence in a work of compensating aesthetic qualities; (2) the necessity in art of an honest view of life. These constitute what the courts have called "redeeming social value." The weakness of the first criterion is apparent in the uncertainty that has characterized the history of court rulings on censorship. It is too subjective and utilitarian to be an adequate guide for Christians. It requires a judge who, though ignorant himself concerning the aesthetic merits of a work, is competent to identify expert witnesses who are knowledgeable and impartial. His problem is complicated by the circumstance that aesthetic values nowadays tend to be subjective and relativistic, easily affected by extraneous considerations. The aesthetic criterion in censorship rests not on absolute moral principles, which Biblical ethics requires, but on the toleration of the social community.

The second criterion—the necessity in literature of an honest imitation of life—is the standard defense by modern writers of the sordid and salacious elements in their fiction. But ideas of the world and of life vary widely. Every serious secular novelist invents fictional worlds that vindicate his moral and religious preferences. Moral libertines nurture private world views that justify and reinforce their licentious lifestyles. Even were there an accurate, Biblical consensus of the nature of life and the world, it could hardly be maintained that literature, while imitating reality, need include all of reality. The Bible speaks of some realities we are to flee (I Tim. 6:11; II Tim. 2:22). Moral considerations must override the aesthetic and mimetic in a Christian's perspective on literature and life. That which threatens the moral and spiritual life cannot be justified on other grounds. Permissivism arrogantly elevates human wisdom above divine.

The **exclusivist** view is held by conscientious pastors, Christian educators, and laymen concerned for the moral preservation of their children and for the moral wholesomeness of their communities. They reason that, because evil is evil, any avoidable exposure to it is wrong for even the most praiseworthy of purposes. It follows, they argue, that one should avoid any work of literature or discard any element of the curriculum that contains any amount of any of these elements. A few hold as a corollary that, since the Bible is a sufficient guide in all important matters of life and since there is peril in other reading, we *ought* not to read anything else.

Our spiritual affinities are with these who hold the exclusivist position, and our sympathies must be also. They are the ones with the sensitive consciences, the zeal for what is pleasing to God, the vigilance toward the moral erosion of society. But they should consider the implications of their position. To reject a work of literature or subject of study because of the presence of any amount of these elements within it is, first, to apply a standard that precludes the possibility of a liberal arts education. We forego the major works of Shakespeare, Spenser, Pope, Swift, Wordsworth, Tennyson, Browning, Hawthorne, Melville, Clemens, Frost, and almost every other standard writer. We do not teach the *Declaration of Independence,* for its arguments are based on the secularist idea of natural rights. Even Bunyan's *Pilgrim's Progress* is suspect, for the key to the outer gate (the iron gate) of Doubting Castle, Bunyan tells us, turned "damnable hard." (Bunyan, of course, meant "able to damn," but he must also have been punning.)

Now if eschewing evil requires foregoing a liberal arts education even in a Christian educational environment, then so be it. No human educational values should be allowed to compete with spiritual. However, we recall that "Moses was learned in all the wisdom of the Egyptians" (Acts 7:22). Paul, we know, had the learning of the Greeks, for quotations and echoes of pagan writers appear here and there in his epistles. He knew Greek poetry well enough to quote from memory the minor poets Aratus and Epimenides of Crete on Mars Hill. Furthermore, of Daniel and his three friends we are told that "God gave them knowledge and skill in all learning and wisdom" (Dan. 1:17). Evidently, in these cases, the divine preparation for leadership included familiarization with the writings not only of the inspired authors of the Scriptures but also of the poets, scientists, and philosophers of pagan intellectual and literary traditions. The exclusivist view, if consistently held, condemns the manner in which God conducted the preparation of these great men of Scripture or implies that God did not approve of it.

An even more serious implication of the exclusivist position is that it precludes the reading of some portions of the Scriptures themselves. Elements of all seven categories of censorable elements appear in certain ways and to certain degrees in the Bible. The following list is illustrative, by no means exhaustive:

1. Profanity: "Say we not well that thou art a Samaritan, and hast a devil?" (John 8:48)
2. Scatological realism: Rabshakeh's coarse language (Isa. 36:12)
3. Erotic realism: Proverbs 5:18-19; Ezekiel 23:20-21; and passages in the Song of Solomon
4. Sexual perversion: the sin of Sodom (Gen. 19); the seduction of Joseph (Gen. 39); the rape of Tamar (II Sam. 13); the liaison in Proverbs 7
5. Lurid violence: Joab's murder of Amasa (II Sam. 20)
6. Occultism: Saul's dealing in necromancy (I Sam. 28:7-25)
7. Religious and philosophical assumptions: the misrepresentation of God by Job's three friends (though in no pervasive sense can such assumptions affect any large portion of Scripture)

Obviously the exclusivist view, consistently held, puts the Bible in conflict with itself and lays its advocates open to charges of self-contradiction.

The exclusivist position is based on a misconstruction or misapplication of certain passages of Scripture. We need to deal briefly with each one.

1. "I will set no wicked thing before mine eyes" (Ps. 101:3). This resolution of David may refer to an idol or to some evil device or scheme. It certainly does not refer to all representation of evil, for David read the stories of moral failure in the Pentateuch and, in his capacity as judge, had to scrutinize wrongdoing continually. The sins described in the Bible— for example, David's own adultery with Bathsheba—are wicked, but the descriptions of them in Scripture are not wicked. The examples of Scripture, both positive and negative, are good in the sense that they are "written for our learning" (Rom. 15:4). "All scripture . . . is profitable" (II Tim. 3:16), even the parts that reveal most vividly the depths of human degradation. What is represented is evil, but the representation of the evil is valuable for Christian moral understanding and is, therefore, good.

2. "I would have you wise unto that which is good, and simple concerning evil" (Rom. 16:19). The Greek word here translated "simple" is translated "harmless" in Matthew 10:16 ("Be ye therefore wise as serpents, and harmless as doves") and in Philippians 2:14-15 ("Do all things without murmurings and disputings: That ye may be blameless and harmless, the sons of God, without rebuke, in the midst of a crooked and perverse nation"). Paul's command echoes a passage in Jeremiah in which the prophet complains of Israel, "They are wise to do evil, but to do good they have no knowledge" (4:22). Elsewhere Paul admonishes believers, "Brethren, be not children in understanding: howbeit in malice be ye children, but in understanding be men" (I Cor. 14:20). The meaning of these passages is clearly that the believer should be clever in ways to do good rather than cunning in ways to do harm. On the other hand, believers should not be "children . . . , in understanding." One of the meanings of *simple* at the time the KJV was translated was, in fact, "harmless," and the KJV translators followed Wycliffe in using it in this sense in this verse. The Bible puts no premium on moral ignorance.

3. "But fornication, and all uncleanness, or covetousness, let it not be once named among you, as becometh saints; Neither filthiness, nor foolish talking, nor jesting, which are not convenient: but rather giving of thanks" (Eph. 5:3-4). Evidently Paul does not mean that such sins as fornication and covetousness should never be mentioned at all, for he has just spoken of them himself, as do the other writers of the Scripture. Mentioning these and other sins is necessary if the preacher is to "reprove, rebuke, exhort with all longsuffering and doctrine" (II Tim. 4:2). Every pastor or parent must mention specific sins by name if he is to fulfill his responsibility to God for those under his care. Paul here, as in Romans 2:24, is insisting that the conduct of God's people give no occasion for these sins to be named *as existing* among them. Their conduct should give cause for thanksgiving rather than for gossip and reproach.

4. "Abstain from all appearance of evil" (I Thess. 5:22). The commandment has been interpreted in two ways. The first is that one avoid giving any appearance or impression of evil doing. The believer's conduct must be above suspicion and

give no occasion to those who would wish to find fault. Paul gives the same command in Romans 12:17 ("Provide things honest in the sight of all men") and in II Corinthians 8:21. Daniel's life was such that his enemies could find no pretext for condemning him in any way to the king. The Bible stresses the importance of reputation as well as of moral character. The more likely interpretation, however, is that one abstain from every form or manifestation of evil. The commandment completes the preceding verse. We are to "prove [test] all things," adhering to "that which is good" and abstaining from all that is evil. One must encounter a phenomenon before he can test it and distinguish the good from the bad.

5. "Finally, brethren, whatsoever things are true, whatsoever things are honest, whatsoever things are just, whatsoever things are pure, whatsoever things are lovely, whatsoever things are of good report; if there be any virtue, and if there be any praise, think on these things" (Phil. 4:8). This grand prescription for mental, moral, and spiritual health expresses the principle that dwelling on good will help to drive out evil. The believer's main subject of meditation should be the Scriptures—for blessing (Ps. 1:2) but also for protection (Prov. 6:20-24). The Biblical commands to center one's mental life on the Scriptures do not exclude those passages in which evil is described, often graphically. On the contrary, those passages, Paul says, were intended to be pondered as negative examples (I Cor. 10:1-14). The Bible uses both positive and negative examples to enforce its message. Good literature does also. A person whose mind has been fortified by such examples against the evil in his moral environment will be better able to live in that environment with his mind focused on the things of God.

More than four centuries ago, William Tyndale, arguing for the common man's ability to make use of Scripture, addressed the issue of the questionable elements in Scripture:

All the Scripture is either the promises and testament of God in Christ, and stories pertaining thereunto, to strengthen thy faith; either [or] the law, and stories pertaining thereto, to fear thee from evil doing. There is no story nor gest [narrative account], seem it never so simple or so vile unto the world, but that thou shalt find therein spirit and life and edifying in the literal sense: for it is God's Scripture, written for thy learning and comfort. There is no clout or rag there, that hath not precious relics wrapt therein of faith, hope, patience and long suffering, and of the truth of God, and also of his righteousness. Set before thee the story of Reuben, which defiled his father's bed. Mark what a cross God suffered to fall on the neck of his elect Jacob. Consider first the shame among the heathen, when as yet there was no more of the whole world within the testament of God, but he and his household. . . . Look what ado he had at the defiling of his daughter Dinah. . . . Mark what followed Reuben, to fear other, that they shame not their fathers and mothers. He was cursed and lost the kingdom, and also the priestdom, and his tribe or generation was ever few in number, as it appeareth in the stories of the Bible.

The adultery of David with Bathsheba is an ensample, not to move us to evil; but, if (while we follow the way of righteousness) any chance drive us aside, that we despair not. For if we saw not such infirmities in God's elect, we, which are so weak and fall so oft, should utterly despair, and think that God had clean forsaken us. It is therefore a sure and an undoubted conclusion, whether we be holy or unholy, we are all sinners. But the difference is, that God's sinners consent not to their sin. They consent unto the law that is both holy and righteous, and mourn to have their sin taken away. . . .

Likewise in the homely gest of Noe, when he was drunk, and lay in his tent with his privy members open, hast thou great edifying in the literal sense. Thou seest what became of the cursed children of wicked Ham, which saw his father's privy members, and jested thereof unto his brethren. Thou seest also what blessing fell on Shem and Japhet, which went backward and covered their father's members, and saw them not. And thirdly, thou seest what infirmity accompanieth God's elect, be they never so holy, which yet is not imputed unto them: for the faith and trust they have in God swalloweth up all their sins. *[Obedience of a Christian Man]*

The **pragmatic** position is held by those who, acknowledging God's standards to be absolute, consider some compromise to be necessary if one is to get along in a fallen world with flawed human beings. Misapplying Paul's concession in I Corinthians

5:10, they allow some degree of exposure to the evil of this world, but not "too much." It is inevitable, they maintain, that passing on our way through the world we would pick up some dust. The pragmatist, seeing the bankruptcy of the permissive view and the impossibility of the exclusivist view, falls back on a rule-of-thumb utilitarianism that makes Christian evaluation entirely subjective. Each person must decide for himself how much evil is too much to be tolerable in a literary work or in material used in teaching. This view is perhaps theologically the weakest of all, for it implies that it is impossible to order our lives according to the will of a holy God or that God will accept from us less than His standards require. In the issue of a Christian response to the censorable in literature or in life, adopting a mean between extremes or a policy of convenience is no solution. Genuine Biblical morality is not a matter of expediency or of proportion and degree, but a matter of principle based on moral absolutes.

Fortunately there is another position, the **Biblical,** which takes the Bible itself as the supreme literary and pedagogical model. It accepts the Biblical purpose of moral education as stated in Proverbs 1:4: "To give subtilty to the simple, to the young man knowledge and discretion." It recognizes that the image of God in redeemed man—Christ-likeness—includes moral understanding and that moral understanding requires an awareness of both good and evil and "the end thereof" (Prov. 14:12). It identifies as spiritually "of full age," or mature, "those who by reason of use have their senses exercised to discern both good and evil" (Heb. 5:14).

The Biblical position adopts the pedagogical method of the Scriptures in teaching moral understanding. The Bible teaches by means of precept and example. Its examples are both positive and negative. The writers of the Old Testament enunciate emphatically the commandments of God and reinforce them with many examples of right behavior and many more of behavior to be shunned. They associate good or evil consequences with good or evil behavior. New Testament writers draw on these examples, positive and negative, for encouragement and warning.

The Lord Himself made full use of negative examples in His teaching and preaching, citing the degeneracy of Sodom (Matt. 11:23), Cain's slaying of Abel (Matt. 23:35), the debauchery of

Noah's generation (Matt. 24:38), and many other instances of wickedness. Paul's warnings to the Corinthians run nearly the full gamut of human depravity, including incest (I Cor. 5:1) and homosexuality (I Cor. 6:9), referring to active homosexuals in "abusers of themselves with mankind," passive in "effeminate." We regard these accounts of wickedness in the same way that the New Testament writers regarded those recorded in the Old Testament: as "ensamples" given to us for our profit (I Cor. 10:11; II Pet. 2:6). Clearly, to exclude the negative example from the Christian educational experience is to depart from the pedagogical method of Scripture.

Does this mean that we must accept in our reading and include in our teaching the full range and extent of the censorable that the permissivist would allow? Not at all. Following the standard of Scripture controls our choice and handling of material in a way that most pragmatists, let alone permissivists, would find over-restrictive. Though defense attorneys in pornography cases can point to portions of the English Bible that seem to violate the Bible's own admonitions concerning preserving the purity of the mind, the Bible is in reality completely self-consistent and purposeful in its presentation of evil. Evil is represented in the Bible in certain ways, for certain purposes, and with certain effects. Understanding the Biblical manner of representing evil is a far surer and more workable guide for the conscientious Christian parent or educator than the subjective criteria and arbitrary lists conceived by some conservative moralists, well-intentioned as they may be.

The basis of a truly Biblical position concerning censorable elements is the following distinction. If a work of literature or other element of the curriculum treats evil in the same way that it is treated in the Scriptures, we regard it as not only acceptable but also desirable reading, listening, or viewing for someone of sufficient maturity as to benefit from comparable portions of the Scriptures (with the qualification that visual or auditory effects are more potent than those of reading). If it does not treat evil in the way evil is handled in the Scriptures, its content is not good. Evil in the Bible appears dangerous and repulsive. Reflections of evil appear in the Bible in the form of negative examples so as to create a defense against what they represent or to give hope to the fallen for forgiveness and recovery from sin.

Criteria of worth

We may draw three criteria from the Scriptures for judging literary and other works with respect to their content.

1. Is the representation of evil purposeful or is it present for its own sake? This is the criterion of **gratuitousness.** We know that "all scripture is given by inspiration of God, and is profitable for doctrine, for reproof, for correction, for instruction in righteousness: That the man of God may be perfect, throughly furnished unto all good works" (II Tim. 3:16-17). Nothing in the Scriptures is superfluous or irrelevant to this high spiritual purpose.

2. Is the representation of evil, if purposeful, present in an acceptable degree? Or is it more conspicuous or vivid than the purpose warrants? This is the criterion of **explicitness.** No one with a high view of Scripture would charge it with inappropriateness or excessiveness in its representation of evil. The presentation of evil in the Bible is realistic enough to convince us of its threat as a temptation but not so realistic as to become for us a temptation. Some sins are referred to but not enacted in the text.

3. Is evil presented from a condemning perspective? Is it made to appear both dangerous and repulsive? What is the attitude of the work toward it? This is the criterion of **moral tone.** "Woe unto them that call evil good, and good evil," says the Lord through the prophet Isaiah (Isa. 5:20). A good work of literature does not glorify human weakness or encourage tolerance of sin. It allows evil to appear in a controlled way in order to develop in the reader or hearer a resistance against it. In literature, "vice," wrote Samuel Johnson, "must always disgust." Its purpose is to initiate the reader through "mock encounters" with evil so that evil cannot later deceive him—so that he will be better able to maintain a pure life in a fallen world.

These three criteria are complementary. None is alone sufficient to justify the censorable in a work of literature or another element of the curriculum. Together they work powerfully, because they work Biblically, to preserve moral purity while providing for a developing moral understanding and judgment.

Let us consider how some censorable elements in Shake-speare's plays appear in the light of these criteria. One of the most violent scenes in English Renaissance drama, and one of the most violent in all dramatic literature, occurs in act three of *King Lear,* when the duke of Gloucester, loyal to King Lear, is charged with helping him escape and is cruelly punished. The cruelty takes place on stage in full view of the audience. Gloucester is tied to a chair, and hair from his beard and scalp is torn out by Lear's daughter Regan. Then her husband, the duke of Cornwall, tips the chair backward onto the floor and with his tall, narrow heel gouges out one eye and afterward the other. The scene, acted realistically, would scarcely survive the liberal television censors of today and, if so, would raise an outcry among conservative viewers. Why did Shakespeare bring this action before the audience and not at least have it reported by a messenger as most other dramatists of his day and before would have done?

In *King Lear* Shakespeare uses parallel plots, the stories of two old men who undergo severe ordeals because of their moral imperception. Each wrongs his loyal child and favors his disloyal child or children, learning too late that he has misread their char-acters. Lear's moral blindness is the consequence of his pride. He involves his loyal daughter in a contest of flattery with her two sisters. When she refuses to participate, he disinherits her, leaving himself at the mercy of his two faithless daughters and their husbands, to whom he has ceded the kingdom. Gloucester's moral and later physical blindness derives, ultimately, from a sin of lech-ery. He has begotten an illegitimate son, who deceives him into disinheriting his legitimate son and eventually betrays him to the enemies of King Lear. Lear's sin is mental, the arch-sin of pride; and his punishment is fittingly mental: he loses, temporarily, his mind. Gloucester's sin is physical, sensuality, and his punishment appropriately is physical: he loses, permanently, his eyes. In the last scene, the loyal son remarks to his disloyal brother, whom he has mortally wounded:

The gods are just, and of our pleasant vices
Make instruments to plague us.
The dark and vicious place where thee he got [begot]
Cost him his eyes.

Both plots depict the unforeseen consequences of a casual, thoughtless immoral act. The audience takes the moral tally as the chickens come home to roost.

The punishment of Lear recalls God's dealing with Nebuchadnezzar, who because of his self-exaltation lost his reason and was, like Lear, turned out-of-doors to live as a beast until purged of his pride. Gloucester's punishment also has strong Biblical warrant. The aged duke has been ruled by the lust of the eyes. As he approaches the hovel in the darkness with his lantern, the fool exclaims, with double meaning, "Look, here comes a walking fire." Though the process of Gloucester's punishment is horrible, we may construe the effect as beneficent; for the Scriptures counsel, "If thy right eye offend thee [i.e., cause thee to offend], pluck it out, and cast it from thee: for it is profitable for thee that one of thy members should perish, and not that thy whole body should be cast into hell" (Matt. 5:29). Indeed Gloucester seems to understand his ordeal in this light when he acknowledges, "I stumbled when I saw." Like Samson's blinding, Gloucester's is not gratuitous, nor is it, in relation to what Shakespeare means to emphasize, overly explicit. It is part of a scheme of moral consequences, and the moral tone is clear.

In the comedy *Twelfth Night,* there is some questionable humor associated with the foolish Sir Andrew Aguecheek. Sir Andrew, unwelcome suitor of the countess Olivia, is a companion of the countess's freeloading uncle, Sir Toby Belch, and Feste, her court jester. Their enemy is Olivia's vain steward, Malvolio. Sir Andrew's surname, like *Belch* and *Malvolio,* has moral meaning. *Aguecheek* indicates the effects of syphilis, known as the pox or the French disease. Andrew's face is evidently pocked and otherwise deformed from lechery. Andrew also has the thinness of hair and the mental debility associated with the later stages of this disease. When Maria reveals her plan to humiliate Malvolio, Sir Toby exclaims, "Excellent. I smell a device." Andrew, understanding as usual only in part, sighs, "I have't in my nose too." His mental debility (evident in his construing of "device" as "vice") and physical deformity (indicated in his reference to the effects of the pox on his nasal cartilage) produce humor, but humor for a moral purpose.

For Sir Andrew is ruled by the lust of the eyes. When he first appears, he stands transfixed by the sight of Maria, Olivia's fair lady in waiting. Sir Toby, reading his mind, encourages him to "accost" her ("Accost, Sir Andrew! Accost!"), knowing full well that the word *accost* is beyond the narrow bounds of Andrew's comprehension. Andrew then addresses her, "Good Mistress Accost, I desire better acquaintance." Maria corrects him: "My name is Mary, sir." Andrew replies, "Good Mistress Mary Accost." In these passages and others, the lust of the eyes is associated, by the intermediate cause of social disease, with physical deformity and mental debility.

The vice of the rotund Sir Toby Belch, as both his name and his amplitude of girth indicate, is gluttony. This vice, one of the seven deadly sins of medieval theology, included drunkenness. Sir Toby detests moral restraints as much as he hates "an unfilled cannikin [can] of ale." He is ruled by the lust of the flesh.

Malvolio's vice is ambition. His name, *mal volio,* means "bad volition"—that is, "inordinate ambition." As Olivia's steward, Malvolio has risen as high in the household order as a commoner legitimately can. He is the chief servant, manager of Olivia's house, answerable only to the countess herself. But he is not content. He aspires to marry Olivia, to be Count Malvolio. Malvolio is ruled by the pride of life.

Each of the three characters is humorously yet purposefully degraded in the play. Each is made a fool by his vice and is punished according to the nature of his vice. The sin of Malvolio is, like Lear's, of the mind, and, like Lear, he is punished mentally. His household enemies expose him to the laughter of the court and, having confined him in a dark room, taunt him to desperation. Sir Toby's and Sir Andrew's sins, like Gloucester's are physical, and they, like Gloucester, are punished physically. At the end of the play they have been thoroughly pummeled and appear before Olivia in humiliation with bloody heads. They have themselves become the court spectacle they delighted in rendering the hapless Malvolio.

The humor of *Twelfth Night* is morally targeted. The references to Sir Andrew's licentiousness, like those to Sir Toby's gluttony and Malvolio's pride, are not gratuitous or, one might argue, improperly explicit, but part of a scheme of moral consequences. Furthermore, they are qualified by moral tone. We are not allowed to admire these characters. The bullying nature of Sir Toby shows itself in the last scene in his ugly repudiation of Sir Andrew's offer of assistance: "Will you help? An ass-head and a coxcomb and a knave, a thin-faced knave, a gull." Olivia, indignant, orders the drunken Sir Toby away.

In both *King Lear* and *Twelfth Night,* the censorable elements are not gratuitous but instrumental to moral purpose. They condemn evil and uphold a Biblical standard of virtue. The pitiable Gloucester and the silly Andrew Aguecheek appear aberrational and absurd in relation to the morally normative Edgar in *King Lear* and Viola in *Twelfth Night.* Reflections of evil in the two plays are a function of their morality rather than of their immorality or amorality. Both plays condemn and enact judgments upon evil character.

Criteria of use

There remains the issue of whether works that do not fulfill the criteria of gratuitousness, explicitness, and moral tone have a place in the curriculum. The same criteria apply to evaluating the censorable *as* literature that pertain to judging the censorable *in* literature. Can a censorable work or part of a work function effectively as a negative example? We can put the questions in this way:

1. Is the teacher's or textbook's use of the censorable material purposeful, or is it presented only for its own sake? This is the criterion of **gratuitousness.**
2. Is the censorable material too potent to serve well as a negative example in the classroom in which it is to be used? This is the criterion of **explicitness.**
3. Will the censorable material be presented emphatically as a negative example? That is, will what it portrays appear dangerous and repulsive, regardless of the author's intentions? This is the criterion of **moral tone.**

If so, including this material is justifiable and desirable, for in the hands of a wise and skillful teacher it will create a defense against that which it represents.

There is therefore a place in the Christian English curriculum for a paganistic poem by Robert Herrick or William Blake or a pessimistic novel by Thomas Hardy or Joseph Conrad, *if* these are taught within a proper context, for a proper purpose, and in a proper way. There is a place in the American-literature curriculum for an essay of Ralph Waldo Emerson or Henry David Thoreau or a story by the naturalists Stephen Crane or Theodore Dreiser, *if* it is intended to show, for example, the result of religious unbelief in nineteenth-century American thought.

We must recognize, of course, that the shocking indecencies of much twentieth-century fiction disqualify it for use as negative examples; for the censorable language and description are often too potently explicit to be offset by a supplied moral tone. For instance, whereas a conscientious Christian teacher might assign a Willa Cather novel to a Christian high school class, he would not assign John Steinbeck's *Grapes of Wrath* or Thomas Wolfe's *Look Homeward, Angel* for the profanity of the one and the sexual explicitness of the other. There are, indeed, many modern fiction works more objectionable than these, not to speak of poetry. The field of choice narrows progressively and drastically as we apply our Biblical criteria to the writings of recent times.

We also must realize that all literary works assigned as negative examples must be taught rather than just listed for class reading. It is the teacher rather than the student who must supply the necessary moral tone. Furthermore, the teaching should precede and accompany the reading of such works by the students, rather than just follow it the next day. Finally, class discussion must be carefully planned and controlled. Only then can the students be certain to experience a censorable work in a way that will ensure their moral and spiritual benefit rather than harm. (See Chapter 6, pp. 94, 101-6, for an account of how such material can be handled in the classroom.)

A useful analogy for explaining the proper handling of censorable materials is inoculation. The moral purpose of Christian teaching is, minimally, to enable the young to escape the infection of evil. There are two ways of escaping an infectious disease: (1) avoiding contact with it, which of course should be done whenever possible, and (2) developing a resistance. There are two ways of developing a resistance: (1) inoculation and (2) having a non-fatal case. Developing resistance is certainly more desirable than assuming one can avoid contact with infection in a world where contagion constantly threatens. Of the two ways of developing resistance, having a nonfatal case is not the sort of experience that one can plan; and even if one happens to be successful, it may leave him scarred and disabled. Clearly inoculation is superior.

The process, and the advantage, of inoculation is familiar to almost everyone today. Inoculation takes place in a disease-free environment. There the recipient receives a controlled exposure to the disease along with the resistance of the donor so as to fortify the recipient against future infection. The sterile environment and controlled dosage ensure present safety. The resistance of the donor ensures both present and future safety.

The factors determining the success of inoculation are three: (1) the strength of the dosage, analogous to the amount of exposure to evil; (2) the resistance of the donor, analogous to the condemning perspective supplied by the teacher; and (3) the strength of the recipient, analogous to the readiness of the student to benefit from the negative example. Inoculation is inappropriate for a recipient who is weak—either too young (the maturity consideration) or too sick (the background consideration). Factors one and three have to do with explicitness; factor two, with moral tone. The very purpose of moral inoculation satisfies the criterion of gratuitousness.

The book of Proverbs inoculates the reader against sexual immorality by a vivid account of an adulterous liaison (7:6-27). The reader's ability to profit from this account depends on his maturity. But such instruction is an important part of the young man's defense against one of the most dangerous temptations he will face in the world. The story of the strange woman and the young fool illustrates the method of Scripture, which offers vivid accounts of sin and its consequences not for titillation of the imagination but "to the intent we should not lust after evil things" (I Cor. 10:6).

Motivation

We need always to distinguish between the educational and recreative purposes of reading and viewing. The Christian cannot read for pleasure works or parts of works whose censorable elements do not pass the Scriptural test. The Christian's enjoyment of a work must be determined by the degree to which its form and content approach the Biblical standard. However, the educational purpose requires at times a greater latitude than the recreative. If we are to obey the Lord's commandment to be "wise as serpents" as well as "harmless as doves," we need to know what we are to be wary of. We need to be conscious of events and developments that have a bearing on our service for the Lord and on the well-being of ourselves and those under our care. One cannot read far in even *National Geographic* or *U.S. News & World Report* without encountering censorable elements. We are justified, indeed obligated, to expose ourselves to some material that is repugnant to our Christian morality and theology so that Satan may not take advantage of us and ours. This latitude does not extend to idle curiosity; it stops where the recreative interest begins.

Genuine moral education

Christian moral education aims at the moral preservation and development of Christian students. This aim entails teaching them to discern and desire good and to recognize and abhor evil, before they encounter the crucial and often subtle moral choices of adulthood. Most often, in literature as in life, good and evil are intertwined. The older the student, the more easily he can separate the strands, categorizing his responses. Christian education, in home and school, has not accomplished its purpose in the mind of the student and prepared him for life until he has learned to discriminate between the good and bad elements of his experience with the world and to choose the one rather than the other. The Christian educator must not only judge but also teach judging if he is to engage in Biblical moral education.

Education, then, is preparation, and preparation implies a process. There are two notions of moral education that are not really education at all, for they involve no process:

1. Immediate immersion (immediate exposure to the evils of the world). The permissivist secular view assumes there exist from the beginning the capabilities it undertakes to teach.
2. Ignorant innocence (complete seclusion from the evils of the world). The exclusivist view provides for no development of discernment and resistance to the evils of the world. This

view is what Christian educators are often charged with holding and what, in fact, some of them actually think they hold.

Neither concept of moral education allows for any process of preparation for confronting and resisting the deceptions of the world. In reality these conceptions are not moral education at all, but moral noneducation. If we wish to educate a person to survive in water over his head, we may, of course, push him in suddenly (the method of immediate immersion) and trust his innate swimmer's intelligence. We can, on the other hand, try to keep him away from the water (the method of ignorant innocence), though we cannot be sure that he may not someday be trapped in a flood or on a sinking vessel. The better way, we think, is to teach him to swim. We will introduce him to the water gradually with someone present to instruct him so that someday he can survive on his own.

In order not to leave doubts unanswered, we need to give special attention to the two censorable elements that are most flagrantly prevalent in the modern moral environment and yet that are not absolutely condemned in the Scriptures: erotic and scatological realism. Occurrences of these elements in the Bible suggest two mutually qualifying principles in the divine attitude toward them: (1) the goodness of nature as God created it and (2) the propriety of concealment because of the fall. The human bodily functions are part of the divine creation that God approved and blessed: "And God saw every thing that he had made, and, behold, it was very good" (Gen. 1:31). Since the fall, the body has shared the corruption of the fallen nature even in redeemed man, and the redemption of the body will be the last step in God's restoration of man to what he has lost. However, it is clear that the human physiology itself and the physical desires created in man by God are not to be despised but to be regarded with respect as part of His handiwork. "I will praise thee," wrote David, "for I am fearfully and wonderfully made: marvelous are thy works; and that my soul knoweth right well" (Ps. 139:14).

Both the procreative and excremental functions are recognized in the Scriptures and are mentioned without any sense of shame. They are, however, regarded as private: in the case of the marriage union, to preserve its meaning to those involved; in the case of the excremental processes, to prevent offense to others. Modern thinking typically supposes, on the one hand, that the goodness of nature justifies the flaunting of nature and, on the other, that the impulse for concealment implies shame. The divine view combines high respect and secrecy. Upon those parts that fallen nature regards as uncomely—those kept clothed—God, says Paul, has bestowed "more abundant honour" (I Cor. 12:23-24).

Erotic realism

Eroticism in the Scriptures is both fervently approved and vehemently condemned. Physical intimacy within marriage is not only tolerated (as in Roman Catholic theology) but also commanded and celebrated (I Cor. 7:3-5; Song of Solomon, passim). Physical intimacy between the sexes outside marriage is fiercely denounced and threatened. "Marriage is honourable in all, and the bed undefiled: but whoremongers and adulterers God will judge" (Heb. 13:4). The measure of the divine approval of the sexual relationship in marriage is the measure of the divine disapproval of its perversion outside of marriage. Also, in the command to "flee . . . youthful lusts" (II Tim. 2:22; I Cor. 6:18) is a recognition of the power of perverse sexual desire to destroy the spiritual life. "Can a man take fire in his bosom, and his clothes not be burned? Can one go upon hot coals, and his feet not be burned?" asks Solomon (Prov. 6:27-28). Divine wisdom in Proverbs juxtaposes accounts of licit and illicit eroticism with exhortations to enjoy the one and shun the other (chapters 5-7).

The Biblical view of the marriage union is both more idealistic and more realistic than the common view today even among Christians. In both Old and New Testaments, the marriage union images the relationship between God and His people. Christians throughout the ages have seen in the celebration of the physical loveliness of the bride and the fervent desire for physical consummation in the Song of Solomon a picture of Christ's love for His Church. The prophets depict the love of Jehovah for Israel and His grieving over Israel's rebellion in terms of the marriage relationship. Ezekiel represents the broken relationship in strikingly erotic terms (chapters 16 and 23). Spiritual infidelity is represented as harlotry from the prophetic books to the Revelation. The defilement of the temple in Jerusalem by the heathen, a consequence of Jehovah's abandonment of Israel to her lovers, is described as a sexual violation of a once-holy sanctuary (Lam. 1-2). The use of this imagery to express the relationship of God and

His people indicates the high value He places upon the marriage union, including the physical experience, and the favor with which He regards those who preserve it undefiled.

But combined with the idealistic perspective of the Scriptures is also the realistic. The Scriptures speak matter-of-factly about the "duty of marriage" (Exod. 21:10), "the natural use of the woman" (Rom. 1:27), and the need to "come together" regularly to avoid the temptation of the devil (I Cor. 7:5). Discussions of marriage today tend to be either idealistic or realistic rather than both. The result tends to be either sentimental or coldly practical. Both the highest idealism and the most practical realism combine in the Biblical view of the marriage union, whose purpose is severalfold: human happiness, the replenishing of the species, and a defense against incontinency. A fourth purpose, often neglected, is to produce "a godly seed" (Mal. 2:15)—in the words of the poet, "Of blessed saints for to increase the count" (Edmund Spenser, *Epithalamion*, l. 423). The function of the erotic in each of these purposes is obvious.

The representation of the erotic in the Scriptures exceeds what in literature would be the tolerance threshold of many moral conservatives but is less obtrusive and graphic than its manifestation in modern literature generally. Its level of explicitness in the Scriptures varies somewhat according to whether the Holy Spirit is depicting virtuous or vicious love, whether (in the case of virtuous love) the perspective is ideal or practical, and whether the eroticism is being rendered metaphorically or is the metaphoric vehicle of another idea—namely, the relationship of God to His people.

In the case of virtuous love in particular, the privacy associated by the Scriptures with the physical union is reflected in a certain tact with which manifestations of it appear in the sacred text. This privacy, as indicated above, is not because of shame but for the protection and honor of an exclusive relationship. The purpose of figurative expression in the Song of Solomon is both to protect from profanation and to glorify the reality to which it refers. There is frank description to a certain degree and figurative representation thereafter. In its affirming the goodness of the marriage union, this description is the very antithesis of the pornographic in purpose and effect.

As the metaphoric vehicle, rather than what is rendered metaphorically, eroticism appears with greater explicitness, particularly in the prophets' denunciation of Israel's disloyalty to Jehovah. Israel, charged Ezekiel, "doted upon their paramours [the Babylonians], whose flesh is as the flesh of asses, and whose issue is like the issue of horses." This Israel did as in "the lewdness of thy youth, in bruising thy teats by the Egyptians for the paps of thy youth" (23:20-21). The loftiness of the ideal of virtuous love in the Song of Solomon permits less explicitness than the searing scorn of Ezekiel toward the profaned relationship of Israel with Jehovah. Idolatrous Israel had nothing left to conceal.

The explicitness of the practical perspective in the Scriptures appears in Paul's commands concerning the physical obligations of the marriage relationship in I Corinthians 7. Paul is straightforward and specific in answering the questions of the Corinthians. The passage is a model of spiritual advice. An even bolder explicitness appears in Paul's discussion of circumcision in Galatians. Angered by the Judaizers' insistence upon circumcising the Gentiles, Paul exclaims that castration might quickly allay their concerns: "I would they were even cut off which trouble you" (Gal. 5:12).

The Christian turns to the Bible for his standard in evaluating erotic realism in literature. Is the Biblical moral perspective present? Is there an affirmation of the good and the true and a condemnation of the evil and the false? If so, is there also a mutually qualifying idealism and realism in the presentation of the good? Is there a controlled and purposeful explicitness? On this basis the Christian can reject the overwhelming majority of instances of explicit erotic description without condemning those instances, rare as they be, that conform to the practice of Scripture.

Scatological realism

Scatological realism, like erotic, is more apparent in the Scriptures than most moral conservatives would find tolerable in literature but less apparent than in much of modern literature. References to excrement or to the excremental functions appear usually in passages implying divine contempt or disgust. Divine indignation appears in the language with which the Lord has the prophet Ahijah address the disguised wife of Jeroboam in I Kings 14:7-10.

> Go, tell Jeroboam, Thus saith the Lord God of Israel, Forasmuch as I exalted thee from among the people, and made thee prince over my people Israel, And rent the kingdom away from the house of David, and gave it thee: and yet thou hast not been as my servant David, who kept my commandments, and who followed me with all his heart, to do that only which was right in mine eyes; But hast done evil above all that were before thee: for thou hast gone and made thee other gods, and molten images, to provoke me to anger, and hast cast me behind thy back: Therefore, behold, I will bring evil upon the house of Jeroboam, and will cut off from Jeroboam him that pisseth against the wall, and him that is shut up and left in Israel, and will take away the remnant of the house of Jeroboam, as a man taketh away dung, till it be all gone.

A similar contempt appears in the Lord's message to the wicked priests through Malachi (2:1-3).

> And now, O ye priests, this commandment is for you. If ye will not hear, and if ye will not lay it to heart, to give glory unto my name, saith the Lord of hosts, I will even send a curse upon you, and I will curse your blessings: yea, I have cursed them already, because ye do not lay it to heart. Behold, I will corrupt your seed, and spread dung upon your faces, even the dung of your solemn feasts; and one shall take you away with it.

Paul, comparing the acquired capabilities and credentials which he once valued so highly (and which, by the way, the Lord continued to use after Paul's conversion) to his present concerns and goals, said that he counted them "but dung" that he might "win Christ." He used some of the strongest available language to express contempt for his former values. Expressing God's contempt for Israel's facade of respectability, Isaiah wrote, "All our righteousnesses are as filthy rags" (64:6). The reference is to discarded menstrual napkins. To the Laodicean church, the Lord Jesus has John write, "Because thou art lukewarm, and neither cold nor hot, I will spue [vomit] thee out of my mouth" (Rev. 3:16).

These and other references assume the obnoxiousness of excrement to civilized man. They also associate moral and spiritual purity with physical cleanliness. To leave human excrement uncovered in the camp of Israel was to offend the sensibilities not only of man but also of Jehovah (Deut. 23:12-14). This offensiveness exists presumably when excremental references gratuitously cover the pages of literature or appear in conversation. Both speaking and writing are social acts liable to moral censure. The most naturalistic of writers have not considered descriptions of urination and defecation necessary, in fiction or nonfiction, to ensure realism. Gratuitous scatological references are quite properly regarded as defilement in verbal communication—all the more so when they are used to degrade and desecrate the pure and noble. By most of today's writers they are not used to portray the vileness of a thing as it appears in the eyes of God.

Should Christians judge acceptable the kind of rough language used by God in the Old Testament in response to Israel's degeneracy? The criteria of gratuitousness, explicitness, and moral tone apply here as elsewhere. Is the occasion analogous to those that elicited this language in the Scriptures? Is the target of the language spiritually and morally detestable to a degree that would be equally disgusting to God and His people and incur a similar rebuke? Is such expression similarly motivated? Will it be similarly received? Are social sensibilities today such that similar expressions will have a similar effect, or will they complicate the impact in a way that will cause confusion? Advanced societies with sanitary conveniences live farther from "nature" than do less well-developed societies and become more fastidious about such matters. The Biblical model together with a sensitivity to social norms will be a sufficient guide for judging instances of this type of the censorable.

These considerations must also control our own practice. Nature, as God created it, is not evil, but neither is concealment, whether for protection of the precious or for accommodation of others' sensitivities. Extreme wickedness merits strong but not reckless language. The believer's speech should be "seasoned with salt," not salty; it should communicate "alway with grace" (Col. 4:6). The enemies of Jesus tried but failed to "catch him in his words" (Mark 12:13)—words that had keen edge but also graciousness (Luke 4:22). The Biblical standard, today as then, is "sound speech, that cannot be condemned" (Titus 2:8).

The Christian concept and practice of censorship is an outgrowth of the Christian philosophy of education. (See Chapters 1 and 2.) All non-Christian material in the Christian classroom functions to make a Christian point. It is godly to present ungodliness in a Biblical manner, for a Biblical purpose, and to a Biblical effect. It is ungodly to use what might seem the freedom of Scripture as a cloak of licentiousness (cf. I Pet. 2:16). Genuinely Christian teaching, permeated with Scripture and directed by the Spirit of God, remains morally and spiritually well-targeted in its choice and use of materials. It meanwhile does not deny accountability to the trustees, administrators, principals, and parents it serves.

P A R T

APPLICATIONS

The Christian teaching of English or science or physical education or music does not happen automatically when a Christian teaches one of these subjects, even with the advantage of Christian educational materials, Christian administrative supervision, and a Christian class. It happens when the study he is conducting supports the growth of a Christian student in the image of God and equips him for the service of God. Performing this educational ministry requires of the teacher mature spiritual perception, since he must understand and embrace the goals of Christian education. It requires of him also sound professional preparation, since he must know his subject well enough to recognize its potentialities for fulfilling these goals and must be sufficiently well versed in the techniques of its presentation to exploit these potentialities. The following discussions reveal the uniqueness of Christian teaching in the standard content areas and the way in which this teaching fits into the total program of Christian education.

THE CENTRAL
STUDY

The Christian Teaching of Bible

5

Teaching the Bible in a classroom setting involves the teacher in a spiritual task that most directly affects the student's growth in godliness. God uses His Word, the Bible, to produce mature believers equipped to serve and live for Him.

The uniqueness of Bible teaching

The nature and purpose of the Bible

The Bible is uniquely God's book, for God inspired it. Inspiration is that act of the Holy Spirit whereby He moved on the human authors of Scripture, causing them to record inerrantly and infallibly in the original autographs the exact words breathed out by God (II Sam. 23:2; II Tim. 3:16; II Pet. 1:21). God, using the personalities of the authors, protected them from error to communicate His own infallible Word. As God's authoritative, verbally inspired self-revelation, it is His written record of His will and purpose for mankind. Thus the Bible is without error, not only in its religious teaching but also in matters of history, science, and chronology.

In a certain sense, God reveals Himself in all creation. His eternal power and deity can be seen in the created universe (Ps. 19:1-3; Rom. 1:19-20). Though this "general revelation" communicates vital information about God, it has serious and inherent limitations. Creation cannot tell a sinner the way to God. The Bible is God's precise revelation of His person, purposes, and plans, including man's redemption. This "special revelation" is preserved in the sixty-six books which constitute the Old and New Testaments and is a perfectly harmonious unity inseparable from the "Living Word," the Lord Jesus Christ, who is the final and complete revelation of the Father (John 1:1-2; Heb. 1:1-3).

The Bible's divine origin gives it unique authority. Although the words of Scripture came through the instrumentality of men, these words are ultimately and uniquely authoritative because God authored them. The Scripture is not the product of human thought, for "holy men of God spake as they were moved by the Holy Ghost" (II Pet. 1:21). Because it is the infallible, inerrant Word of God, it must be received "as it is in truth, the word of God" (I Thess. 2:13) and not simply as the words of men. Since the Bible is the Word of God providentially preserved (see Ps. 119:89; Isa. 40:8; I Pet. 1:25) and ordained to accomplish God's purposes (Isa. 55:11), it must be the supreme authority for the Christian in faith, doctrine, and practice.

Scripture reveals, therefore, what man is to know and believe about God. It also reveals what God requires of man. It is this Word which God has exalted above His own name (Ps. 138:2). It will abide forever and must be fulfilled (Matt. 5:18; Isa. 40:8). Specifically, the Bible is the means by which people are saved, for "faith cometh by hearing, and hearing by the word of God" (Rom. 10:17). The Bible convicts and humbles the sinner (II Chron. 34:18-19, 26-28) and leads him to Christ (Acts 8:27-39). It enlightens man (Ps. 19:8) and strengthens him against temptation (Ps. 19:11; I Cor. 10:11). It builds up the believer in grace (Acts 20:32). The Bible directs man to personal appropriation of the truth it reveals (Ps. 119:4).

Although there are many specific concerns in Scripture, the supreme purpose of the Bible is to reveal Jesus Christ as the only Redeemer and King (cf. Luke 24:25-27; John 5:39). The purpose of Bible teaching must conform to the purpose of the Bible itself. Effective Bible teaching will include those elements necessary to make sinners aware of God's provision of salvation in Jesus Christ (Acts 4:12) and to conform believers to the image of Christ (Rom. 8:29-30; II Cor. 3:18; Rev. 5:9-10), who is supreme King and Lord.

Spiritual factors in Bible teaching

The following powerful factors combine in the spiritual process of communicating God's Word.

1. The spiritual capacity of a regenerated mind—A regenerated mind is requisite to proper comprehension of spiritual truth. The Scriptures teach that the unsaved or natural mind cannot accept the things of God (I Cor. 2:14-16). To be spiritually discerned, truth must be received by a person indwelt by the Holy Spirit through regeneration. Christian Bible teaching demands not only Christian teachers who understand God's truth but also Christian students who have the capacity to receive, believe, and act on the truth.

2. The Bible as a living book—In their classroom study of the Bible, students must understand that the Bible is unique among their textbooks and among all the books ever written. Because the Bible is God's *living* and *active* message to mankind (Heb. 4:12-13), students cannot deny its truth or disregard its application without suffering the consequences of being disobedient to God's revelation. Believers who feast on it and delight in it are promised God's blessing (Ps. 1:1-3; I Pet. 2:1-3).

3. The work of the Holy Spirit—As the "Spirit of truth" (John 14:17) and the teacher of believers (John 14:26; 16:13; I John 2:20, 27), the Holy Spirit empowers the human teacher and illumines the student in the Bible-teaching process. The Holy Spirit functions specifically through the gift of (Bible) teaching. As one of the gifts sovereignly given by the Holy Spirit (Rom. 12:7; I Cor. 12:28; Eph. 4:11), the gift of (Bible) teaching is not simply the natural ability to communicate. It is not a gift of fluency nor the ability to funnel facts to a student's mind. It is rather the God-given ability to interpret, communicate, and apply God's written revelation, the Bible, to edify or profit God's people (cf. I Cor. 12:7). In performing this function, the Holy Spirit takes God's Word as taught by the teacher and applies the truth to specific areas of the student's need. The Holy Spirit prompts and empowers the student to be a doer of the truth and not simply a hearer (James 1:22-25).

Thus, whereas the Bible acknowledges that the Holy Spirit illumines individual believers in God's truth (I John 2:27), it also establishes the need for human teachers through whom God's revelation may be communicated by instruction. The Great Commission, for example, includes a teaching mandate (Matt. 28:19-20), and the early church leaders indoctrinated new converts in the Christian faith (Acts 2:42; 14:21-22). Paul gave a specific command to Timothy to commit the truth to faithful men who could teach other faithful people (II Tim. 2:2). Being ''workers together with God'' includes teaching the Bible to others (I Tim. 4:11) and indicates that God uses human instruments as well as His divine power to accomplish His work of edification toward godliness.

Common concerns with other disciplines

Bible teaching shares with other disciplines a concern for goals, academic quality, and thoughtful lesson preparation. Teacher qualifications should be no less demanding for those who teach God's Word than for teachers of science, English, mathematics, or history.

Conformity to the goal of Christian education

The goal of Bible teaching is that of all Christian education—godliness of life and character. Because Christian school training is directed primarily toward professing Christian students, the main task of the Bible teacher is to impress on redeemed students the need for godliness as taught in the Scriptures. This concern does not preclude frequent references to the gospel by the teacher in various lessons and specific invitations for students to receive Christ as Saviour. But the teacher's major thrust will be teaching God's Word so that Christian students will grow in Christ (Col. 1:28; II Pet. 3:18). The Bible teacher will also seek to equip students for Christian service, since being ''throughly furnished unto all good works'' (cf. II Tim. 3:17) is God's will for the maturing believer.

Dedication to academic quality

Although the gift of (Bible) teaching is of divine origin (I Cor. 12:4-6, 11), those gifted of God must also dedicate themselves to academic excellence. Strong academic preparation complements and enhances what God has already entrusted to the Bible teacher. School administrators will guard against attitudes that contribute to shallow and ineffective Bible classes.

A systematic and comprehensive approach to the subject matter—If the Bible is to be an integral part of the Christian school curriculum, it must be studied on a systematic basis. To rely on weekly chapel messages alone to supply facts, principles, and application of the whole counsel of God for every student is to miss the benefits of planned instruction. If students are to know God's truth (James 1:22-25), teachers must adopt a comprehensive plan of study which the Bible itself commends. The "form" of sound words Timothy was to maintain (II Tim. 1:13) literally means a "pattern" of wholesome teaching. Luke wrote his Gospel from the perspective of "having had perfect understanding of all things from the very first" and thus set out to "write . . . in order" so that Theophilus would have clear teaching about the ministry of Christ (Luke 1:1-4). Jesus Himself spent time with two disciples after the resurrection, showing them all that had to be fulfilled regarding the Messiah (Luke 24:44). The Bereans "searched the Scriptures daily" (Acts 17:11), and Aquila with his wife Priscilla instructed Apollos more thoroughly in God's Word when it became apparent he needed more systematic teaching (Acts 18:26).

Old Testament precedents for a systematic teaching of God's Word can also be found. Israel's kings were to keep a copy of the law in a book and read it all the days of their lives (Deut. 17:18-20). Before entering Canaan, Moses commanded Israel to gather to hear and learn the law (Deut. 31:11-13). As Ezra read the law to the returned exiles (Neh. 8:1-8), the priests and Levites moved among the people and "gave the sense, and caused them to understand the reading" (v. 8). These Old and New Testament examples, together with the direct commands to teach and study God's Word, obligate Christians to study systematically God's written revelation, the Bible. With sound, Biblically centered curriculum materials, intensive classroom instruction in Bible contributes directly to the developing of Christ-like students. Learning is enhanced when the classroom instruction is correlated with Bible teaching in Sunday school and youth-group meetings.

Careful and thorough class preparation—Thorough preparation and spiritual power in teaching are not mutually antagonistic. Although the gift of (Bible) teaching is divine in origin, Bible teachers must take the time for careful and thorough preparation of the lesson. Spiritual gifts and power are enhanced through proper preparation. A prepared teacher can be more flexible in response to the varying needs of his class and determine the direction the lesson should move from class response. The unprepared teacher who has failed to draw on resources adequate to meet the deeper needs of the students, touches only the obvious and the superficial.

Attention to teacher qualifications

Academic background and training—Because most Christian school teachers have a general knowledge of God's Word, many administrators succumb to the notion that "anyone can teach the Bible." While every Christian should have a sound testimony for Christ and be able to speak intelligently of his relationship to Christ, it does not follow that all Christians are equally well qualified to teach the Bible in a structured classroom environment. Qualifications extend beyond Bible knowledge to the ability to form lesson aims, assign student-learning activities, maintain discipline, evaluate student progress, and determine student need for additional instruction.

Those who teach Bible in both elementary and secondary schools should be among the most effective communicators in the school and possess positive and enthusiastic personalities. While allowing time for a school to attain the goal of a qualified staff in every teaching field, school administrators should give priority to hiring Bible teachers who are both spiritually mature and professionally qualified. Academic training as a Bible major in combination with educational methods courses helps equip a person to teach the Bible, particularly on the secondary level. Knowledge of the original languages is a definite advantage to the Bible teacher, although a lack in this area can be overcome through the use of curriculum helps that take the languages into consideration. Administrators should also expect interesting and enthusiastic Bible classes from their elementary-grade teachers. These teachers, who are in constant contact with their students, need to be encouraged to meet the special needs of the age group they teach. Many personal and group problems can be addressed through relevant Bible study on the elementary level.

Personal example of godliness—The Bible teacher teaches as much by his example as by his words in the classroom. The Christ-like character and conduct of the Bible teacher provide the model by which young believers grasp the reality of the Christian faith. The Apostle Paul testified of the Thessalonian believers that they first followed him, then God (I Thess. 1:6). In Ephesus, Paul "shewed" as well as "taught" the believers (Acts 20:18-20; cf. I Thess. 2:1-12). Life example as well as spoken teaching is essential to effective Bible teaching. Hypocritical teaching which, like that of the Pharisees, says, "Do as I say, but not as I do" is to be condemned as Jesus condemned the Pharisees (Matt. 23:3). The Bible teacher, to be a discipler of others, must also be a disciple himself. That is, he must grow in Christ personally while teaching others how to grow. The teaching of godliness clearly demands a godly example: a spiritually minded, dedicated teacher who lives the truth he teaches.

Special concerns

Christian teachers of the Bible sense a special burden to teach God's Word so that students will grow in Christ. Elementary and secondary teachers must incorporate several factors into lesson-building if effective Bible learning is to occur in the classroom.

Emphases

Focus on the Scriptures—The Bible teacher must take sufficient time for prayer and reading of the passage to be taught before turning to specific helps in the teacher's manual. He must recognize his need to turn his own heart toward God and to have the Lord speak to him through the passage. As the teacher reads and re-reads the Scripture portion and as he studies his teaching resources, he should seek to determine "What does this passage say?" He should study further to understand "What does this passage mean?" Only then may he proceed to discern "How does this passage apply to my class?" Since Bible teaching is primarily a spiritual task, effective teaching comes through presenting truth that has first gripped one's own soul.

The teacher should not jump to the application of the truth without proper exposition of the text. In the effort to be practical and relevant, he should not substitute application for the truth itself. He must base all practical application on the principles of God's Word and draw these principles from a careful study of the text and context. Biblical principles are the universal, timeless truths revealed in Scripture. The principle, extracted from the Biblical historical context, gives authority to the application made within the current context of life.

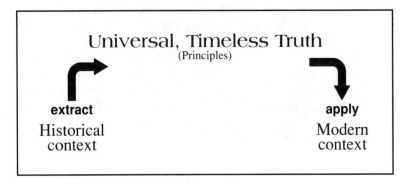

For example, that God's people are to be holy or separate from the world and sin is a timeless truth (Lev. 19:2). Nehemiah 13 gives a historical context for that truth. Nehemiah strongly rebuked those who had married women from Ashdod, Ammon, and Moab. This intermarriage with pagans violated God's demand for separation, and Nehemiah applied the principle of personal separation to this definite problem in his day. From this Biblical example, the Bible teacher can extract the timeless truth of separation and apply it to the present need of his students for guidance in their social relationships. More than simply declaring that Christian youth should not date or marry unsaved people, the teacher should stress the timeless truth that requires that rule of life.

Focus on Jesus Christ in the Scriptures—Jesus said of the Scriptures, "They are they which testify of me" (John 5:39). The sixty-six books of the Bible center on the person and work of Christ—His plan of redemption of fallen mankind and the ultimate rule of His kingdom. The Old Testament prophesies and typifies His first advent. The Gospels verify His sinless life, perfect sacrifice, and bodily resurrection. The Acts of the Apostles records the work of the risen Christ through His Holy Spirit. The Epistles expound the gospel of Christ and teach godly living. Revelation prophesies the Second Coming of Christ. To the disciples on the road to Emmaus, Christ "expounded . . . in all the scriptures the things concerning himself'' (Luke 24:27). To the apostles Christ opened the Scriptures that they might understand He is the one revealed therein (Luke 24:44-46). Peter taught that Christ's sufferings and glory were the subject of Old Testament revelation (I Pet. 1:10-12). Bible teachers must focus, therefore, on the lovely person of Christ and show their students how all the Bible focuses on Him.

Bible teachers must not be guilty of teaching facts or even principles without teaching Christ. Paul expressed the desire to ''know Him'' (Phil. 3:10), which is more than knowing about Him. To know Christ is to develop a personal relationship with Him through His Word so that His fellowship and presence determine our attitudes and actions in life. The Lord expressed this relationship in the figure of the vine and the branches: ''Abide in me, and I in you. As the branch cannot bear fruit of itself, except it abide in the vine; no more can ye, except ye abide in me'' (John 15:4).

Focus on students' living for Christ and serving Him—The Bible teaches that the believer's way of living is a result of personal faith in Christ and an obedient walk in His will. Only saved people who are living under the control of the Holy Spirit can please God (Rom. 8:8). Christian graces and virtues are presented as the natural ''fruit'' of knowing Christ (Gal. 5:22-25; II Pet. 1:1-11). This does not mean that a Bible teacher presents no serious explanation and application of Scripture (since ''the Spirit will lead'' anyway), but is rather a recognition that the Holy Spirit will lead a believer to do what is pleasing to God through the written Word of God He has inspired. Students will not please Christ until they are saved and walking obediently with Him. Student conformity to imposed discipline or even principled teaching without a Christ-centered focus is mere human religion, moralism, and asceticism. All of these fall short of genuine Christian experience. Christian school Bible teaching must do more than enforce rules in the halls. It must establish Christ as ruler in the hearts of students.

Christian Bible teaching must focus on equipping God's saints to live and serve in every area and relationship of life. The Scriptures are given ''that the man of God may be perfect, throughly furnished unto all good works'' (II Tim. 3:17). When Christians are right with God and striving to live for Him, they will also be right in their relationships to others. For example, all the human relationships found in Ephesians 5 and 6 are prefaced with the guiding principle "Submitting yourselves to one another in the fear of God" (Eph. 5:21). The wife's submission to her husband is to be "as unto the Lord" (Eph. 5:22). The husband is to love his wife "as Christ also loved the church" (Eph. 5:25). Children are to obey their parents "in the Lord" (Eph. 6:1). Fathers are to bring up their children "in the nurture and admonition of the Lord" (Eph. 6:4). Servants are to be obedient to their masters "as unto Christ" (Eph. 6:5). Masters are to be aware "that your Master also is in heaven" (Eph. 6:9). Bible teaching must keep the focus on living the Christian life not merely for the purpose of doing right for right's sake, or avoiding the consequences of sin, or avoiding embarrassment by getting caught. Bible teaching must focus on pleasing Christ and obeying His Word from the heart.

Focusing on the need to equip students to live for Christ and serve Him will offer the Christian-school Bible teacher the opportunity to inform and challenge young people about full-time vocational Christian service. Students should be taught the privilege of serving God through missions; pastoring; Bible teaching on the secondary, college, and seminary levels; Christian education; and youth work. Paul exhorted the Corinthian believers to "desire spiritual gifts, but rather that ye may prophesy," for "he that prophesieth speaketh unto men to edification, and exhortation, and comfort" (I Cor. 14:1, 3). In much the same way, the Bible teacher can present to young people the privilege of communicating God's Word to others through vocational Christian service. Specific training courses for young men can enable them to consider seriously God's call to the ministry.

Balance

In addition to maintaining its unique emphases, Bible teaching preserves a balance between factors competing for emphasis.

A balance between presenting the gospel and stimulating Christian growth—The Bible teacher must be aware of those students who are not yet converted to Christ. Before their basic spiritual need is met, little can be done to provide the Bible instruction relevant to the class as a whole. Sessions at the beginning of the year or lessons on the days following an evangelistic chapel service provide opportunities for the teacher to include the plan of salvation in the lesson. Old Testament survey courses include many opportunities to give the plan of salvation. God's provision of animal skins for Adam and Eve, Noah's building of the ark, Abraham's sacrifice of Isaac, and Moses' construction of the brazen serpent are examples of lessons that can be used specifically for salvation emphasis. Studies in the life of Christ, especially His crucifixion, and lessons from Romans, Galatians, Philemon, and Hebrews should be used to present the gospel. Studies of the doctrines of salvation, the end times, and the Christian life also give ample opportunity for teaching salvation. An alert teacher can also create other teaching opportunities to present the gospel when the lesson is not specifically structured for evangelism. Often an emphasis on sin and its effects will bring conviction to a student, resulting in his turning to Christ for salvation.

In their need for spiritual growth, students will present varying challenges to the Bible teacher. Some students will be spiritual leaders, and others will be followers or imitators. Some students will come from strong Christian families; others will receive little or no support from home in their spiritual training. Each of these students has definite spiritual needs that must be met through relevant Bible study.

Since students reveal their spiritual needs most often in a warm, accepting, and loving atmosphere, the Bible teacher will discover that genuine Christian love is the link that establishes contact with their hearts. Discerning student needs is not an easy task, but loving and caring teachers can make themselves available to observe their students away from the classroom—during recess, on the athletic field, at school functions, and even in their homes. Contacts during these informal times reveal much about spiritual needs and emotional problems needing answers from God's Word.

A balance between facts and application—Bible facts are important and should be taught, reviewed, and tested. Paul, for example, argued a point of authority from the historical fact that "Adam was first formed, then Eve" (I Tim. 2:13). Paul argued that God's order in the home is not inconsistent with His act of creation and cited the sequence to prove God's consistency. With an accurate understanding of the facts of Scripture, the Christian teacher and student can make necessary deductions from Biblical statements. Christ's rebuke of the Sadducees who denied the resurrection shows the need to make such deductions. Christ claimed the Sadducees were ignorant of the Scriptures because they did not deduce the doctrine of the resurrection from the words "I am the God of Abraham, and the God of Isaac, and the God of Jacob" (Matt. 22:29-32). Through careful deduction, principles may be extracted from otherwise inapplicable statements. For example, the instruction of Leviticus 19:19 that "a garment mingled of linen and woollen" should not be worn has little application to the modern Christian whose wardrobe consists primarily of blended fabrics. But the principle of separation involved in the prohibition is strongly applicable to today's church.

Seldom do facts alone change conduct. Facts must be transmuted into principles and principles applied to life situations. God revealed His Word to us that we might respond to Him. Revelation demands response. God revealed to Israel that He was the one true God (Deut. 6:4-6). But that fact was not sufficient for Israel's obedience. Israel must respond to that one true God with hearts of love. If Bible teachers expect no more from students than that they learn a few basic facts from Scripture or memorize selected portions of the Bible, then little spiritual change will take place. If, however, the Bible teacher understands the true nature of God's Word and believes that people can and do change as they study God's Word, then exciting changes can take place. Pupils will begin to evidence wisdom—the ability to apply Bible facts and principles to everyday problems.

Young people studying the life of Joseph, for example, could be encouraged to write their own set of principles drawn from Joseph's victory over temptation in Potiphar's house (Gen. 39:1-23). As they study the passage, several keys to victory will become evident. (1) Young people should "Flee . . . youthful lusts" (II Tim. 2:22). Joseph literally ran from the temptation. (2) Young people should never forget that God sees them. Joseph knew he lived in the sight of God. (3) Young people need to make up their minds to do right before the onset of temptation. (4) Young people must realize that all sin is "great wickedness" in God's eyes. As young people see these principles for themselves and make their own personal applications, they are more likely to regard them as God's message to them and to practice these principles.

A balance between teacher and student activity—Effective Bible classes blend teacher direction and control with student participation and investigation. Most Bible teachers were taught the Bible through the lecture method, which is designed to communicate information and maintain teacher control. But Bible teachers also need to assist students in thinking through truths and applying them to life. Through participation and investigation, students internalize the truth and are directly involved in the learning process. Therefore, in addition to lecture, the Bible teacher will use a variety of approaches to involve students in class activity.

A lesson on soulwinning for high school students would normally include exposition of various verses teaching the necessity of evangelism as well as examples of soulwinning efforts. Christ's own example would also likely be studied from the Scripture. But this teacher-oriented study should be complemented with student interaction and involvement in the lesson. The teacher might challenge the students to give their testimonies to two unsaved people during the next week. These two people should be persons who are close to them—a father or mother, a sister or brother. They could be neighbors or friends. To reinforce the activity, the teacher could distribute small cards and instruct the students to write on them the names of the two people to whom they will testify. Then he should have them place these cards in their Bibles as a prayer reminder. Time could be spent in class interceding for the people named. The teacher could also call on several students to give their salvation testimonies to the class to show others how to testify. Student activities such as these implement the lesson concepts, involve the student through direct learning activities, and provide students opportunity to put the lesson into practice.

Regardless of the method used, the teacher must be in control of his classroom. He should be alert to students' verbal and nonverbal reactions. When seeking student involvement, a teacher may say, "Have you found these things to be true in your own life? If so, I'm sure the class would want to hear what you have experienced." He may say, "Do you understand what I'm saying? If not, please ask me about anything you think needs more explanation." A hypothetical question that begins "What would you do if . . . ?" prompts student thought. Often questions students ask can be turned back to the class for response before the teacher elaborates on the answer. In answering questions or discussing concepts, the teacher must give Bible answers, not personal opinion.

Teachers who plan for student involvement in Bible learning will find that they can teach more by talking less. That is, when teacher-centered communication through lecture is reduced, student involvement through interaction is increased, providing opportunity for students to think through the truth and begin to practice it in their lives.

False assumptions and misconceptions

That spiritual and intellectual stimulation are the same—Teachers must not assume that the cure for classroom dullness is novel and ingenious interpretation. While recognizing the need for creative teaching techniques to avoid sameness in the classroom, the teacher should not be reluctant to review and repeat needed emphases. Students benefit from hearing concepts explained again even though they may have studied them in earlier years or previous lessons. Their developing needs continue to make these truths relevant to students.

Scripture memorization, for example, should not be minimized. Hiding God's Word in the heart is God's way for us to avoid sin (Ps. 119:11). Meditating on the Word of God (Ps. 1:2-3) brings spiritual endurance. It is true that there is a danger of overemphasizing memory work to the exclusion of more intensive learning activities, especially in the elementary grades. But memory work and creative teaching approaches are not mutually exclusive.

That Bible teaching must be forced to fit a particular theological system—Wise Bible teaching recognizes those areas of interpretation where committed Christians have differed while not denying the Bible's authority, inerrancy, and inspiration. Since most Christian schools are committed to a definite doctrinal stance, care must be exercised that Bible teaching not be limited to the support of a particular system, whether that of the institution or of the individual teacher. In any case, the Bible should control the system and not the reverse. Denominational distinctives must, of course, be taught, but the Bible should not be made to serve as handmaid to any system. Sound Bible teaching fits all special emphases into the overall emphasis of the Bible in a way that transcends denominational or individual systems.

That all sowing of the seed of God's Word will produce convictions in students—Teachers must be aware that Christian school students tend to parrot Bible truth rather than appropriate it for themselves and be committed to it. It is false to assume that all sowing of the seed of God's Word will produce deeply rooted convictions. Much in this world inhibits students from bringing forth fruit when the seed is sown (Matt. 13). Teachers should not be surprised by incomplete success. Aware of the hard, stony hearts and the thorns that choke the Word, teachers can work at preparing the ground so that students will be more prone to receive the Word and make it part of their experience.

Points of Conflict

The Christian Bible teacher rejects the following concepts as inconsistent with Biblical Christianity and thus as having no part in the Christian teaching of the Bible.

The claims of higher criticism—Higher criticism is a rationalistic approach to Scripture that rejects the supernatural and attempts to reduce Scripture to the limits of human understanding. In attempting to explain those parts of Scripture which seem contrary to reason, higher criticism questions both the authorship and inspiration of the books of Scripture. The book of Isaiah is a case in point. Although Isaiah prophesied between 740 and 680 B.C., he accurately predicted events that would not occur for hundreds of years. Denying the possibility of predictive prophecy, higher criticism insists that those prophecies could not have been written until after the event. Accordingly critics have dissected Isaiah and distributed the parts between two and even three different authors in defiance of New Testament statements affirming the unity of Isaiah (John 12:38-41). The Bible teacher must reject the claims of higher criticism wherever they occur and never elevate reason above revelation.

The veneration of the Bible only as literature—Whereas the written Word of God deserves a place of preeminence in the library of the literature of the world, the Bible teacher rejects any view of Scripture that attributes worth to the Bible solely on its literary merit. The Lord Jesus Christ condemned the rich young ruler for acknowledging only the Lord's goodness, not His deity (Matt. 19:17). Similarly, unless a person receives the Bible as God's inspired and authoritative Word, he cannot honor it in any way acceptable to God. To praise the Bible as a great literary monument and stop there is to demean its sacred and supernatural character.

Conclusion

Through His own act of self-disclosure, God has given us His divine Word. God intended that His people study His Word and grow through obeying its precepts. Christian-school Bible teachers bear the heavy responsibility of communicating the message of God's Word faithfully to others (cf. James 3:1-2).

Basic to the success of this ministry is a recognition that the Holy Spirit must teach and apply the Word of God to the human heart. Yet He also uses human instruments—prepared teachers yielded to the Holy Spirit. These teachers must be sensitive to the needs of those taught, desirous of facilitating changes in understandings, attitudes, appreciations, values, and motives. Though the Holy Spirit alone can bring about spiritual change, Bible teachers, seeking His guidance, plan and conduct Bible instruction according to their perceptions of student needs. Learning to work with and through the power of the Holy Spirit is the key ingredient of successful Bible teaching in the Christian school.

THE LIBERAL
ARTS

The Christian Teaching of English

6

Definition

English studies pertain to the process and product of human communication, particularly in the English language. Improving the process of communication requires study in language and in the art of personal expression. Learning to understand and appreciate the written product of communication requires study in literature (writing distinguished for its excellence or for its cultural significance). Traditionally, English also includes the methods, conventions, and ethics of discovering, analyzing, and reporting information. English education from kindergarten onward takes the form of instruction in reading, penmanship, composition, speaking, listening, grammar, persuasion, literature, and library skills.

Justification

Reflection of God in the subject matter

The study of English can serve the purpose of Christian education—to conform redeemed man to the image of God—because the subject matter reflects the character and works of God. Verbal communication is an attribute of God. Creation was a verbal act: God spoke the universe into being (Gen. 1:3 ff.). God's revelation to man is primarily verbal. He has revealed Himself not only by His spoken word in ancient times but also through His written Word, the Scriptures (Heb. 1:1-3).

In the process of communication—Man, created in the image of God, was given the power of verbal communication. Man, therefore, was intended to imitate God in the process of his communication. However, man's power of verbal communication, like the other parts of the divine image he bore, was marred by the fall (Rom. 3:13-14). It is true that unregenerate man is capable of true and beautiful utterance, for the divine image in man was not entirely destroyed by his disobedience (James 3:9). Still, linguistic cultivation cannot in itself restore the godliness of verbal communication lost by man. "You taught me language," Caliban tells Prospero, "and my profit on't / Is, I know how to curse" (*Tempest* 1. 2). However, supported by the ministry of the Holy Spirit in the regenerate mind, linguistic cultivation can help improve the Christian student in the image of God. This improvement results from the student's imitation of the character and works of God as they appear in the subject matter of English.

Christian English education finds in the Scriptures the divine ideal of human verbal communication. The Christian English teacher draws upon Biblical examples of effective oral and written expression. The poetry and prose of the Scriptures offer inspired examples of the whole range of human communication: impassioned oratory (Jeremiah and Ezekiel), close reasoning (Romans, Galatians, and Hebrews), tactful persuasion (Philemon), sublime lyricism (the Psalms and Isaiah), artfully shaped narratives (Ruth and Jonah), and abundant instances of ordinary discourse perfectly suited to subject, audience, and situation (e.g., John 4:1-26). Of course, the Bible as a record of unregenerate as well as of regenerate man contains negative examples also. The coarse reviling of Israel by Rabshakeh (Isa. 36:1-10, 12-20) and the pretentious flattery of Tertullus (Acts 24:2-4) are certainly no models for Christian discourse, either in content or in form. But the positive examples of Scripture furnish patterns for discourse of all kinds, and the recommendation of these examples is a direct means of developing the student's verbal capacities in the image of God.

The Christian English teacher also recommends to the student noninspired human examples of oral and written communication that reflect the Biblical standard in both ethical and rhetorical integrity. Worthy thoughts delivered suitably and well by fallible human creatures are encouraging models for students who must learn to speak and write acceptably without the support of divine inspiration. Formal oratory such as Lincoln's Gettysburg Address or Edmund Burke's *Reflections on the Revolution in France,* tender personal expressions such as John Winthrop's letters to his wife, the lyricism of Milton's "Ode on the Morning of Christ's Nativity," the sustained argument of the Declaration of Independence, the crisp conversation recorded in Boswell's *Life of Johnson* and in John Wesley's *Journal*—these and many other examples of expression in the English language reflect some of the divine qualities of verbal communication supremely exemplified in the Scriptures.

In the product of communication—The product as well as the process of man's communication can reflect the character and works of God. That is, language shaped into permanent literary form, as well as instantaneous verbal expression, can exemplify divine attributes and actions. Whether directly, as in poetry of praise to God, or indirectly, as in plots showing moral consequences or in themes expressing Biblical wisdom, human literature may contain reflections of God and His works. When beauty of literary form combines with truth and goodness of content, literature most fully reflects the divine nature. For example, there is Biblical integrity of content as well as of form in such plays as *The Merchant of Venice, King Lear,* and *The Tempest* of Shakespeare; in many an essay of Francis Bacon, Samuel Johnson, and John Ruskin; in the epic poetry of Edmund Spenser and John Milton; in the lyric poems of George Herbert, Edward Taylor, and Christina Rossetti; in Jane Austen's *Emma*; and of course in the fictional writings of John Bunyan. Paul's citation of pagan writers in various places—twice in his sermon on Mars' Hill—shows the ability of human literature to reflect and illustrate the truth of God.

Even literary works which are deficient in these qualities but which collectively represent the history of man's thinking about himself and the world reveal the consequences of belief and unbelief and, therefore, the work of God. For this reason, the Christian English teacher sees spiritual value in a historical survey of literature that includes works representative of the character of each age, whether or not these works are specifically Christian or philosophically sound. A Christian intellectual and cultural history helps the student discern the moral causes that underlie fashions of thought and behavior. It is instructive, for example, to trace the intellectual line of descent in American literature from Emerson through Thoreau and Whitman down to today's apostles of moral and theological libertinism. Such a study reveals that human thought, without the recognition by man of his responsibility to God, degenerates into intellectual and moral confusion.

The Christian English teacher draws the student's attention to these reflections of God. He recommends the virtues of effective oral and written communication as characteristic of the verbal communication of God and shows them to be epitomized in the Scriptures. He remarks that since God is a God of order, creation is orderly, and that it is therefore no wonder that language is systematic also. He points out that the truth, beauty, and moral goodness that determine greatness in literature are attributes of God and are supremely exemplified in the Scriptures, the written revelation of God. He explains that the history of man's thought recorded in literature reflects man's responses to his Maker and the moral, intellectual, and spiritual consequences of those responses. In short, the teacher derives from the subject matter of English a pattern of godly character and conduct corresponding to that revealed in the Scriptures and, setting it before the student, encourages him to be conformed to the image of God.

Manifestations of godliness in the resultant knowledge, attitudes, and skills

Since the subject matter of English contains these reflections of God, the teaching of English may support the student's development in the image of God.

In general Christian character and service—Man in the act of uttering his thoughts in words exercises the gift that most obviously distinguishes him from the lower creation and reveals in him the image of his Maker. The more distinct, logical, truthful, beautiful, and appropriate his utterance, the more completely it reveals in him the image of God. No Christian can be irresponsible in his use of language and fully follow the example of his Lord. Jesus' listeners at Nazareth "wondered at the gracious words which proceeded out of his mouth" (Luke 4:22). By cultivating his personal expression, the student more fully exemplifies in his utterance the winsomeness of God's appeal to man in the Scriptures.

By improving his ability to comprehend and interpret what he reads, the student can see more clearly the reflections of God in what he reads and, especially, in the Scriptures. Seeing these reflections more clearly, he is able to be conformed more completely to the divine Original. The ability to read with understanding also gives the student greater access to human knowledge, which, directed by spiritual wisdom, is valuable in the service of God and lends luster to godliness of moral character. The acquisition of genuine knowledge provides a fuller and more accurate view of reality, a view more like God's. The improvement of reasoning skills—particularly of the logical processes involved in critical reading—helps the student to follow a complicated argument, like that of Paul in Romans. It helps him to analyze and judge more accurately not only what he reads but also the situations of life. In so doing it makes him more able to view himself and the world objectively and therefore, within the limits of finite reason, to adopt the perspective of God.

By exercising his aesthetic judgment in the analysis of literature, the student improves his ability to imitate God in his discrimination and preferences, to "approve things that are excellent" (Phil. 1:10). To scorn good poetry and prose is certainly no recommendation of a person's spirituality. It shows on the other hand, a different view from that of God, who deemed it wise to put much of His sacred revelation to man in the form of poetry and exquisitely shaped narratives, who used metaphor and symbol and patterned expression to touch man at the deeper emotional levels of his being and allure him to a love of the good. Likewise, by developing his aesthetic creativity, the student can become more like God; for God has spoken in poetry, and beauty is one of the divine works. Both aesthetic taste and aesthetic creativity are part of the image of God in man.

By observing the work of God in the cultural history of his nation, the student may more readily adopt the mind of God toward his own age. Certainly Paul's wide educational background gave him insights not only into the Hebrew mind but also into the Roman and Greek minds and those of other nationalities. Writing to Titus, Paul quotes a poet of Crete, Epimenides, to reinforce his judgment of the Cretian national character. "One of themselves, even a prophet of their own, said, The Cretians are alway liars, evil beasts, slow bellies" (Titus 1:12). Having the mind of God toward his own age helps to insulate the student against the moral and religious deception in the cultural myths of contemporary life (e.g., inevitable progress; self-sufficient, self-serving individualism; the fatherhood of the state) and against the pessimism that underlies modern thought and expression. An adequate Christian view of the present requires a Christian understanding of the past. Both help the student not to be conformed to the thinking of his age but to think with the mind of one being transformed into the image of God in Christ (Rom. 12:2).

By acquiring a knowledge of literary culture, the student will gain points of contact for his testimony to unbelievers. New Testament writers used concepts of rabbinic and Greek thought as vehicles for conveying the truth of the gospel. Paul quoted directly from Greek writers in his sermon on Mars Hill and elsewhere. Christ, wrote John, is the divine Logos, the eternal Word of God (John 1:1). The ceremonial law of the Hebrews was a "shadow" of a higher spiritual reality (Heb. 8:5; 10:1). These men of God, writing under the inspiration of the Holy Spirit, drew analogies, intellectual vocabulary, and even quotations from a literary inheritance possessed in common by the cultivated men of their age. Furthermore, the cultural background gained by the study of literature enhances one's testimony to the uneducated as well as the educated. Biblical evangelism—whether personal or congregational—generally proceeds from a point of common knowledge or interest to a presentation of the facts of the gospel. So Christ dealt with the woman at the well. So Paul preached in the synagogues and marketplaces. The greater one's cultural awareness, the more adaptable one's approach to the lost. The Christian student cannot afford to ignore his literary heritage if he wishes to witness with the greatest impact to the widest range of society.

By learning accuracy, objectivity, honesty, and conventional procedure in research, a student may gain a higher sense of responsibility for truth in details and in perspective, as well as a more disciplined and objective approach to factual investigation. Slanting factual evidence and failing to control personal bias are inconsistent with the imitation of the God of truth. Honesty and diligence in factual investigation and reporting reflect the character of the Author of the infallible written revelation, who could not violate truth and righteousness to save mankind. Such discipline is a part of studying to show oneself approved unto God, who ''cannot lie'' and who died that He might remain just while being the justifier of those who believe (Rom. 3:26; II Tim. 2:15; Titus 1:2).

The perfecting of all the faculties engaged by the study of English makes the student more like the One after whose attributes his capacities were fashioned. This process of perfection also enables the student to reveal his Maker more fully and convincingly to the unbelieving world.

In special vocational service—The study of English is not only valuable for preparing the student to reflect the image of God in his personality and conduct but also essential for certain kinds of vocational service. These kinds of vocational service include such English-related ministries as teaching, writing, editing, and secretarial work. They also include all kinds of vocational service that require formal education. The knowledge, attitudes, and skills developed through the study of English underlie general academic achievement and therefore are fundamental to all vocational service that depends upon academic training. By increasing the scope and effectiveness of these ministries, English studies enhance their reflection of the character and work of God.

The Christian English teacher capitalizes on these potentialities in the teaching of English for developing the student in godly character and conduct. He gives constant attention to the student's oral and written expression so that it becomes more like God's in clarity, truth (accuracy, honesty, and precision), efficiency, winsomeness (including acceptability of grammatical usage and spelling as well as of strategy and tone), and persuasive force (both logical and emotional). He exerts a continuing effort in the disciplining of the student's mind to think logically and objectively so that his thinking will more nearly resemble God's. He forms the student's judgment, both linguistic and aesthetic, according to Biblical criteria so that his discernment and preferences will conform to the judgment of God. He helps the student improve his ability to comprehend and interpret what he reads so that he will have greater access to the most important agency in his growth toward Christ-likeness, the written Word of God, as well as to other works that are supportive of his development in the image of God. He orients the student to his cultural tradition from a Christian point of view so that he may be reinforced in his spiritual convictions and be strengthened against the influences in his cultural climate and tradition that could hinder his growth in godliness. He holds up to the student high standards of accuracy, objectivity, honesty, and correctness in researching, analyzing, and reporting information and also in handling information as evidence in argument, so that the student will understand his responsibility to truth and develop a habit of careful investigation and candid presentation of facts. The result of these concerns and emphases is greater godliness of character and, consequently, a more powerful influence for God.

The Christian English program gives future writers and editors a fuller and more intense experience in the discipline of writing and in the procedures of publication. It provides future English teachers with a more comprehensive instruction in the theoretical and practical principles underlying effective verbal communication and with a wider, more intense study of literature. It ensures their understanding of the structure and history of the English language. It requires all students for whom English education has a particular vocational application to demonstrate their grasp of both the professional and the spiritual principles necessary to the success of their service for God.

Distinctiveness

It should be obvious by now that Christian English teaching, from the foundation up, is different from secular English teaching. It is true that some functions of the Christian English teacher are not essentially distinct from those of the secular English teacher. The Christian teacher simply performs them for a different purpose and, therefore, with a special conscientiousness. For example, he tries to teach reading skills more thoroughly and expertly than his secular counterpart since he realizes that spiritual growth as well as intellectual and social development is affected by the ability to read. But his teaching of reading may utilize the instructional techniques that secular education has proved to be the most effective. His teaching of grammatical structure and usage likewise has a singular urgency, for he realizes the importance of clear, forceful, and appropriate expression to the student's witness for Christ. But as means to this end he welcomes the insights of recent grammars where they are helpful as well as those of the more traditional Latin-based system.

Other functions of Christian English teaching are distinctive in mode as well as in purpose. The Christian teacher conducts his teaching of rhetoric so as to impress upon the student the truth that the standards of clear thought and effective expression (including forceful and proper persuasion) are God's as well as man's and have a moral and theological as well as practical basis. He shows them to be taught and exemplified in the Scriptures. He insists on discipline—of thought, speech, writing, listening, and reading—and brings a disciplining pressure to bear on the student's work, realizing that progress in verbal communication requires effort on the part of the student and careful criticism of the product of his effort. He conducts the teaching of literature so as to emphasize the fact that true literary criteria originate with God and have a moral and theological as well as historical and philosophical basis. He shows these criteria to be fulfilled in the Scriptures. He emphasizes certainties rather than ambiguities in his discussion of literature and does not raise moral and religious questions for which he has no answers. He uses literature to show the intellectual and moral consequences of rebellion against God. He differs therefore from his secular counterpart in teaching literature not merely for the aesthetic and mimetic pleasure of the moment but for the promotion of the student's growth in the image of God.

Practical application in the classroom

The distinctiveness of Christian English teaching derives from its Biblicism. An observer acquainted only with secular English teaching would doubtless be struck with the way in which the Bible is a constant point of reference in the Christian classroom. A unit on persuasion might take as a starting point the speech of Stephen to the Sanhedrin (Acts 7), emphasizing its adaptation of approach to audience and situation and its avoidance of unethical emotional appeals. It would note the establishment of rapport and common ground ("our father Abraham"); the gradual revelation of the thesis in order to secure a hearing with a hostile audience; the patient building of the case by references to Israel's history; the climactic structuring, both logical and emotional; the use of clear, direct language; and the avoidance of such dishonest rhetorical techniques as intimidation, begging the questions, diversion (red herring), slanting of evidence, and gratuitous abusive language. The discussion might then turn to non-Biblical examples of persuasion—positive and negative; ancient, recent, and contemporary; literary and ordinary—to illustrate further the principles previously defined from the Scriptures. It would eventually apply these principles to the conduct of the believer in moral and religious controversy and to his witness to the unsaved, showing Christ's differentiation of tactics according to whether the audience happened to be, for example, an ignorant, uncommitted lost person (John 3-4) or a self-important, defiant religious fraud (John 8:21-58).

A unit on late Victorian and early modern poetry might divide the authors into poets of religious faith and poets of religious doubt. The distinction is conventional, but the Christian teacher's approach would differ entirely from the secular approach. The immediate objective would be to show the depressing effects of Darwinism on late-nineteenth-century thought. The ultimate objective would be to help the Christian student recognize an element in his cultural environment that can hinder his development in the image of God and to provide him with an antidote. The teacher might begin by directing the student's attention to Matthew Arnold's well-known "Dover Beach," a poem that epitomizes post-Darwinian gloom. Looking out on the Straits of Dover on a clear night with the sea at full tide, the speaker muses:

> The Sea of Faith
> Was once, too, at the full, and round earth's shore
> Lay like the folds of a bright girdle furled.
> But now I only hear
> Its melancholy, long, withdrawing roar,
> Retreating, to the breath
> Of the night wind, down the vast edges drear
> And naked shingles of the world.

Doubting the ability of Christianity to offer him comfort or certainty, he turns for consolation and ultimate value to human relationships:

> Ah, love, let us be true
> To one another! for the world, which seems

To lie before us like a land of dreams
So various, so beautiful, so new,
Hath really neither joy, nor love, nor light,
Nor certitude, nor peace, nor help for pain;
And we are here as on a darkling plain
Swept with confused alarms of struggle and flight,
Where ignorant armies clash by night.

A proper survey of English literature would by this time have established the fact that genuine Christian faith has never been so universal nor is doubt so exclusively modern as the poem implies. The teacher would recall instances of skepticism that preceded Darwinism and refer to the words of Satan to Eve in the Garden of Eden as the prototype of all religious doubt. He would stress the blindness of modern man, who likes to think that religious doubt is of recent date and springs from incontrovertible scientific findings. On the other hand, the teacher would point out that there has been a trend away from a Biblical world view since the time of Darwin and that Arnold's poem expresses vividly the melancholy pessimism that results from questioning the existence of a benevolent Creator. He would add that man questions the existence of God in order to relieve himself of his responsibility to God and become "free," but that having done so he pays a terrible price—in this life as well as in the next.

At this point, the teacher might proceed to a poem of religious faith written about twenty-five years later (1877), "God's Grandeur" by Gerard Manley Hopkins. "The world is charged [bursting/flashing] with the grandeur of God," the poem begins. The goodness and greatness of God shine through His creation, declares the poet, despite its continual defilement by man. Obviously, religious faith survived Darwinism and inspired a splendid poem by a first-rate poet. The teacher would be careful to represent Hopkins as a poet of religious rather than Christian faith, since as a Catholic priest he did not profess the saving faith of the Scriptures. He would explain, however, that the truth affirmed in the poem is accessible to the natural as well as to the spiritual mind (Rom. 1:20) and that we may, following the example of Paul, value the truth uttered by unbelieving as well as by believing writers. The teacher would conclude that those who do not see God in His creation fail to do so because they prefer not to, not because He is not visible there. Analyzing the structure of the poem and demonstrating the power and precision of its imagery, he might take opportunity to improve the student's attitudes toward the aesthetic. Since most modern literature has been written by authors who have no sympathy with what Christians believe and since much of what has been produced by Christian writers is artistically feeble, students tend to dismiss the whole realm of the aesthetic as either irrelevant or hostile to spiritual concerns and as of trivial importance in the general business of life. In Hopkins's poem, aesthetic form powerfully supports didactic purpose, in this case a most worthy purpose: to remind the reader that the old verities of God's power and love are just as certain and obvious in a skeptical age as they have ever been.

The teacher might then turn to Psalm 19, the probable inspiration of Hopkins's poem, to clinch these points. The central affirmation of Hopkins's poem is stated at the beginning of the psalm: "The heavens declare the glory of God, and the firmament sheweth his handiwork." The opening verses speak of a silent, continuous language of creation, uttering forth without interruption its testimony to the glory of God. The psalm's three sections present the witness of the physical universe (vv. 1-6), the witness of the Scriptures (vv. 7-11), and the impaired witness of the human creation, the psalmist (vv. 12-14). The parallelism of thought, characteristic of Hebrew poetry, varies in strictness according to the clarity and completeness of the testimony of these that bear witness. The parallelism of the central section, referring to supernatural revelation, is the strictest; that of the first section, referring to natural revelation, is less strict; that of the last section, expressing the imperfection of the human creature, is the least strict, in fact scarcely evident. The gradation of the parallelism associates regularity with divine rule and supports the idea of the psalmist's prayer: that the divine nature and works may be manifested in him as in the other agencies of God's self-revelation, the universe and the Scriptures. As creation was pronounced "good," he desires that he also may be "acceptable" to his Creator and therefore give a satisfactory witness to the glory of God. The teacher would remark that this reflection of the character and works of God by the Christian—his godliness—is the goal of Christian education. The teacher might note the progression from outward (the physical universe) to inward (the meditations of the heart), ending with the supreme question of the individual's acceptability to God. He might also call attention to the circular structure, beginning and ending with references to God, signifying His work as Creator and Redeemer (the two acts making possible the condition the psalmist desires). As a result of this discussion, the student is fortified against the pessimism in his environment and is directed to the Bible for the solutions to man's intellectual and spiritual problems. Furthermore, he has been shown that the aesthetic in literature can and should be a vehicle of truth and that the Bible is the supreme model for our aesthetic as well as moral and spiritual standards.

A more thoroughgoing discussion of the nature of the aesthetic, suitable for an upper-level college class, would find a model in the elaborate inverted parallelism of Matthew. About midpoint is the account of Christ's transfiguration on a mountain (ch. 17). Toward either end are two long discourses delivered on mountains, the Sermon on the Mount (chs. 5-7) and the discourse on the Mount of Olives (chs. 24-25), both addressed to Jesus' disciples. Preceding the first discourse and following the second are corresponding elements in opposite order: the predecessors of Christ (ch. 1) and His successors (ch. 28); His birth (ch. 1) and His resurrection (ch. 28); His rejection in Jerusalem by the political and religious leadership (Herod, etc.) with an attempt to destroy Him by sword (ch. 2) and His rejection in Jerusalem by the political and religious leadership (another Herod, etc.) with an attempt to destroy Him by crucifixion (ch. 27); His acknowledgment by John (ch. 3) and His nonrecognition and abandonment by the disciples (ch. 26); the temptation in the wilderness to avoid the cross (ch. 4) and the temptation in a garden to avoid the cross (ch. 26); the calling of the twelve disciples (ch. 4) and confirmation of the eleven disciples (ch. 26). The symmetry is not gratuitous but functional. It centers the narrative on the revelation of the King in His heavenly glory and uses contrast within similarity to point up the progression in His earthly ministry, in which a developing pattern of rejection by the world and of failure by the disciples is counteracted by an unfolding program of divine redemption. The progression culminates in Christ's farewell to His disciples, also on a mountain, and the opening up of a new vista of service and fellowship in the coming age.

From this analysis the student comes to understand that the major elements of the aesthetic are unity and progression and that both are supremely exemplified in the Scriptures. It could be shown that they are fully realized not only in individual portions like Matthew but also in the Scriptures as a whole. The book of Revelation picks up the themes and motifs of Genesis, bringing the history of man's redemption full circle, though with a difference. There is a new creation "wherein dwelleth [remaineth] righteousness" (II Pet. 3:13; Rev. 21:1-4, 27). There is a garden with a river bordered by trees of life without the presence of temptation. Satan, "that old serpent," cannot spoil this garden, for he, rather than his victim, has been "cast out" (Rev. 12:9). A second Adam has repaired the ruin caused by the first Adam, and man is restored to paradise. Thus the Scriptures, like many great works of human literature, carry us from a state of order (the original creation) through a disruption and disintegration of that order (by sin) to a new state of order (by the suffering and death of the Creator) with encouraging potentialities. The process of redemption, God's masterwork, is thus the prototype of that aesthetic form, including full resolution and closure but also joyful promise, which human beings require for complete satisfaction from narrative art. On the simplest level of applicability to the student, it underlies the teacher's insistence that his compositions have a beginning, a middle, and an end and that, if possible, the end link up with the beginning.

The amount of Biblical analysis in the preceding account is not meant to imply that the Christian English teacher spends a great deal of class time in detailed discussion of Scripture. Such analysis is necessary at key points in any Christian course of study. But most of the teacher's references to the Scriptures are of the brief, occasional sort that reflect a presiding purpose, framework of assumptions, and point of view. This purpose, this framework, and this perspective are rooted in the Scriptures, from which the Christian teacher derives his authority and his commission. Also, it should be clear that the Christian English teacher who turns to the Bible for models of literary and rhetorical form is not in any way detracting from the primary importance of its content or encouraging the students to classify it with the works of writers who were not supernaturally inspired. On the contrary, it reflects his belief that the Scriptures are the supreme guide of the believer in all areas of his faith and conduct.

Points of conflict with secular English-educational philosophy

Distinctively Christian English teaching requires the rejection of certain approaches to its subject matter that derive from the climate of modern thought. These approaches not only are avoided by the Christian English teacher but also are explicitly condemned.

Unrestraint in oral and written expression—Some contemporary rhetoricians favor unfettered spontaneity of expression. In language usage this preference appears in a nonjudgmental point of view. A student is regarded as being entitled to his own mode of expression as long as he can make himself understood. "I don't got no money" is not thought to be inferior to "I don't have any money"; "between my wife and I" is considered to be as respectable as "between my wife and me." It is true that language does change and therefore that an unacceptable expression today may have been acceptable in the past and may be acceptable at some time in the future. It is also true that appropriateness varies to a considerable extent with geographical, social, and situational differences. Nevertheless, there exists a rough consensus about what is standard and nonstandard usage, and English teachers traditionally have believed that a student is entitled to the personal advantages of being able to speak and write in an acceptable way, whether or not he perceives these advantages while he is being taught. Of special importance to the Christian is the fact that educated usage opens doors for his testimony, whereas uneducated usage distracts the cultivated mind from the message of the truth of Christ. He therefore disciplines his expression so as to "give none offense," striving like Paul to "please all men in all things," not seeking his own profit "but the profit of many, that they may be saved" (I Cor. 10:32-33). He recognizes that appropriate language usage enables his verbal communication to be more like God's in winsomeness and, therefore, in scope and intensity of impact.

In style the preference for unfettered spontaneity of expression manifests itself in a dislike for deliberate planning and careful revision. The student, it is felt, improves simply by discovering his personal voice rather than by subjecting his first thoughts and expressions to rigorous discipline. However, continuity and method characterize the formal utterances of the Scriptures. Even Biblical poetry generally conveys the impression of thoughtful design. Structured oral and written composition more closely conforms to the Biblical standard. Surely we learn from the Scriptures as well as from common experience that inventiveness and discipline are mutually supportive rather than mutually opposing powers in the creative act. In style, as in other things, discipline releases, not represses, individuality.

In content, the preference for unfettered spontaneity of expression permits frivolous, depressing, and even sordid writing. It stems from the romantic concept of literary creativity as an essentially nonrational process conducted in a state of intellectual and moral suspension. Freudian literary criticism has given a sort of scientific respectability to this view of the artistic process by associating literary creativity with fantasizing. The successful literary work, according to Freud, is illicit wish fulfillment, the disguised expression of a desire that the better judgment would not permit the artist or his reader to act out in real life. This view is clearly un-Christian, for it disallows any check on human depravity in verbal communication. The Bible emphatically declares that the evil conceptions and impulses arising from the inner man are to be denied expression (Eph. 4:29; II Tim. 2:22; Titus 2:12). A consciously self-critical attitude is necessary to both Biblical morality and Biblical artistry. It is morally perilous and un-Biblical to encourage students to record the raw flow of mental images or impressions in a written assignment or journal, for it is morally perilous and un-Biblical to relax the control of Christian conscience and will. Christian writing is different in content from non-Christian, and moral deliberation must be part of the creative process if the product is to be pleasing to God.

The subordination of reading to nonverbal sensory apprehension—Some educational theorists advocate substituting learning through direct sensory impressions for learning through reading. Although Christian education welcomes a variety of teaching media—both the electronic and others that appeal legitimately to the various senses—it opposes the displacement of reading by direct sensory experience. The suppression of reading, were it possible, would impair man's access to the Scriptures, the chief revelation of God, and therefore limit the believer in his attempt to know and imitate God.

Aestheticism in literary criticism—Although artistic creativity is one of the noblest of man's capacities and the appreciation of beauty one of man's richest and worthiest enjoyments, the pursuit of beauty cannot preoccupy the Christian so entirely as it does the artists and connoisseurs of the world. He cannot make art, literary or otherwise, his religion. The veneration of art for art's sake is a form of hedonism in which aesthetic pleasure is sought as an end in itself. In such veneration, physical manifestations of an attribute of God, beauty, are worshiped rather than God Himself. Aestheticism is therefore a kind of idolatry in which the creation replaces the Creator as an object of worship. Aestheticism is pervasive in recent literary criticism. The realm of art is viewed as morally neutral. The work of art is regarded as existing for itself rather than for some purpose beyond itself. Didacticism is rejected as nonartistic—as irrelevant, if not indeed hostile, to the concerns of art. Content, by this view, is not legitimately distinguishable from form. Aestheticism therefore excludes the moral criteria that Christians must apply in evaluating literature. A work of literature may deserve very high recommendation by purely aesthetic standards and yet be detrimental to the believer's development in the image of God. As a school of criticism, aestheticism offers an incomplete and therefore erroneous basis for literary judgment. As a way of life, it is a false religion.

Relativism in literary criticism—Modern unbelief in the possibility of being sure about anything produces an attitude of relativism in interpreting and evaluating literature. Recent criticism has tended to regard the question of the author's meaning as irrelevant to criticism and to focus on the significance of the work for the individual reader. The extreme of this tendency is the notion that all interpretations are equally valid, that there are no right or wrong interpretations. An interpretation is considered legitimate if it links the work in some way with the experience of an individual reader. A work is considered to be as good as the number and variety of interpretations (even conflicting interpretations) it can support. An inconclusiveness or even contradictoriness of meaning is considered essential to good literature, and therefore to pin down the meaning of a work with any assurance is to threaten its integrity as art. Christian criticism, in contrast, views the literary work as fundamentally a vehicle of meaning, recognizing that beauty is not degraded by service to goodness and truth. This meaning exists independent of the individual reader and is not affected by the diversity of private significances for various readers at various times. The goal of interpretation is to ascertain this meaning as fully as possible. Good interpretation accounts for more of the features of a work and reveals the work as a more coherent whole than does poor interpretation. It also accords better with what is known of the author's life and times, especially as these are revealed in the totality of his works. Poor interpretation reads into a work what it wishes to find there. For example, some modern critics read twentieth-century cynicism into great works of the past that celebrate ideal virtue. They justify their subjectivism by maintaining that it is impossible to know an author's intentions or by affirming the primary importance of the reader's personal response. Their justification is a rationalization of their emotional bias. Such interpretation is irresponsible and pernicious not only in its particular bias but also in its principles of justification. Interpreting literature, like interpreting the Bible, requires objectivity and must assume the possibility of arriving at the truth. Understanding true principles of interpretation is important; for accurate interpretation is essential to accurate evaluation of literature, and accurate evaluation is part of the Christian's conformity to the image of God (Phil. 1:10).

Relativism in the evaluation of literature derives from the assumption that literary value depends solely upon the idiosyncrasies of the individual reader. The Christian evaluates literature, like everything else, according to external, objective, permanent standards: those of the Scriptures. In fact, the model to which Christian criticism refers all work of literature and on which it forms its judgment is the Bible itself. The Bible exemplifies to perfection—both in the deliberately aesthetic portions and as a whole—the qualities of beauty, truth, and moral goodness. These qualities of the Scriptures are reflections of the attributes of God. They are also recognized in traditional criticism as the ends of art. Literature historically has been judged by aesthetic, mimetic, and didactic criteria—that is, according to its reflection of beauty, truth, and moral goodness. In the moral view of art—the Biblical view—they are complementary and mutually qualifying principles. Furthermore, they appear in a certain rank: the mimetic principle (consideration of truth) and the aesthetic (consideration of beauty) serve the didactic (consideration of the reader's good). Christian criticism regards a work of literature as good to the extent that it conforms to the Biblical example in the presence and proper relationship of truth, beauty, and goodness within it. For this reason the Christian must bring his judgment to bear on content as well as on form and bring considerations of morality and religious truth into his evaluation of all works of literature. The goal of Christian literary criticism is to see the work as it appears in the view of God.

Permissivism in the selection of literature for reading or teaching—Secular attitudes toward censorship justify works with objectionable elements on either aesthetic or mimetic bases; that is, either on the grounds of compensating artistic values or on the basis of the necessity of an honest view of life. A Christian philosophy of education regards the didactic consideration as an absolute principle of exclusion. If the reading or teaching of a work threatens a student's growth in godliness, assigning it cannot be justified on other grounds. The question of whether certain elements of a work are objectionable can be resolved by consulting the examples of the Scriptures. Vice does appear in the Scripture but only in certain ways, for certain purposes, and with certain effects: namely, in the form of negative examples. Moral questions, in literature as elsewhere, must be decided on moral grounds: on the basis of the principles and according to the example of the Bible.

Pragmatism in persuasion—Contemporary rhetoric sets the student an amoral example of the arts of persuasion. Motivational research provides advertisers with scientifically gathered and analyzed data showing how consumers may be induced to buy their products whether or not they need them or even want them. Public relations firms contract with individuals or organizations to sell a public image. Public influence is available to the client who can afford it, without regard to the worthiness of his cause. In such an amoral climate, even Christians may drift toward expediency in the handling of evidence or in the candor with which they reveal their intentions. Christian English teaching inculcates Biblical ethics as well as Biblical methods of persuasion. Christian persuasion imitates the logical integrity, emotional urgency, and absolute honesty of the divine appeal to mankind in the Scriptures.

Conclusion

The English teaching described above is the response of Christian education to its Biblical mandate and also to certain specific Scriptural injunctions. For example, the Bible commands, "Let your speech be alway with grace, seasoned with salt" (Col. 4:6). The salt analogy implies that the language of the child of God must be (1) pleasing, not in itself obnoxious, and (2) morally pure, free of corruption. Salt was required with the offering of an animal in Old Testament times (Lev. 2:13). Likewise, the salt of gracious words must accompany the "living sacrifice" of the believer today (Rom. 12:1). The Bible also commands us to "prove all things" and "hold fast that which is good" (I Thess. 5:21). Aesthetic and linguistic, as well as moral and religious, discernment and discrimination are necessary to fulfilling this commandment. Finally, the injunction "Be ye therefore perfect, even as your Father which is in heaven is perfect" (Matt. 5:48) is a mandate for teaching all the verbal and intellectual skills traditionally known as English studies, for it requires the development of every capacity with which man has been endowed in the image of God.

The Christian Teaching of History

7

Definition

A description of the discipline of history must center on what is essential in the concept of history but also allow for the diversity of subjects conventionally taught under the designation of history studies. Let us therefore define history as the study of the record of the past acts of man on the earth from his creation to the present, based on surviving evidence. Let us also recognize that, as an academic study, history includes or partakes of the related disciplines of politics, economics, and geography. History education begins in kindergarten and continues in courses designed to teach fundamental history facts and heritage truths and also includes studies in citizenship, law, political functions, economic principles, geographical features, social (family, community, national, and international) relationships, and cultural distinctives.

Justification

History can contribute to the student's growth in godliness if it is taught in the light of the Scriptures. Here we must recognize the basic difference between Christian and secularist thinking about the human past. All historical study begins with a concept of the nature of man. A historian tries to discover not only what actions occurred at a particular time but also why they occurred and what principles, if any, governed their occurrences. The Christian teacher of history, unlike his secular counterpart, begins with a Biblical view of man and interprets his actions according to Biblical principles and insights. He understands that the actions of man, though willed by him, are always under the superintendence and sovereign control of God and therefore that the facts of history are actions either directed or permitted by God. As such they are God's doings, while man's. Whereas man chooses to act in a certain way and bears responsibility for his action, God controls man's action and its consequences. In short, the Christian teacher presents a providential view of history, and this view governs his specific emphases and interpretations. The genuinely Christian teaching of history assists the Christian student toward his goal—conformity to the image of God—because it finds in its subject matter reflections of the character and works of the Creator.

Reflections of God in the subject matter

Within the complex web of events, conditions, and forces with which history must deal, the spiritual mind can trace the character of the divine Maker of the ages and discern His ways. God's character and ways are also visible in the actions of the human agent of history. Created in the image of God, man, though fallen, still reveals in his actions and ways something of the qualities and capacities with which he was originally endowed. His appreciation of beauty, his concern for order and harmony, his desire for knowledge and wisdom, his moral sense, his creative inventiveness—all appear in his record of himself and point to his divine Author. His power of choice reveals God as one who invites, but does not force, submission to His will. Family ties and other expressions of natural affection testify to the close attentiveness and protective love with which the heavenly Father observes and provides for His children and the jealous ardor with which He preserves His love relationship with His saints. In unselfish acts of heroism we may see reflections of the great self-sacrifice of the Redeemer. Particularly in the biographies of godly men these and other reflections of God appear.

The nature of God is especially apparent in the rules and systems by which He governs His creation and according to which He has ordained it should operate (Ps. 96:10; 104; 107:21-42; Col. 1:15-17). These rules and systems appear in the study of history and reveal a God of order and justice. Political history portrays the guidelines God ordained to protect the affairs of a people in a city, state, or nation in response to man's need for law and order after the fall. Economic history reveals principles for the responsible use of God-given natural resources, which man cannot afford to squander. It reveals a work ethic which, if obeyed, leads to physical sustenance and blessing. (Although man's need to work for a living is a judgment on his original disobedience [Gen. 3:17-19], it is also a means of God's promised provision of his physical needs.) The study of geography reveals the infinite wisdom and special forethought of God in planning a suitable habitat for man and regulating it for man's benefit and blessing. The study of human social relationships and emotional behavior brings to light the divine principles of personal discipline and submission to authority that man must observe to live in peace and happiness. Here, as elsewhere, the student is impressed with the truth that obedience to God's rules and established order brings blessing, whereas disobedience results in privation and ultimate destruction.

When we pass from the secular to the Biblical record, the testimony of history to the nature and laws of God comes into much sharper focus. Here we need no allowances for human fallibility or distorting viewpoints. The Biblical accounts raise history to its highest function: the revelation and demonstration of the facts fundamental to Christian belief and godliness. Old Testament history illustrates divine precepts by showing the consequences of obedience and disobedience. The Gospel narratives establish the basis of Christian belief and hope. Indeed, it may be said that history is the cornerstone of the Christian faith. "If Christ be not raised, your faith is vain; ye are yet in your sins" (I Cor. 15:17). God Himself is a historian and holds man responsible for obeying the truth taught by the inspired record.

The Christian teaching of history is therefore especially consequential for the student's growth in godliness. It shows God at work in behalf of and in response to man. It shows the results of submission, indifference, or resistance to the commands of God. From such reflections of God in history the Christian student derives a pattern of righteous character and conduct to imitate. Meanwhile his studies shore up his doctrinal beliefs and reinforce his Christian view of the world.

Manifestations of godliness in the resultant knowledge, attitudes, and skills

Attending to these reflections of God in history produces certain qualities of spiritual maturity in the character and life of the Christian student.

In general Christian character and service—The Christian study of history satisfies the human need to learn from past experiences. God allows memory of the past for our learning and commands us not to forget our heritage (Ps. 78; Prov. 22:28; Jer. 7:23-28; Rom. 15:4; I Cor. 10:11-13). The memory of man's past follies and failure helps us avoid error, while evidence of God's constancy in the past gives confidence of solid moorings in a changing world. There emerges from the Christian study of history a conviction of divine control (Prov. 21:1): the earthly course of events was begun by an act of God; it is progressively unfolding, revealing God's good purpose in His good time; and it will be brought to an end by God. This conviction of providential control over human affairs is transferable to the student's personal experience, strengthening his confidence in the wisdom and goodness of God's unfolding plan for his life.

The Christian study of history will give the student a proper toleration for those who have followed God with the light they had. He will see the error of assuming that an earlier age possessed and is responsible for the same illumination and understanding as a later period. He will observe that truth and righteousness, in the long run, tend to triumph and that error and unrighteousness are eventually destroyed, often containing within themselves the seeds of their own destruction (Prov. 14:34). This realization teaches patience and a willingness to let God execute correction and vengeance in His own good time (Heb. 10:30).

The study of history encourages a more detached, objective view of human events—a view more like God's. It is especially valuable for what it helps prevent: a narrow provincialism that either assumes the absolute uniqueness of its own times or blindly assimilates all other periods to its own. History study combats the twin errors (1) that the present is so different from the past it owes nothing to the past and can learn nothing from it and (2) that the past was just the same as the present and that to learn of other nations or times we need study only our own. From history we may learn, for example, that as a society we have reached neither the millennium of perfection nor the nadir of degradation. From history we become aware that "the past is a foreign country; they do things differently there"—sometimes more successfully than in our own time and place. The student of history thus becomes less susceptible to the prejudices of the tribe, cave, theater, and marketplace, as Francis Bacon describes them. The Christian study of history adds to this breadth of view a framework of providential purpose. The student comes to see that the events of his own time are part of a much larger panorama of God's unfolding scheme than what appears in his own time-bound perspective. Christian history thus fills in and fleshes out with details the Biblical account of man's creation and redemption so that the student can look at himself and his own age in the context of God's will for man on earth—in the way that God Himself looks at human history. The pattern he sees provides him encouragement for facing the future and challenges him with the goal of a life of fruitfulness and ultimate blessing (Acts 17:26-27).

More specifically, as a student sees reflections of God's nature and of God's laws in history, and as he observes man's response to God's revealed will, he learns to emulate qualities of godly character and action and avoid their opposite. He learns the principle of submission to government as ordained by God and exemplified by Christ (Rom. 13:1-7; I Pet. 2:13-17).

He condemns violence and lawlessness. He recognizes his obligations both to "Caesar" and to God (Mark 12:17) and understands what to do when they conflict. He learns to take advantage of his legal rights and resources. He understands that he must sometimes rebuke a godless ruler (Matt. 14:3-4; Luke 13:32) but also seeks to convert rulers and prays for those in authority over him (I Tim. 2:1-4). He learns, when necessary, to suffer patiently for righteousness' sake.

With respect to nations and governments he learns that they are accountable to God (II Chron. 19:6; Ps. 75:7; Rom. 13:1; Heb. 13:17) and that God uses them for His own purposes: to preserve and to punish other nations (Isa. 44:28-45:4; Jer. 27:6-8; 48:2; Hab. 1:5-6) and in other ways to accomplish His will in the world (Gen. 12:17-20; Exod. 7:3; I Sam. 2:8-10; Rom. 9:17). He sees that God often raises up wicked nations as instruments of judgment and lets them appear to prosper for a while before eventually judging them—the principle of deferred judgment. In economics he learns the principle of sowing and reaping (Gal. 6:7)—that is, the responsibility of laboring to earn one's sustenance. He learns the principles of stewardship with respect to all of God's gifts (Prov. 27:23-27), recognizing that God distributes His gifts differently among men as it pleases Him (Rom. 9:20-21). He applies stewardship also to geography, realizing man's duty not to abuse what God has given, but to conserve and care for it and to exercise a responsible dominion over it.

In his study of human relationships he learns of the dignity and sanctity of the family as an institution of God and finds a pattern for the home as well as for the school, church, community, and nation (Deut. 6:6-7; Prov. 4:1; 22:6; Eph. 5:22-33; Titus 2:4-5). Here he also learns to reject philosophies that teach human perfectibility and essential goodness (Ps. 62:9) and that offer false solutions to society's problems. From his study of the lives of the human makers of history, he derives an appreciation for the heroic qualities of sacrificial devotion, patient endurance, and constancy in hope. His conformity to the character and will of God revealed in these examples, patterns, and standards is the result of the Christian teaching of history.

In addition, study of history encourages a godly concern for truth (Prov. 3:3): a sense of caution in the presence of sweeping generalization and exaggeration and a corresponding sense of obligation for meticulousness and objectivity in the handling of evidence. The study of human interpretations foisted on history shows the bankruptcy of human wisdom and the superiority— indeed, the exclusive accuracy—of the Biblical view of the past. While learning these lessons, the student will also be acquiring a knowledge of the common stock of historical ideas that marks him as an educated person to the non-Christian world and adds luster to his testimony.

In special vocational service—The study of history and its related disciplines is important preparation for such diverse occupations as those of teachers; lawyers; elective and appointive governmental officials; guides and consultants at state and national parks and monuments; participants in personnel services, public relations, and community service; journalists; writers of military or institutional history or of historical fiction; archivists;

curators of historical collections; and research librarians. God calls His witness in every legitimate area of man's activity; and the opportunity for witness in these occupations, when viewed as Christian vocations, is enlarged through competent Christian preparation in the historical disciplines. Historical study has a special value as preparation for preaching and pastoral ministries, providing a fuller and more accurate sense of the unfolding plan of God in human affairs and a wealth of examples for the instruction of God's people. By increasing the scope and power of these ministries, history studies enhance their reflection of the character and work of God.

Distinctiveness

It should be clear by now that the Christian teaching of history is fundamentally different from and frequently at variance with the secular teaching of history. Technically, the "facts" are the same for both the Christian and the non-Christian. Both must strive to see things "as they really were." But the Christian is able to see more clearly. Beginning from Biblical presuppositions and with the advantage of confidence in the Biblical record and a humility arising from his awareness of human limitations, he is prepared to see better what may be seen from the writings of history.

The Biblical view of the past helps the Christian teacher of history avoid the complete self-assurance of some secularists and the complete skepticism of others. Unlike the Epicurean, the Marxist, and the Darwinist, the Christian does not believe in the *knowable schema* of history. Though God has a plan for the whole course of human existence on earth, man can know only so much of it as He has revealed. Historians, even Christian historians, have been poor prophets in the short run because the events of history do not repeat themselves; they only "rhyme."

Nevertheless, while acknowledging these limitations and maintaining a proper tentativeness concerning details, the Christian teacher of history emphasizes certainties. He insists that although history is not predictably repetitive and prophetic, it does illustrate the constancy of God's responses to man. He denies purposelessness in the events of history and teaches a unity and continuity to man's story that leave no room for accidents or chance happenings. He affirms moral causation, pointing out that nations, like men, have enjoyed the rewards of virtue without having had a knowledge of revealed truth, as for instance in the case of pre-Christian Rome with its early respect for personal morality, family honor, and duty to country.

Meanwhile, the Christian teacher of history selects and orders his facts differently from his secular counterpart. He insists on considering the whole man in history; for interpretations that emphasize a single sphere of experience—whether economic, social, philosophic, or even religious—limit God's motives and are out of balance. He reminds students of the selectivity of historical writings, showing how selectivity is necessarily and legitimately influenced by the historian's purpose and framework of interpretation. The historical books of the Old Testament, he notes, specifically disclaim the recording of even all the "important" facts about the reigns of the various kings (e.g., II Chron. 28:26), selecting their facts according to a spiritual purpose. The Apostle John remarks that, though a world of books could hardly contain a complete account of Jesus' acts, "these are written, that ye might believe" (John 20:30-31; 21:25). The Christian teacher condemns secularist distortions of history not because they are selective and refer to an external framework of interpretation, for these are necessary. He condemns them because of their imbalance, dishonesty with the facts, and unbelief concerning the Biblical record. The Christian teacher of history, in his own practice, is careful not to distort his subject by arbitrarily slighting some period in favor of others he considers to have been more receptive to Christian beliefs and values. There are Christian lessons to be learned from every period, and a knowledge of each period contributes importantly to a Christian understanding of the whole. Christian selectivity and interpretation are therefore an outgrowth of Christian belief but are not dishonestly biased. They result from the attempt to represent reality with the greatest clarity and insight—to show the course of human events from the view of God.

Practical application in the classroom

The Biblical starting point and frame of reference of Christian history teaching determine course content and objectives. Their effect on the student is to bring vast tracts of knowledge within the compass of his Christian world view and to give him principles for life. A class discussion of the sixteenth-century Protestant Reformation would likely observe the Lord's propitious ordering of events on the eve of that century, making possible the "success" of that movement, in contrast to the fate of similar movements in earlier centuries. Movable-type printing had been introduced in the fifteenth-century, permitting rapid and inexpensive distribution of ideas and writings, including the Bible. National states and princes were in competition with one another, fiercely resisting interference by foreign powers, including the papacy of Rome. The papacy itself was filled by a succession of men either flagrantly immoral or amazingly ignorant of the theological issues raised by the reformers. The reformers, for their part, had been inspired by a desire for personal assurance of salvation and for a restoration of the primitive Christian church. To the latter end, the Renaissance had fashioned the tools of lay education, fostered the study of classical and Biblical languages, and generated a spirit of examination and constructive criticism. All these together God prearranged and then used for His own purposes of destroying the European ecclesiastical monopoly of Rome, reasserting individual responsibility, and restoring individual liberty, both spiritual and political.

A course in the history of the United States would emphasize the providential circumstance of its founding and associate its prosperity with its obedience to God. The Reformation was used by God to bring a prepared people to a prepared land as a model of God's blessing upon the obedience of His people. God protected this people and blessed them with religious, civil, and economic freedom. He also chastened them, using two wars, the "Revolution" and the "Civil War," to punish disobedience and faithlessness in the midst of economic prosperity. Bringing healing after their suffering, He united the people around a Constitution after the first war (in spite of those who preferred state sovereignty or loose confederation) and reunited the nation after the second. Thus a nation—born, in part, of Christian principles—was formed and preserved in spite of factors, both external and internal, that should have caused it to fail. During the latter part of the nineteenth century, Christians found their society overwhelmed by materialism, secularism, big statism, humanism, and denominational apostasy. As a result of their concern the nation became a leader in world evangelism and was blessed by great revival movements. Desiring to make available to the rest of the world the material as well as spiritual blessings of their society and to protect the freedoms of the peoples of other lands, the United States fought two world wars. Though its cause prevailed by providential favor, it trusted in its military might rather than in God, and so the peace was lost. In the history of this nation God has once again illustrated the truth that obedience to Him brings prosperity, and disobedience failure.

Points of conflict with the secular philosophy of teaching history

History teaching that is distinctively Christian rejects certain philosophical attitudes and approaches that stem from modern unbelief. In particular it opposes humanism, which denies the existence of a personal God, rejects all value systems external to man, and trusts in human self-sufficiency. Humanism believes in progress on the basis of rational (particularly scientific) principles. It determines ethical behavior situationally, relative to service to fellowmen, rather than by principles deriving from moral absolutes. It pragmatically assumes that the end justifies the means. The following errors reveal the fundamental conflict between the Christian and the humanist teaching of history.

Cynicism—Even professional historians sometimes treat history as if it had no value other than for academic credit or professional employment. The Christian teacher presents history, both oral and written, with the conviction that it is not without meaning or value beyond itself. He also, however, rejects the belief that all topics are equally worthy of historical study—from jackknife carving in ancient Egypt before the middle of the Old Kingdom to the history of pornography in Keokuk. There are some topics that are not "good" or "profitable" for the Christian student and should not be assigned. The Christian teacher avoids and condemns another kind of cynicism: the practice of debunking genuine heroes and creating unwholesome ones, of debasing good men and exalting sinners. "Woe unto them that call evil good, and good evil," wrote the prophet in a time of moral declension too like our own (Isa. 5:20). Similarly the Christian teacher rejects an egalitarianism that attacks as evil the exceptional endowments and achievements of the few. Gifts of leadership are to be recognized and valued by society rather than questioned and ignored. Moreover, behavioral norms are not, for the Christian, to be drawn from statistical aggregates; average conduct, in moral matters such as heroism, is not the divine ideal for men. The depreciation of individual excellence is an expression of the moral pessimism of a spiritually bankrupt age.

Relativism—Common in modern historical study is the belief that there is no correct interpretation of the historical record or even degree of correctness. The Christian teacher of history recognizes, however, that explanations are not equally true or false. He has an infallible historical record by which to judge human writings of history and systems of interpretation. Furthermore, he is not so entirely skeptical of the reliability of the human senses and reason as to conclude that nothing can be known from human observation and inference. Good interpretation, he believes, accounts for more of the facts of history, and accounts more fully for them, than does poor interpretation, and conforms more closely to the statements and perspective of Scripture.

The Christian history teacher also understands that the inevitable differences in separate historical accounts of a particular event need not imply the impossibility of certainty but that separate perspectives may be complementary rather than contradictory. Highly individualistic angles of perception control the narratives of the four Gospels. And yet as complementary, corroborative accounts of the earthly ministry of the Saviour, they illuminate brilliantly, rather than distort and cloud, the divine subject they consider from their separate vantage points. Other parallel accounts, such as those in the Old Testament books of Kings and Chronicles, illustrate the truth that individuality and multiplicity of perspective need not validate relativism or encourage skepticism. Cumulatively, in converging fashion, the accounts of Biblical history provide perfect knowledge of the nature and works of God necessary to man's fulfillment of divine purpose.

Pragmatism—Sometimes propaganda masquerades as responsible history. Modern instances of such propaganda include pseudodocumentaries on television and "new leftist" interpretations narrowly based on the author's revolutionary presuppositions without regard to historical accuracy. Political parties and candidates evidence pragmatism when they cite Thomas Jefferson, Washington's Farewell Address, or even passages of Scripture out of context in order to win votes. In the Christian's hands, history should be an ax at the root of manmade theoretical systems. It should emphasize the exceptions to the rules of these systems—stubborn facts that their authors ignore. The Christian teacher of history does not claim omniscience, the ability to interpret every event. He acknowledges the limitations of finiteness. He resists comfortable interpretations, both simplistic and narrowly partisan.

The Christian teacher must also, for the sake of honesty and consistency, be careful to guard against similar aberrations in his own historical interpretation. The blood of the martyrs is not always the seed of the church (as, for example, in France after the revocation of the Edict of Nantes and in modern China). Economic collapse does not necessarily bring about religious revival; in fact, the opposite is more often true. The Christian teacher of United States history must resist the temptation to identify the American nation as God's particular chosen people and its history as a peculiar and ultimate fulfillment of the purpose of the incarnation of Jesus Christ. While he appreciates a political environment in which the gospel may prosper and a legacy of divine blessing for the obedience to God of past generations, he does not consider the characteristics of American society a list of Christian essentials. Whereas the concept of limited government and the principle of checks and balances reflect the need to place restraints on man because of his depravity, they are not peculiarly Christian. Likewise, separation of church and state has been a congenial setting for American religious liberty, but the doctrine is not specifically a Biblical teaching. On the contrary, theocratic monolithic government was the political means of God's blessing upon ancient Israel and will be reinstated during the millennium with the reign of Christ. It was also the form of government instituted by the Puritan settlers of New England. American Christians can argue the merits of their political system and way of life on more accurate and substantial bases than their fidelity to a supposed Biblical archetype. They are thankful for their political system principally because it safeguards their freedom to serve God.

Conclusion

The kind of history teaching just described enables the Christian teacher to carry out the general purpose of Christian education and to fulfill for his students the specific function of history in the life of God's people. History, to the Christian, has a warning function: "Now all these things happened unto them for ensamples: and they are written for our admonition, upon whom the ends of the world are come" (I Cor. 10:11). But it also comforts: "For whatsoever things were written aforetime were written for our learning, that we through patience and comfort of the scriptures might have hope" (Rom. 15:4). The consequence of this twofold ministry in the life of the Christian student is his increasing conformity to the image of God in Christ, his godliness of character and service.

The Christian Teaching of Mathematics

8

Definition

Mathematics as a discipline comprises (1) the symbols and operations used to represent quantitative characteristics of the physical world and (2) the principles and relationships found in an analytical examination of those symbols and operations. Successful mathematical study requires not only computational skills but also an understanding of the way the computed quantities relate to one another. Many of these abstracted relationships are so thoroughly interrelated and so frequently recurring that studies of them have been grouped into separate subject areas, such as arithmetic, algebra, geometry, trigonometry, and calculus.

Mathematics is not usually considered an empirical science—that is, an experimental discipline like physics or chemistry. It is almost always classified as a deductive, or rigorous, science—one that does not involve experimental technique. For example, the development of calculus by men like Gottfried Wilhelm von Leibniz and Sir Isaac Newton sprang from a need to study physical processes and obtain practical answers. It was more than one hundred years later that calculus was placed on a sound deductive basis by men like Augustin Louis Cauchy and Georg Friedrich Riemann. Mathematical ideas, for the most part, spring from the natural sciences. It seems to be their nature, however, to grow into the purely deductive and aesthetic to such a point that their original roots are obscure. The definition recognizes the close tie between mathematics and the physical world.

Justification

Of all the subjects in the curriculum of the Christian school, mathematics may seem to be the one least affected by religious presuppositions. It also may seem to have the least potentiality for serving the spiritual education. This is a misconception. The Christian teaching of mathematics, like that of any other subject, advances the student in Christ-likeness by teaching him to know God and to imitate Him. The student learns about God from reflections of Him in the subject matter of mathematics and then incorporates what he has learned of God in his character and service.

Reflections of God in the subject matter

Mathematical study points to the underlying structure of the universe and therefore to its intelligent design. This design is evidence of a wise, all-powerful Creator. Even though mathematical systems are products of human reasoning, they reveal the outer world; for both reasoning ability and the physical universe are the work of the Creator.

In the functioning of man's mind—God has given man the capacity to reason mathematically. This reasoning is common to all mankind and, though marred by the fall, reflects its Creator's orderly thought. God in the Scriptures is said to reason. In Isaiah 1:18 the Lord urges, ''Come now, and let us reason together.'' In the Gospels Christ used reason to reveal truth and combat error. He countered the Sadducees' teaching against life after death by reasoning deductively from the Old Testament and from a self-evident truth. ''Have ye not read that which was spoken unto you by God, saying, I am the God of Abraham, and the God of Isaac, and the God of Jacob? God is not the God of the dead, but of the living'' (Matt. 22:31-32). He left the Sadducees to draw the obvious conclusion, and the multitude was ''astonished at his doctrine [teaching]'' (v. 33). The Christian study of mathematics finds in human reasoning a reflection of the divine.

Man in his reasoning need not follow a previously existing logical development; he can also create that development himself. Mathematicians, for example, distill their perception of physical relationships into mathematical "models," or simplifications of observed operations and principles. Behind these constructs is a type of thinking that is far more imaginative than pure inductive and deductive proof. God, the original and primary creator (Gen. 1:1), has placed in the mind of man an intricate and fascinating capacity to observe reality and then to explore and formulate relationships and consequences that both explain and predict. This mathematical way of thinking the American mathematician George Polya called "plausible reasoning." He explained it in terms of clever guessing, formulation of hypotheses, and the inductive attitude. Unregenerate men would like to explain this reasoning process as mere "genius," but the image of God in man and the orderly touch of the Creator are the only explanations satisfactory to the Christian.

Another characteristic of human thinking that is interwoven with the ability to formulate mathematics is the attraction to structure, form, beauty, and orderliness. Although some may scoff at the idea of beauty in mathematics, the twentieth-century English mathematician G. H. Hardy compares the mathematician to the painter and the poet and regards beauty as "the first test" of a mathematical system. The aesthetic consideration in mathematics is but another of its reflections of the character of God; for man, like God, desires that the mathematical products of his mind be aesthetically pleasing.

In the structure of the physical universe—It is proper to tie mathematics, though an expression of the human mind, with the physical universe; for both the human mind and the physical universe are the work of the same Creator. Since God has designed a relationship between the two, human mathematical systems correlate with the physical reality to which they are applied. The psalmist exclaims, "The heavens declare the glory of God; and the firmament sheweth his handywork" (Ps. 19:1). The Christian should find his mathematics making a similar declaration as he uses it to study creation. The study of mathematics reveals a world of complexity, harmony, and precision—qualities befitting the handiwork of God.

Complexity—With its ability to derive models of the phenomenon of creation, the mathematics of even some very elementary physics can be extremely complicated. Every student of atomic physics, for example, has had the traumatic first experience of solving the Schrödinger equation for the quantum description of the hydrogen atom. If this, the simplest of atoms, strains man's mental powers, what must be the mathematical model of the uranium atom? Mathematics demonstrates repeatedly the awesome complexity of creation. There is thus no possibility that blind chance and evolutionary ages put our universe together; it is far too complex. It must be the work of an infinite intelligence.

Harmony—Harmonious mathematical structures and patterns occur abundantly in nature; the French mathematician Pascal, having recognized such patterns, said "God is the great geometer." Man himself has borrowed from this harmonious structure. The Parthenon of ancient Greece, for example, had a rectangular shape that the architects found artistically pleasing. The ratio of the length to the width of this rectangle was approximately 1.618, the so-called "Golden Ratio." This irrational number, precisely rendered $\frac{1}{2}(1 + \sqrt{5})$, shows up repeatedly in nature: in the spiral of the nautilus shell, in the whorls of the pineapple, in the arrangement of seeds in the sunflower, and in the geometry of the pentagon, the five-pointed star, and the regular icosahedron. Once again, the harmonious unity of creation shines forth in the study of its mathematical relationships.

The relationship of mathematics to art and music appears in their natural harmonious structure. The concepts of symmetry, pattern, perspective, tone, and texture in art and those of volume, pitch, timbre, blend, harmony, and rhythm in music can all be expressed to some degree mathematically. A vibrating string or tuning fork moves in a simple harmonic motion that most students of trigonometry and physics know as the superposition of several sine waves. Mathematically we can predict that certain sounds will be dissonant because they are not in accord with the natural harmonics of creation. The artist's creative possibilities are vast, but the further he moves away from the intrinsic mathematical principles of nature, the fewer will be the human minds with which he can effectively communicate his ideas. Thus the harmony-within-complexity of the universe is like the orderly complexity of mathematics. It shows the infinite wisdom and care of a master designer and a divine concern for both utility and beauty.

Precision—The heavens further declare the glory of God by their precision. This precision is well illustrated by the experience of the late physicist and author Professor Samuel R. Williams of

Columbia University and Amherst College. As a young college student Williams made his first trip to the college observatory to view a particular star whose position had been carefully calculated. All of the equipment was meticulously in place, and the sidereal clock was running. With his eye to the eyepiece, he waited in suspense as the seconds ticked by. Then, at precisely the right moment, the star came into the focal plane. He tells of his excitement as he observed once again the precise order of God's universe. This experience, Williams said, was instrumental in his conversion. God's heavenly timepiece ticks on, kept in perfect regularity by divine omnipotence and wisdom. The mathematics required to study the heavens is very complicated and very often crude, for there are so many forces acting and so many directions of motion that it is nearly impossible to account for them all. But our mathematical abilities and systems, however short they fall, still reveal the omnipotence of our Lord and the infinite precision of His handiwork.

Manifestations of godliness in the resultant knowledge, attitudes, and skills

The reflections of God in mathematical studies, when recognized by the student, encourage his growth in Christ-likeness.

In general Christian character and service—The study of mathematical structures and procedures can improve the student's own mental clarity, helping him think less like the world and more like God. The study of logic will lessen the chances of his using or falling prey to such fallacies as the false dilemma, begging the question, and guilt by association. He will develop an appreciation for correctness of procedure and accuracy in dealing with the facts. In so doing, he will be fulfilling the Apostle Paul's command to "provide things honest in the sight of all men" (Rom. 12:17). In studying algebra and geometry especially, he will learn perseverance in a difficult task, perhaps failing several times before obtaining the solution to a difficult problem. This training in discipline and faithfulness to an assigned task will help him "faint not" amidst the difficulties of serving Christ in this world (Gal. 6:9; Heb. 12:11-13).

The study of mathematics will also keep the student aware of his own limitations. As he strains his mental faculties to their utmost, he will realize that there are many truths—in the physical as well as the spiritual realm—that are simply beyond his ability to understand. He will appreciate the Scripture's warning against reliance upon human reasoning to the exclusion of the work of the Holy Spirit: "Trust in the Lord with all thine heart; and lean not unto thine own understanding" (Prov. 3:5). Thus warned, he will learn not merely the proper use but also the proper place of human reasoning. He will exercise his reasoning ability as a vehicle of, rather than as a substitute for, the work of the Holy Spirit in and through his life.

The habit of proceeding by principles, so necessary in mathematics, is transferable to the moral and spiritual life. To be successful in his profession, the mathematician must imitate the consistency of creation in practicing mathematical principles. To be successful as a person, he, like everyone else, must practice this consistency in his moral life. This he often does not do. The Christian student, recognizing that the universe operates by principles, realizes that he must establish a principled life as well. He learns to make his decisions not on the basis of an emotional "hunch" or the circumstances of the moment, but by careful consideration of principles of Christian behavior and growth. He understands that just as disobedience to mathematical principles incurs a penalty (whether the academic penalty for wrong answers or the more serious professional and public consequences of carelessness in collapsed bridges and buildings), so a disregard for moral and spiritual principles brings humiliation and ruin. The principle of punishment for disobedience and reward for obedience is a consequence of Christian mathematical, as well as Biblical, study.

In special vocational service—Mathematics is not only an aid to general character training; it is also the key that opens doors of opportunity into many vocations. God calls many Christians into fields of service that are not necessarily "the ministry of the gospel" as practiced by a preacher or a missionary. Faithful Christians are needed in every legitimate profession to be the salt of the earth and the light of the gospel to a lost world. What many young people and even their counselors do not realize is that mathematics is a prerequisite to many vocations, especially those that involve some degree of technology. Does a young person feel called to serve as a Christian doctor or engineer? Sound training in mathematics is a critical prerequisite. Most sciences and many business fields require a strong background in mathematics. Mathematics thus is essential for the service of God in a variety of fields.

Distinctiveness

It should be obvious by now that the Christian teaching of mathematics and the secular are fundamentally different. Christian belief permeates the Christian mathematics classroom. Though the wise Christian teacher of mathematics does not turn his classroom into a Bible class, his teaching reveals that he has made the Bible his intellectual and spiritual home. His teaching is distinguished from the secular by certain emphases.

For example, the secularist assumption that mathematics is solely the product of the human mind tends to glorify man's intellectual prowess and to inflate his ego. It views man as the master of his own destiny, able to lift himself out of chaos and to develop a utopian world. It denies any distinction between the divine and the human mind and any role of God in determining the mathematical relationships that prevail throughout the universe. Secular educators, for the most part, want their students to become practical atheists. On the other hand, the Christian mathematics teacher emphasizes that the source of wisdom and knowledge is the Lord and that a keen mind is a gift from God—in other words, that there is no justifiable cause for intellectual egotism (I Cor. 4:7; James 1:17). He also reminds his students constantly that in mathematics, as in any other subject, they cannot rely entirely upon their innate abilities.

The Christian mathematics teacher, unlike the secular, emphasizes the evidence of purposeful design in the universe. He illustrates this design by such means as pictures and diagrams that point out natural geometric patterns and their functions. The geometry of the honeycomb, for example, provides the most efficient structure for strength against collapsing. Although the circle is slightly stronger than the honeycomb's hexagon, it leaves small apertures of wasted space; the hexagon, on the other hand, wastes no space at all. A demonstration of the Fibonacci numbers, or the Golden Ratio, and of occurrences of these in the geometry of nature shows the mathematical consistency of nature, another evidence of intelligent design. This consistency supports the Christian view of creation while facilitating scientific activity of all kinds. A teleological view of the universe is integral to Christian mathematics teaching and indeed is inherent in the Christian definition of mathematics.

Practical application in the classroom

The study of mathematics provides many opportunities for promoting spiritual understanding and growth in godliness. In nearly every class period the Christian teacher of mathematics can reinforce such moral habits as diligence, honesty, precision, and perseverance. For example, many an elementary or secondary school student, when struggling with a problem that involves application of newly learned principles, "invents" a rule that seems to simplify the problem. In the process, however, he violates principles he has already learned. The Christian teacher will see in the student's confusion an opportunity to emphasize the importance of acting on principle rather than according to feelings or circumstances. Procedure by principle is no less necessary in the moral and spiritual life than in mathematics. Principle-based decision making is the only way that a person's life can have any degree of order or consistency.

An advanced class, particularly of future mathematics teachers, could benefit from an expanded discussion of this topic. For several decades mathematical training consisted largely of the memorizing and practicing of certain computational functions: the multiplication table, long division, and so forth. But this purely "skill-and-drill" approach, sometimes referred to as "traditional math," has definite weaknesses. The students often attained only superficial knowledge and sometimes acquired a distinct distaste for mathematics in general. Many were incapable of applying their mathematical learning to real-life situations. And when they reached upper-level mathematics courses such as trigonometry and calculus, they did not have the principled foundation they needed. The stupefying effect of this approach was one of several motivating factors in the rise of the so-called new math, which was most popular in elementary and secondary school programs in the early 1960s. This mathematics overemphasized the study of set theory, alternative bases (i.e., bases other than ten—most commonly two, five, and twelve), and other theoretical ideas. Because of the extremes to which the teaching of theory was carried, teachers, parents, and students were all confused. The entire program was fraught with mistakes.

The supposed dichotomy between rote memorization (championed by "traditional math") and principled analysis (promoted by "new math") has brought about the often bitter battles between advocates of the two. But the Christian philosophy of mathematics is not on one "side" or the other. Both "new" math and "skill-and-drill" math are distortions—albeit in opposite directions—of proper educational technique. The principled foundation that new math overemphasizes is essential to a thorough understanding of mathematics in general; it introduces the student to the mathematical way of thinking and thus increases his chances for success in upper-level mathematics courses and in applying his mathematical knowledge to real-life situations. But the student also needs to learn and master computational skills; without them he cannot apply the principles that he has learned. New math's one-sided emphasis on principles was the main reason for its dismal failure; students learned theory to the virtual exclusion of application. The Christian teacher of mathematics lays an appropriate theoretical foundation for computational skills, teaching the student *why* as well as *how* mathematics functions. In so doing he is not only exercising sound Christian judgment but also returning to the best pedagogical practice of a century ago.

In the process of teaching the principled basis that underlies mathematics, however, the teacher will introduce material that might be misunderstood if it is presented carelessly. When "new math" began teaching the principles of alternative bases, for example, many parents were angered by what they thought were attacks on absolutes; students began to learn, apparently, that two plus two no longer equals four. New math made the mistake of failing to teach clearly a perfectly valid principle. Computation with alternative bases demonstrates that whatever numeration system is used, the idea underlying an equation remains constant. In base four, for example, "2 + 2" stills equals "four"; but "four" in base four is written "10," not "4." The absolute truth has not changed, even though the method of writing it has. Rather than destroying absolutes, the teaching of principles helps to confirm them by demonstrating that the concept "two" plus the concept "two" always equals the concept "four," regardless of the numeration system used to indicate it. We engage in this sort of thinking every day when we tell time. Eleven o'clock plus two hours is one o'clock, not thirteen o'clock, according to the common method of computation. Obviously we do not believe that $11 + 2 \neq 13$; we simply numerate "13" differently.

The Christian teacher can use these ideas (adapted, of course, to the appropriate grade level) to develop in his students an appreciation for the importance of learning and abiding by principles in real life as well as in mathematics classes. The math teacher does not seek unthinking computations any more than God seeks mindless obedience.

Points of conflict with the secular philosophy of teaching mathematics

The Christian teaching of mathematics is at odds with the secular-humanistic point of view with respect to the neutrality of mathematics and the nature of mathematical reality.

The neutrality of mathematics—Some secular mathematicians have maintained that mathematics is neutral, or amoral, neither influencing nor influenced by religious beliefs. Even a brief look at the history of mathematical development, however, bears out the fact that many facets of this discipline were conceived amid stormy religious discussions that were anything but "neutral." The mathematical calculations of Galileo and Copernicus brought them into conflict with religious authorities, for their conclusions challenged—rightly—the erroneous concepts of the Roman Catholic church. Recent mathematician-philosophers such as Bertrand Russell and Alfred North Whitehead used mathematics to project world views at odds with the Scriptures. Accordingly, in the elementary, secondary, or college classroom mathematics is a convenient instrument for projecting and reinforcing either a secular or a Christian view of physical reality.

The subjectivity of mathematics—To hold to what is called the "neutrality postulate" of mathematics is not only out of step with reality; it has a disastrous consequence as well in that it leads to the belief that certain mathematical ideas have no real existence in themselves. Such a belief is completely at odds with the Christian teaching of mathematics.

The question "Does mathematical reality exist apart from the human mind?" leads to the key distinction between Christian and secular mathematical philosophy. Proponents of the idea that mathematics is solely a human construct—that mathematical laws and relationships exist only because man sees them—claim that there is absolutely no mathematical reality outside the human mind. This philosophy, which is akin to the suggestion that a tree falling in a forest makes no noise unless someone hears it, militates against the idea of a nonhuman logical being—God. The Christian mathematics teacher, on the other hand, believes that mathematical structure is an intrinsic characteristic of the creative works of God. It may be predicated of the universe on the basis of human perception because God is the author of both the universe and the human mind. For example, man has invented a formula as a model for simple harmonic motion: $x = c_i \cos(\omega t + \phi)$. The formula is useful because it is an honest description of a mathematical reality in creation as well as an outgrowth of careful systematic thought. Faith in God enables the Christian student of mathematics to believe that mathematical systems can be both self-consistent and consistent with the realities of the physical world.

Conclusion

The differences between Christian and secular mathematics teaching amount to more than petty professional quibbling. They arise from the fundamental philosophical conflict between those who accept the authority of God's Word and those who reject it. In a truly Christian curriculum the student learns mathematics with a respect for divine truth as revealed through God's Word and God's universe. Indeed he learns that because all truth is of God, even the simplest mathematical equations are gifts of the Creator. The Christian mathematics teacher, unlike the secular, recognizes and acknowledges his indebtedness to God for the truth he teaches. The reward for such teaching is a student intellectually well trained, yet very much aware of his dependence upon his Maker, whose designs are ever flawless.

The Christian Teaching of Science

9

The Christian teaching of science requires not only a good command of basic subject matter but also the spiritual perception to discern truth from error in a great variety of contexts. As a prerequisite for this, the Christian teacher of science must be thoroughly grounded in the Word of God. Moreover, he must have firmly implanted in his mind a Biblical framework of truth which serves as the touchstone for his decision making. True science will fit that framework; anything that fails to fit the Biblical framework must be rejected as erroneous. The present discussion demonstrates the need for a distinctively Christian philosophy of science teaching and surveys the differences between Christian and secular science education.

Definition

Science is the systematic study of nature, based on observations. If a phenomenon cannot be observed by man's senses, either directly or with the aid of instruments, it cannot be dealt with scientifically. For example, all speculations concerning ultimate origins are excluded from the lawful domain of science, since the necessary observations cannot be performed. Closely akin to science is technology, the practical application of scientifically acquired knowledge. Science and technology are often intertwined to the extent that it is impossible to teach the one without touching upon the other.

True science, diligently studied and carefully taught, will dispel a multitude of myths. Unfortunately, it has become fashionable in today's media to erase the line of demarcation between true science and science fiction. The Christian teacher of science can render a valuable service to his students by reestablishing that line and stressing its significance.

Justification

Reflections of God in the subject matter

In the study of nature—The Christian can gain an enhanced appreciation for the God he serves by studying His creation (Ps. 19:1; Rom. 1:20). With the present level of sophistication in scientific instruments and techniques, we are in a position to appreciate more fully than ever before the majestic splendor of His handiwork. Moreover, we can ascertain several of God's attributes through a study of His workmanship. His wisdom is displayed in the marvelously contrived design of the universe and its parts; His omnipotence is manifested in the sheer vastness of its structure; His sovereignty as lawgiver is seen in the ordinances that govern it. His benevolence is attested by His abundant provision for the needs of His creatures. Though it is now flawed by the fall, nature still bears God's distinct and indelible imprint.

Another benefit of modern research has been an increased cognizance of some remarkable scientific statements contained in Scripture—statements that can be attributed only to the author of the universe Himself, for they manifest an understanding of the intricate workings of nature far in advance of the day in which they were written. Among these are the assertion of Jeremiah 33:22 that the stars cannot be numbered and the declaration in Ecclesiastes 1:6 that the wind follows a cyclic pattern.

The above perspectives, properly taught, can heighten the student's awareness of God's greatness and goodness. Moreover, they should draw him closer to the Lord and encourage him to emulate the one who "hath done all things well" (Mark 7:37). The student with a fuller, more accurate understanding of reality— a view more like God's—may be conformed more readily to the mind of Christ.

In the history of science—It is instructive for the modern Christian to study the lives of great scientists who were believers and to note the evidences of the Creator's hand they looked for and found as they studied nature. Such venerable researchers as Robert Boyle, Michael Faraday, Lord Kelvin, Johannes Kepler, Matthew Maury, and James Clerk Maxwell approached their work with an attitude of extreme reverence and humility. These men, in a tradition that has been all but lost in scientific circles, reported their findings in a manner that placed the emphasis on the greatness and goodness of the Creator, rather than on the theoretical or experimental prowess of the researcher. It was Kepler who set the example for all who followed him in attempting to ''think God's thoughts after Him.'' As an astronomer he believed that God had given scientists in that field of study the special privilege of learning about His glory by studying the heavens. These men then had the responsibility of disseminating this knowledge of His majesty by making their findings known to men. It is an enriching experience indeed to glean insights from men of keen minds who were rightly oriented to God's truth.

Manifestations of godliness in the resultant knowledge, attitudes, and skill

In general Christian character and service—A student who seriously pursues some area of experimental science will find that it requires and develops self-discipline. Instead of taking a casual, hit-or-miss approach to making observations, he learns to be precise and meticulous, carefully controlling his operating conditions, proceeding in logical steps, and recording his data neatly and efficiently. This organization is transferable to other areas of the student's life, developing him into a better-regulated person. To a limited degree a student of science is required to mirror God's activity. This is manifested in a general way in the care and concern he must exercise for his work; it is also manifested in certain specific operations, such as measurement, synthesis, purification, and evaluation.

Second, science can be a tool to aid a student's understanding of Scripture. For example, a knowledge of the chemical composition of the salt used by the ancients enables one to comprehend how it could lose its savor (Matt. 5:13; Mark 9:50). (The salt, a mixture of sodium chloride and impurities, loses its strength with exposure to moisture, as the sodium chloride dissolves, leaving impurities.) A knowledge of early metallurgical processes provides insight into the meaning of purging away the dross from the life of an individual or a nation (Prov. 25:4-5; Isa. 1:25; Ezek. 22:18-22). A study of the properties of gold drives home the meaning of the analogy of a vessel that is pliable in the hands of its Creator, capable of repeated refining (Job 23:10).

Third, the Christian student who receives a thorough grounding in true science develops his defenses against a number of "isms" that are built upon "science falsely so called" (I Tim. 6:20)—evolutionism, communism, fascism, scientism, modernism, liberalism, humanism, and environmentalism. Our young people are continually bombarded with a variety of pseudoscientific claims—on television and in newspapers, books, and magazines. Many of the statements they hear have religious overtones. The science courses in the Christian school provide an antidote for such onslaughts, furnishing continuing guidance for our students at various levels of instruction, helping them to stay "on course."

Fourth, a knowledge of science can enhance the Christian's testimony by giving him a point of contact with a sizable segment of the population. Almost everyone possesses an appreciation, at least, for the *results* of science, if not for the intricacies of its inner workings. The nature of our society dictates that every citizen know *some* science. Other things being equal, it is a better testimony for a Christian to be knowledgeable about such matters than to be ignorant. Today even the so-called common man whose vocation has nothing to do with science (if that is in fact possible) must have a working knowledge of basic scientific terms to understand even his daily newspaper. Slightly more erudite reading can make considerably greater demands upon his scientific vocabulary. A knowledge of metric units (taught in science courses) is important for many kinds of purchases; a knowledge of physical principles can often assist in making intelligent choices of tools, appliances, and other household commodities. The life of the Christian becomes incalculably more useful to God as well as more enjoyable to himself when he understands something about the earth he lives on, the objects he views in the night sky, the plants he cultivates in his garden, the food he eats, and the physical body he inhabits.

In special service—It is not unrealistic to expect that a certain percentage of the students we educate will feel called to scientific vocations. In addition to the obvious benefits of having Christian witnesses in the scientific community, the infusion of qualified Christian personnel should have a salutary effect on both the quality of the research that is performed and the philosophical interpretation of that research. More than once in the past a believing scientist has been in a position to lay an ungodly theory to rest before it had the opportunity to gain more widespread support.

If the Christian school has performed its role faithfully, its graduates not only will be able to compete favorably in their higher-education or specialized-training programs but also should perform better in general than students who have been educated in secular schools. There are at least two reasons for this. First, the Christian student has been taught *true* science, more clearly and realistically. Second, many of the character traits he has acquired during the course of his Christian training—orderliness, diligence, patience, perseverance, honesty, and dependability—will stand him in good stead for the work that lies ahead. When he occupies his post in industry, in the teaching profession, or wherever he might be called, other things being equal, he should do so more capably than his secular counterpart. This superiority will strengthen his testimony and help defeat the notion that Christian faith and scientific achievement are mutually exclusive.

In fact, in a very specific way, Christian character facilitates scientific achievement. Most technological advances have resulted from team effort. When a member of a scientific community bases his work on the amount of recognition he can receive, he creates jealousies within the community that tend to stifle exchange and generous collaboration. Theories that have outlived their usefulness may be vehemently defended in disregard of scientific evidence, to the detriment of science as a whole. A scientist working unselfishly gives preference in honor to his scientific colleagues and, if he is a Christian, refers all glory to God.

Distinctiveness

The Christian who labors in the field of science or science education does many things the same way that his secular counterpart does. To a great extent he uses and teaches the same facts and laws. His research equipment and instructional aids are much the same. Where, then, does the difference lie? Ironically, a major distinction is the fact that the Christian is more consistently committed to the key ingredient of the scientific method—observation—than is his unregenerate counterpart. The latter is often prone to rely more heavily on human speculations than on the data themselves, especially when they are inimical to his evolutionary-humanistic beliefs. The Christian is specially motivated to be scrupulously honest in both the recording and the interpretation of his data, for he does his work as unto the Lord rather than unto men. Other distinctives have to do with certain erroneous beliefs and practices to which the Christian does *not* fall victim. These will be enumerated in the section on the limitations of science and the section on the points of conflict with the secular philosophy of teaching science.

Practical application in the classroom

A discussion of the empirical method in a Christian classroom would differ markedly from its presentation in a secular school. It might proceed in the following manner.

Despite its frequent abuses and many limitations, the fact remains that, apart from divine revelation, the empirical approach (i.e., methodology based on observation and experiment) is the most reliable means available to man for gaining basic information about nature. Actually there are a few alternatives—intuition, guesswork, extrapolation from known data, and prediction based on theory— all of which are demonstrably deficient in their reliability.

The so-called scientific method is nothing more than a sophisticated technique for finding answers to questions. There is no single set of procedures or standardized list of steps that constitute the scientific method. There are probably as many variants of the method as there are researchers. All, however, would (or should in principle, at least) agree that *observation* is the key ingredient of the method. If a phenomenon cannot be observed, it cannot be dealt with scientifically. As creationists—those who hold that the universe was spoken into existence in substantially its present form by the miraculous acts of God described in Genesis 1 and 2—we contend for faithful adherence to the actual observations in every area of science. We oppose the trend of licentious theorizing that has invaded too many disciplines, much of which runs directly counter to the observations. In genetics the empirical data indicate that each organism breeds true, reproducing after its kind (Gen. 1:11, 12, 21, 24, 25). Yet theorists imaginatively postulate "molecules-to-man" evolution. In astronomy, only degenerative processes are observed in stars and interstellar clouds. Nevertheless, it is speculated that such clouds are capable of organizing themselves into stars, a suggestion that flies squarely in the face of three and a half centuries of telescopic observations. Regrettably, evolutionary theory has been exalted to the point where men trust it more than their own eyes.

Observations are made using one or more of the senses. As with any human activity, there is an element of fallibility involved in this operation. Optical illusions and other misinterpretations of sensory information are a definite possibility and must be carefully guarded against. To this end investigation involves numerous observations with as many different instruments and by as many independent observers as possible. In spite of these precautions, spurious observations do occasionally find their way into the scientific literature. A classic example of this was the so-called canals of Mars, attested by many astronomers in various parts of the world. It is now realized that the "canals" were an optical illusion. Does this invalidate observation as an acceptable tool of science? Not at all, for when the error was corrected, it was done by again using observations. Space probes photographing the Martian surface from close range provided the detail and clarity that had been unobtainable with earth-based telescopes. As can be readily seen, data vary widely in the error they contain.

The use of observation is not without Biblical endorsement. Under Old Testament law the testimony of two or three witnesses was sufficient to condemn a defendant to death (Deut. 17:6). This quite obviously placed a heavy premium on sense-derived information. In the New Testament the Lord invited Thomas to both see and feel the nail prints in His hands (John 20:27). As a result of what he observed, Thomas was instantly convinced that he was in the presence of the crucified and risen Lord. The early Christian argued the truth of the Resurrection from empirical evidence: the experience of more than five hundred witnesses (I Cor. 15:3-8). John commends the message of his First Epistle on empirical grounds: "That which was from the beginning, which we have heard, which we have seen with our eyes, which we have looked upon, and our hands have handled, of the Word of life . . . declare we unto you'' (I John 1:1, 3).

Once there is agreement on scientific observations, the weightier problem of their interpretation must be confronted. Here certain arbitrary decisions must be made. The researcher's judgment, and often his prejudices, will come into play in this phase of the work. In a very real sense, not only scientific theories but scientific laws as well are *chosen* rather than discovered. Thus there is a human element involved, and the generalizations that derive from an investigation often bear the personal imprint of the researcher himself. Since his conclusions may be challenged and eventually overthrown by other investigators at some future date, it is apparent that scientific conclusions are not absolute and final, but probabilistic and tentative. The probability that a result is essentially correct will increase with added confirmation. With enough support the probability will approach, but never fully arrive at, certainty. In principle, no tenet of science is completely immune to reappraisal and reformulation. While this constitutes a definite limitation from one standpoint, the ability of the scientific method to provide continuing correction and refinement is one of its most valuable features.

Thus there is nothing inherently anti-Christian in the methodology of science if it is properly executed. We can teach its merits in good conscience, provided that we temper our presentation of it with a careful enumeration of its limitations. The perceptive teacher will also point out to his student how evolutionary-humanistic bias can enter into the interpretation of scientific data, and he will be able to cite specific examples, often from firsthand experiences.

Some of the more conspicuous limitations of science are listed below.

1. Science is fallible. The discipline of science is human activity and is therefore subject to all the limitations of human nature (Isa. 55:9; I Cor. 1:18-21; 3:19-21). The history of science is rife with blunders and blind alleys—the phlogiston theory, the caloric theory, the preformation theory, the pangene theory, the planetesimal hypothesis, the tidal hypothesis—the list could be extended almost indefinitely. These aberrations, often deliberately

glossed over in many science courses, can be the most instructive for the student.

2. Science is changeable. One need only read the science textbooks of fifty or one hundred years ago to observe the change-ability of science; not only the theories but even the ''facts'' themselves are subject to change. Today the atom is no longer indivisible, the number of human chromosomes has shrunk from 48 to 46, and the coelacanth is no longer extinct. It is clear that absolute truth cannot be as flexible as the content of science has been and continues to be. This consideration alone should be sufficient to disqualify science as an object of worship.

3. Science cannot properly deal with ultimate origins. Since no human observer was present at the origin of the world, no scientific observations about its origins could be made. While the unregenerate scientist congratulates himself on his clever detective work in deciphering the remote past, the Christian researcher finds the evidence to fit far more satisfactorily into a creationist frame-work. Further, his faith in the revealed Word of God provides him with definitive statements concerning the creation, while his evo-lutionary counterpart is forced to engage in fanciful guesswork.

4. Science is totally unable to deal with the spiritual realm of existence. Since it is restricted to observations using one or more of the senses, science can deal with only the physical or material world. Thus the knowledge that science gives us is incomplete at best, and the missing information is ironically of the most im-portant sort—that having to do with eternal verities.

5. Science cannot prove a universal negative, or a blanket statement of denial. The statement ''There are no sea monsters'' is one example of a universal negative. In order to prove such a statement scientifically, we would have to look for sea monsters in all parts of all the oceans at the same time. This is impossible, because observers cannot be stationed in all of these places si-multaneously. The unbeliever's statements ''There are no mira-cles'' and ''There is no God'' are in this same category. Though many of its false practitioners seem to think that science can establish such universal negatives, it can, by its very nature, do nothing of the kind.

6. Science cannot make value judgments. There is nothing inherent in its methodology that allows it even to distinguish right

from wrong. Through science we obtained atomic energy but not moral ideas for its use. The science of heredity provides ideas for improving the human race genetically, but it offers no plan for deciding who should select which couples will have children. We have here, then, a further argument against scientism: anything as amoral as science obviously is, is clearly unworthy of worship.

7. Science is frequently forced to deal with models rather than reality. For example, since the real atom is inaccessible to observation, scientists use a mathematical model to represent it. They know the model to be inaccurate, but it works reasonably well for certain applications. For other applications they use a different model, and again the results are only approximate. The interior parts of the sun and stars cannot be observed; so a geometric model is used to represent them. When tested experimentally, the model proves to be quite unsatisfactory; yet it is the most sophisticated approach to stellar interiors known to man. Other models in science are more successful. But the point for the Christian teacher of science to emphasize is that science regularly concerns itself with something other than reality; this fact comes as a genuine surprise to many students.

8. Science has been unable to develop a satisfactory understanding of some of the most basic things with which it deals. What is *matter*? It is usually defined as "anything which occupies space and has mass." But this "definition," rather than stating what matter is, merely describes two of its properties. It is a *description*, not a definition. What is *energy*? Energy is usually defined as "the ability to do work." But again, this only tells us what it does, not what it is. We can calculate the amount of energy in a certain situation, and we can follow it through various transformations. But the true "essence" of energy is not known. What is *gravity*? It is a force that pulls objects toward the earth. How does it work? Again, we must plead ignorance. We can calculate the strength of the force at a given instant and how long an object will take to hit the ground. But to explain how the earth "reaches up" and pulls the object down is beyond the knowledge of present-day science. In fact, no more is understood today about exactly how gravity works than at the time Sir Isaac Newton set forth his law of gravitation three hundred years ago. The same is true of magnetism and electrostatic forces (attraction and repulsion of electrical charges). Their strength can be calculated, but

the details of their operation are not yet understood. If science is this inadequate at describing the *basic* phenomena of nature, how absolute can its pronouncements be when they describe more complex phenomena?

Points of conflict with the secular philosophy of teaching science

The distinctively Christian teaching of science requires the rejection of certain approaches to its subject matter that derive from the modern climate of unbelief. Six specific areas are discussed below.

Scientism—Past and present scientific and technological achievements are often overrated in their philosophical significance. Some scientists cite these as evidence of man's rapid evolution toward total mastery of his environment. But any improvements in the quality of life attributable to such advances should be viewed as God's blessings channeled to man through science or technology, rather than man's bringing it to pass by his own cleverness. Whatever abilities man uses in his scientific endeavors are given by God; hence, God should receive the glory.

Secular science teachers frequently place an undue measure of confidence in what science is destined to accomplish in the future. The Millennium, unregenerate theoreticians inform us, will be ushered in not by the Lord Jesus Christ but by science. The Bible makes it clear, however, that there are some things man will *never* be able to do. Genesis 8:22 places definite limits on how far we can go in modifying our weather. Matthew 26:11 (cf. Mark 14:7 and John 12:8) establishes the fact that poverty will never be eliminated, and Hebrews 9:27 precludes any medical triumph over death.

The belief that science potentially holds the answer to every human problem is one facet of the heterodox position called *scientism* ("science worship"). The scientist is depicted as a godlike being who is motivated solely by an unselfish desire to serve mankind. He is held to be the very quintessence of moral and intellectual excellence. Students are thus conditioned to reverence the scientist and his every pronouncement. This is most unfortunate, for the public statements of the typical unregenerate scientist are often arrogantly evolutionary and anti-God in their tenor. The Christian teacher of science has an urgent mission to counter this worship of science, for it is promoted by all the public media to which his students are exposed.

The Christian approach places man in the proper perspective. It depicts the scientist as a fallen creature in need of salvation. As such he is fallible—prone not only to experimental errors but also, and more significantly, to judgmental errors in the interpretation of his data. Since most scientists are evolutionary by choice, a strong evolutionary bias pervades the reports of most experimental investigations. This is carried over to the editorial policy of the standard scientific journals; so rigid is the editorial bias of such publications that it is virtually impossible to publish any findings that oppose evolution. The depraved nature of unregenerate man manifests itself with great clarity when he attempts to drive a wedge of conflict between the truth of nature and the Word of God.

Blind chance as an ordering principle in nature—The secular teacher of science often feels constrained to attribute many clearly designed features of nature to blind chance. This is done, presumably, in the interest of maintaining a strictly "objective" approach to the subject matter. The Christian teacher of science is not afraid to use a teleological approach at any point. Teleology, the idea of purpose or design in nature, is an intuitively simple concept, and even at an early age we begin to "make sense" out of the world around us by trying to ascertain just what the Creator had in mind when He made various structures. But the public-school educational process leads children away from this kind of thinking. Students are told that it is unscholarly and unscientific and that the things we see in the world about us exist by happenstance rather than by creative design.

All structures in nature have a definite divine purpose for their existence (Col. 1:16, 17; Rev. 4:11). In some cases the purpose is obvious. For example, the eye is for vision, the ear for hearing, and the heart for pumping blood. Much can be done in the way of giving glory to the Creator as these marvelously contrived mechanisms are discussed in the classroom (Ps. 139:14-16). Other objects in nature whose purposes are less well understood (quasars, for example) can be used to show how little we really know about the universe we live in. The futility of speculating about the origin of the universe when we do not even understand the present universe should be obvious. Our failure to understand some features of the physical world, however, in no wise discredits the principle of teleology. Whether or not we understand the specific purpose of a structure, we can still be assured that it exists for the Creator's pleasure and operates in accordance with some part of His overall plan.

Belief in brute facts—The Christian realizes that there are no "brute facts"—that is, facts that lack meaning until man gives them an interpretation. Every fact in the universe is already known to God. Whether any man attempts to interpret it or not, every fact of nature already exists and operates as a part of God's creation. This, of course, represents a major philosophical difference between the positions of the Christian and of the unregenerate scientist. The supreme arrogance of the latter should be apparent, for he claims that no fact of nature can have meaning until some man assigns it one!

Evolutionism—We live in an evolution-crazed world. We are told that everything we see—stars, galaxies, planets, and living organisms, including man himself—has evolved spontaneously out of primordial self-existent matter, is still evolving, and will continue to evolve in the future. This in essence is the view called atheistic evolution. Such fanciful theorizing is both un-Scriptural and unscientific. The compromise position known as theistic evolution represents no improvement, however, for it likewise contradicts the Word of God. Furthermore, it is thoroughly inconsistent, for it represents a welding together of two diametrically opposed world views.

In Matthew 19:4 the Lord Jesus Christ taught the Pharisees that man and woman were divinely created *as such* from the very outset: "Have ye not read, that he which made them at the beginning made them male and female?" (See also Gen. 2:7, 22.) In a parallel passage (Mark 10:6) we read, "But from the beginning of the creation God made them male and female." In this regard it should be noted that Christ at no time disallowed the teachings of Moses. He in fact endorsed them in their entirety. "For had ye believed Moses, ye would have believed me: for he wrote of me. But if ye believe not his writings, how shall ye believe my words?" (John 5:46-47). The writings of Moses and the teachings of Jesus are so closely tied together that it is impossible to accept the one and reject the other.

Moreover, the writings of Paul agree perfectly with the Old Testament concerning the creation of man and his original state. First Corinthians 15:45 speaks of "the first man Adam." First Timothy 2:13 states, "For Adam was first formed, then Eve." And in II Corinthians 11:3 we have a reference to the temptation and subsequent fall of man: "But I fear, lest by any means, as the serpent beguiled Eve through his subtilty, so your minds should be corrupted from the simplicity that is in Christ." These verses demonstrate Paul's literal acceptance and endorsement of Genesis 2 and 3. The argument, used by some, that because Paul antedated Charles Darwin he was ignorant of evolution, misses the mark. The Greeks, beginning around the sixth century before Christ, had already promulgated the satanic doctrine of evolution. Thales, Anaximenes, Anaximander, Empedocles, and Democritus were all evolutionists who taught their many disciples that the world and its inhabitants developed spontaneously out of primordial chaos. Paul was by no means unschooled in the teachings of these Greek philosophers; yet the Holy Spirit, who guided his pen, kept him free from this error as he wrote.

From a scientific standpoint, evolution is at best an unsupportable and unworkable hypothesis, at worst a reprehensible lie that has misdirected the thrust of both theoretical and experimental science for over a century. Ironically, the hypothesis runs exactly counter to the actual observations. Organic evolution, if it were ever to occur, would require the violation of certain well-established principles of genetics and thermodymanics. Paleontology (the study of fossils) likewise militates strongly against evolution: the mediating links required by the hypothesis are systematically missing from the fossil record. Laboratory experiments designed to force plants or animals to change from one distinct kind to another have failed completely. Even if researchers were to succeed in changing one kind of organism into another under these highly artificial conditions, they would not have proved that the same thing could have happened without manipulation by an intellectual power.

Uniformitarianism—One of the major doctrines taught in conventional science courses today is *uniformitarianism*. According to this doctrine, "the present is the key to the past." Present processes, in other words, have been completely responsible for shaping the earth, the solar system, and the universe in the past.

Along with a measure of truth in this concept is a large amount of error. The creationist geologist does not deny, for example, that many presently observed processes, such as erosion, have been going on in the past. The problem comes, however, when unregenerate scientists attempt to use this doctrine to rule out God's supernatural intervention in the past. Because there are no worldwide floods today, they say, there could *never* have been a worldwide flood at any time in the earth's history. Because no miraculous creative processes are observable in the world today, evolutionists refuse to believe that the world could have been formed by the miraculous creative acts described in Genesis 1.

Uniformitarianism is bankrupt as an explanation for the origin of the galaxies, the stars, the planets, and many of the geological features of the earth. Many evidences in the earth's crust speak of at least one major catastrophe in its past. The events described in Genesis 6-9 provide a satisfying explanation for such evidences.

The Bible warns against the error of uniformitarianism in II Peter 3:3-4—"Knowing this first, that there shall come in the last days scoffers, walking after their own lusts, And saying, Where is the promise of his coming? for since the fathers fell asleep, all things continue as they were from the beginning of the creation." All things do *not* continue as they were, regardless of how loudly the scoffers of today might wish to protest. God has intervened in a supernatural way many times before, and He may do so again at any moment. Even our belief in the Lord's return is a rejection of the uniformitarian doctrine.

Environmentalism—The Christian teacher of science is genuinely concerned about the quality of his physical environment, but his motivation and the emphasis of his approach differ from those of his secular counterpart. The Christian recognizes that he is to be a responsible steward of the world God has entrusted to his care, for the earth, as well as everything in it, is the Lord's (Pss. 8:6; 24:1; 50:10-11; 89:11; Hag. 2:8). He is moreover mindful of the command in Genesis 1:28 to "subdue" the earth. This injunction carries an implied mandate to learn about nature and to harness its forces in a way that will serve man's needs. Though man subsequently fell from his first estate, the command to subdue the earth has never been rescinded. Bulldozers, dams, oil wells, copper mines, fluorescent lights, steamships, and communications satellites are all fulfillments of this command, though in most cases those responsible have been unwitting participants in its outworking.

The Christian is in favor of reasonable environmental measures, but he opposes hasty and hysterical legislation that too often not only misses the mark but also imposes outrageously unreasonable burdens on industry and society in general. In addition, the Christian has a greater concern than the non-Christian for the problems of drug, alcohol, and tobacco pollution. He further perceives the importance of the *spiritual* environment for today's youth. The Christian teacher of science regards *mind pollution*— the indiscriminate infusion of false and ungodly ideas that muddy the thinking process and render the mind easier prey for additional heresies—as the most serious potential problem for his students.

The modern environmentalist movement has its roots in pantheism, materialism, and evolutionism. Since it is "Nature" that has produced us, this philosophy says, it is "Nature" ("the Environment") to which we should pay our respects. Since the physical earth is regarded as the only world in which we will ever live, we should make it as utopian as possible. Moreover, since factors in the environment allegedly produce evolutionary changes, theorists maintain that man can influence the course of evolution itself either positively or negatively by altering the environment. Thus the motivation behind the humanist's concern with the environment is poles apart from that behind the Christian's. Only when we realize that environmentalism is part of the humanist's religion can we begin to understand the zeal with which he pursues it.

Conclusion

There is much to engage the talents of even the most gifted Christian teacher of science, for he is called upon to do more than his secular counterpart. He must not only pass on to his students that basic body of knowledge which is essentially noncontroversial; he must also be able to point out to his students where the unregenerate scientist goes astray and to expound successfully the Biblical antidote for each error. Another factor, of course, is that one does not overtly hold to a creationist view in today's world without provoking certain repercussions, and it will happen on occasion that the Christian teacher of science is persecuted for his "antiquated" and "unscientific" beliefs. Thus, in addition to the intellectual requirements for this high calling, the Christian teacher must also possess a greater measure of moral character than his secular counterpart. But though the demands placed upon him are greater, so too are the resources available to him, for the dedicated Christian will find that the same Lord who called him to his teaching post will strengthen him and enable him to carry out his ministry in a manner that brings glory to His name.

THE FINE ARTS

The Christian Teaching of Speech Communication

Definition

Speech communication is the process of conveying ideas and feelings through verbal and nonverbal means. In this context verbal refers to the spoken word. The nonverbal includes those visual and aural elements of communication such as setting, physical appearance, bodily movement, facial expression, vocal pitch, vocal quality, and inflection that interact with the verbal to create the message. As an academic study, speech communication includes public speaking, oral interpretation, dramatic arts, radio and television, and interpersonal communication.

Two overall principles are recognized in a comprehensive speech program. First, speech training is systematically implemented and carefully monitored. Speech must be taught. Effective speech habits do not just "happen" any more than sound habits of grammar and spelling "happen." Second, all teachers, regardless of grade level or subject, must be speech teachers in the sense that they exemplify good speech and that they make effective communication a goal for their students.

Effective speech training begins on the elementary level, primarily through the example of the teacher. He must be a model in voice and diction, nonverbal skills, organization, and delivery. In addition, the teacher plans specific projects and assignments which foster communication. Book reports, discussions, show-and-tell, plays, and chapel programs incorporate speech into the elementary curriculum. The well-prepared elementary teacher recognizes speech defects and recommends professional help.

In the general curriculum on the secondary level, speech projects and principles of effective communication are carefully planned into the content of each course. An overall question each teacher asks is "How can I teach the students to communicate what they learn in this class?" Administrators can facilitate effective speech communication by insisting that courses include activities requiring oral communication: for example, oral reports that are evaluated on the basis of effective delivery as well as content.

A sound secondary-school curriculum provides a separate course in speech communication in addition to the speech emphasis indicated above. The course is taught by a qualified speech teacher with a college major or minor in speech. Since speech is an art as well as an academic subject, the teacher demonstrates a high level of proficiency as a speaker or performer. The content of the speech class focuses on the major areas of speech communication: public speaking, oral interpretation, dramatic arts, radio and television, and interpersonal communication. Assignments in each of these areas are developed to test mastery of the communication principles. In addition, analytical skills such as listening, outlining, evaluation, and criticism are fostered. Every attempt is made to apply Biblical principles of communication to the Christian's daily life and walk.

Justification

The hallmark of our age is "communication." We are in the midst of an information explosion. We are inundated with videotapes, computers, teleconferencing, radio, and television. In the nonelectronic dimension we are stressing improved interpersonal relations through participatory management programs with their discussion groups and quality circles. The Christian as never before has been called upon to speak out in his community not only to propagate the gospel but also to defend his Biblical values against an increasingly antagonistic secular society. The demand today for clear, forceful oral communicators is unmistakable.

Leadership is impossible without excellent communication skills; and, in our age, success, and perhaps survival, in the home, church, and work place demand that we develop solid skills in speech communication.

Reflections of God in the subject matter

The study of speech is an important element in the overall purpose of Christian education—to conform redeemed man to the image of God—because the subject matter reflects the character and works of God. God is a communicating being. He chose to communicate to us His will and plan of redemption. He created man as a communicating being, who, by virtue of regeneration, is capable of using speech to glorify God and to proclaim the gospel of His Son, Jesus Christ, to a lost world.

God's works are reflected in the study of speech in that He chose to use the spoken word to accomplish certain of His purposes. Creation was a verbal act: God spoke the universe into being (Gen. 1:3 ff.; Heb. 11:3). God used speech as a primary means of revealing Himself through the ministry of the Old Testament prophets (Jer. 1:4-7; Heb. 1:1). The inspiration of the Scriptures often involved direct discourse between God and His chosen spokesmen (II Pet. 1:21). God spoke directly from heaven when He gave verbal affirmation of the ministry of His Son (Matt. 17:5; Luke 3:22). God not only spoke directly to reveal Himself but also sanctioned and ordained speech communication as a primary tool to be used by His servants to communicate His messages and truth. Moses and the prophets proclaimed to Israel God's blessings and judgments (Deut. 1:1; Isa. 7). The apostles preached the gospel of Christ with boldness (Acts 2:14 ff.), and God ordained preaching as a primary means for proclaiming His Word in the Church Age (I Cor. 1:18-21; Rom. 10:17). God's use of the speech discipline is not limited to the public-speaking mode; dramatic elements are clearly present in the Scriptures. The book of Job is written in dramatic form. The Song of Solomon is written as a dialogue, and its use of a chorus of women is similar to that of ancient Greek drama which followed later. Jeremiah and Ezekiel occasionally ''acted out'' the messages from God through visual demonstration (Jer. 27:1-22; Ezek. 4:1-17; 5:1-12).

God is further reflected through the study of speech in the ministry of Jesus Christ. Indeed, the Christian teacher of speech looks to Christ as the perfect example of effective speech communication. Christ's speech reflected wisdom and caused those who heard it to be astonished (Matt. 13:54-56). His speech was characterized as gracious (Luke 4:22), for His words were carefully chosen, appropriate for the occasion, and reflective of God's grace. In direct contrast to the manner of the scribes, Christ spoke with authority and power (Matt. 7:29). His manner of speaking reflected the urgency and importance of His teachings; He often "cried out" His messages (John 7:37). Christ varied His style of speaking to meet the demands of each speaking situation, and He utilized many different teaching techniques. Among these are preaching (Luke 4:44), questioning (Luke 9:18-22), and illustrating with stories and parables (Luke 15:3; Matt. 13:3). Christ's interpersonal communication skills are clearly displayed in His interviews and encounters with individuals such as Peter (John 21:15-22) and the rich young ruler (Matt. 19:16-22). We can infer that Christ was an effective oral interpreter because His reading of the Scriptures in the synagogue aroused comment and provided clarity to the passages (Luke 4:16-22). Christ's effectiveness as a speaker is best attested by enemies who said, "Never man spake like this man" (John 7:46).

The character and attributes of God are reflected in His specific commandments to us regarding speech communication. The commandment to "preach the gospel to every creature" (Mark 16:15) demonstrates the love of God for His fallen creation. The commandment to speak "the truth in love" (Eph. 4:15) reminds us that God is truth as well as love. The injunction that we should avoid corrupt communication (Eph. 4:29) reflects God's purity and holiness. Thus, the teaching of speech in the Christian context is grounded in the principles of holiness and illustrated through the example of Christ, the Master Speaker and Teacher.

Manifestations of godliness in the resultant knowledge, attitudes, and skills

In general Christian character and service—God has much to say in His Word about the power of the tongue. In an extensive passage in James 3:1-18, He warns the believer about the dangers of the tongue. "The tongue is a fire, a world of iniquity," and "out of the same mouth proceedeth blessing and cursing." Christian instruction in speech makes the student keenly aware of the enormous power for good or evil that resides in man's speech. The student realizes that control of the tongue will come only as he yields his "members as instruments of righteousness unto God" (Rom. 6:13).

The study of speech helps to develop in the student those qualities he has been taught to admire in the example of Christ. The student develops confidence, poise, control, and fluency as he sharpens his delivery skills through public speaking and other performance situations. The student also gains valuable analytical skills, which aid him in the evaluation of messages and in the logical organization of his own ideas when communicating. A solid speech communication background prepares the student to participate effectively in a variety of communication contexts and better equips him for active involvement in a democratic society where decisions are made through speech discourse. In short, speech training is valuable in the development of competent, thoughtful, and active communicators equipped not only for personal success but also, and foremost, for the service of Christ.

The study of speech also develops the aesthetic tastes and imaginative abilities with which God has blessed man. We are creative creatures made in the image of God, the Creator of all. In His divine creation, God revealed a love of beauty. Solomon declares, "He hath made everything beautiful in his time" (Eccles. 3:11). As we strive for beauty in utterance of poetry or beauty in the action of drama, we imitate this creative impulse of the Lord of heaven. David is an example of one who values artistic expression. He sang unto the Lord, and he was described by others as "cunning in playing" and "prudent in matters [words]" (I Sam. 16:18). Participation in the dramatic arts stimulates and strengthens the student's imaginative faculties and develops in him a desire for and appreciation of wholesome aesthetic experience.

The Scriptures declare that God is a God of judgment and discernment. He is a righteous judge and a discerner of the thoughts and intents of our hearts. In His earthly ministry, the Lord saw past the outward facade of the Pharisees and recognized the purposes of their hearts. Not only is God a God of discernment, but He also commands His people to be discerning. In Philippians 1:10 believers are exhorted to "approve things that are excellent," and in I Corinthians 2:15 the Lord reveals that believers are to judge all things. Thus, when the speech student develops critical skills through argumentation and literary analysis, he is developing skills that will enable him to conform more closely to the image of God.

For the Christian, the most important result of studying speech is that it significantly expands his potential ministry for Christ. Most Christian ministries depend on effective proclamation of the Word. Personal witnessing, an activity to which all Christians are called, can be enhanced and strengthened through the interpersonal communication skills that are a part of speech training.

In special vocational service—The study of speech communication is not only valuable for preparing the student to reflect the image of God in his personality and conduct but also essential for certain kinds of vocational service. These include such speech-related ministries as teaching, broadcasting, law, marketing, public relations, and community service. Speech training also gives the Christian an advantage in gaining positions of special usefulness and influence within a particular vocational area. Numerous studies have indicated that the most important factor in obtaining employment with a major corporation is the ability to communicate orally. Conversely, the inability to communicate is one of the most frequently cited reasons job candidates are rejected. Moreover, speech communication is cited as the most important personal skill considered in decisions of job success and promotion.

The Christian speech teacher is especially concerned with the training of future Christian workers such as preachers, evangelists, pastors, missionaries, and teachers. He is aware that the proclamation of the gospel is the highest calling of God (I Cor. 1:21; Rom. 10:13-17) and that this calling emphasizes a speaking forth of the Word of God (Matt. 28:19-20; Mark 16:15; Acts 4:29, 31). By increasing the scope and effectiveness of these ministries, speech-communication studies enhance their reflection of the character and work of God.

Distinctives

The English language, like other languages, is a code of generally accepted symbols. The General American dialect is a consistently accepted guide to pronunciation in the United States. Thus the study of the effective use of English words in speech must be governed by certain universal principles, principles that are neither peculiarly sacred nor secular.

For this reason, a high-quality approach to the Christian teaching of speech has much in common with a high-quality secular approach. The Rhetoric of Aristotle is as valid and as valuable to the Christian persuader as it is to the secular rhetor. And even the secularist would recognize parts of the Bible as ancient and practical principles of communication. The Golden Rule, for example, is a generally accepted principle of interpersonal relationships for most cultures. Many of the basic principles of speech are universally accepted.

However, there is a key difference between a purely secular program and one that could be properly labeled "Christian." This difference is a conflicting view of truth. Christian communication assumes an absolute standard, the Bible, while the secularist assumes that truth is relative to the individual. This Biblical perspective forms the taproot from which a uniquely Christian approach to speaking grows. The speaker without Christ is like a tumbleweed swept aimlessly across the landscape by winds of culture. He is unable to found his communication on anything larger than his own experience, opinions, and observations. The Christian speaker, anchored in the Word of God, communicates with an assurance of which the unsaved speaker knows nothing.

One of the most distinctively Christian aspects of any speech communication program is its emphasis on selection of appropriate material for use in performance situations. Care must be taken in choosing support material for public speaking, literature for interpretation, and plays for dramatic production. As an example let us consider how a Christian drama teacher might select a play for performance in his school.

First, a thorough play analysis must be made. Such analysis incorporates knowledge of dramatic construction and critical interpretations. The Christian director assumes the presence of objective meaning in the script he is about to analyze. Every play contains a set of values: certain concepts are affirmed, while others are condemned. The Christian teacher-director must measure a play's value system by Biblical values. Since a play may contain a number of themes, it is up to the director to select those he will emphasize in his production. *Hamlet,* for example, presents the director with a complexity of themes which are fascinating for academic investigation; but a production cannot possibly communicate all of these ideas. Choices must be made. A Christian director strives for integrity in his choices by maintaining a healthy respect for the dramatic text. In the case of *Hamlet* the once-popular Freudian interpretation forced directors to read into the text many meanings which are not defensible in a historical-cultural context. It also required overlooking much of what the text of the play has to say about the political scene.

In selecting themes from the text for his production, the director is functioning in his interpretive role. This does not preclude the possibility that a director may enter into a creative role as an artist. He may either create a text through collaborative rehearsal periods or take an existing piece of literature and adapt it through cutting, voicing, or additional writing. Biblical prohibitions against lying and stealing demand that the creative director acknowledge both his literary sources and his own ''literary'' work. This is most often done by listing himself on the program as adaptor as well as director.

No list of guidelines can ever be complete, nor can it ever answer all the questions which will arise in the selection of plays for performance. There is no substitute for a spiritually mature director-teacher relying on the leadership of the Holy Spirit and exercising Christian discernment in any choice of play. The Bible does contain many valuable principles, but these must often be applied in situations not specifically addressed by the Word of God. The ability to apply principles to specific choices requires the director to seek wisdom from above and to exercise discernment at all times.

One consideration for play selection is the intended use of the drama. The Christian director analyzes the potential audience and setting. For instance, informal classroom dramatics might use selected scenes from a play unsuitable as a whole for public performance. This educational value may lie in the content or the technique of the drama. A play embodying a non-Christian world view might serve as a negative example if a scene were enacted and then its unacceptable philosophy discussed. In this way the students could be taught to recognize and guard against such content. Sometimes the technical merits of a play commend it to a student actor or director. In such a case, his teacher is careful to impose on the drama an explanatory framework which sets the drama in the light of Scripture. Tennessee Williams's *Glass Menagerie* is a play that might be studied in class solely for its technical merit. The teacher could use Williams's superior technique to challenge student actors and directors while disavowing the play's content. In contrast to these informal uses of drama, the formal presentation of a play (which typically does not carry a framework of any kind) requires selection of dramas which are philosophically in line with the Scriptures.

Another aspect of intended use which must be considered is the participants' maturity. Even in classroom settings, with an educational framework, some subjects or styles might cause a student to stumble in his spiritual growth. Particularly noteworthy in this regard is the large body of existential drama, primarily the absurdist drama. The writings of the absurdists are exceptionally subtle in their embodiment of the existential viewpoint. Teaching from content or technique is never an excuse to throw a stumbling block in the path of a spiritually immature Christian student. The Christian director-teacher is always obligated to edify, not tear down, his students.

A Christian teacher evaluates a play on theological grounds. Every work of literature expresses a world view, and the Christian director must analyze carefully to find the particular world view of the play in question. He should consider whether the play glorifies (gives a right opinion about) God. A seemingly innocuous play with no drinking, swearing, or sexual innuendo may be unacceptable for Christian production because it either fails to recognize the existence of God or gives a false picture of God. The drama must also be analyzed to determine whether hope and meaning, rather than despair and chaos, predominate. Leonard Bernstein's definition of art as "Cosmos in Chaos" is incorrect; only God can give order to the chaotic world in which we live. Shakespearean drama presumes an orderly (moral) universe, one in which life is given value. Existential drama, in contrast, presents a meaningless, mindless universe in which man can only despair. In an ordered universe the consequences of evil are depicted and the rewards of righteousness are at least assumed. In a chaotic world view there is no such morality.

Arthur Miller's *Death of a Salesman* is an example of a technically well-written play which embodies an objectionable world view. It is often hailed as the greatest American drama of the twentieth century. Conceivably, Christian actors and directors could learn from Miller's techniques of characterization and plot construction. But to take this play out of the classroom into public performance would hurt the Christian testimony of the sponsoring school. Miller gives his audiences a hopeless world of shattered ideals and hostile, meaningless circumstances. Even if the play did not contain frequent vulgarity, the very universe the author presents would discredit it for Christian production. There is no God in this play. The audience is presented a picture of fallen man hopelessly struggling toward death.

Some dramas go beyond the embodiment of a world view to an explicit, programmatic didacticism. "Didactic" dramas, or thesis plays, are written to communicate an objective message to the audience. Much contemporary Christian drama is strongly didactic in nature. In selecting a play for performance, the director must analyze what message is being communicated by studying the statements of the characters, the title of the play, other works by the author, and above all, the action of the play.

But evaluating statements of characters is not enough. A good didactic drama will rise above discursive argumentation and embody the objective message in the action (the spine) of the play. Only by means of thorough analysis can the director arrive at an evaluation of the action. He should be sensitive to the author's use of sympathetic and unsympathetic characters. The plays of didactic dramatists such as George Bernard Shaw and Henrik Ibsen must be evaluated carefully before a decision is made for public production. For example, in Henrik Ibsen's play *A Doll's House,* the dominant character, Nora Helmer, is trapped by the insensitivity of her husband, Torvald. Ibsen elicits our sympathy for Nora and then, at the climax of the play, has her walk out on her husband—a solution we would reject. Not only is the world view of this play objectionable to Christians, but the objective message is also unacceptable.

In evaluating plays on theological grounds, the director must also criticize the presence of objectionable elements. Objectionable material must, of course, not be gratuitous or explicit and, if present at all, must be cast in the proper moral framework to be acceptable for production. But the Christian director also considers the actor. He would not ask the actor, for example, to use profanity on the stage.

After thoroughly analyzing the play on theological grounds, the director must evaluate it on theatrical grounds. He does so by studying the play's audience appeal, quality of content, and practicability. Many plays which are acceptable theologically are not desirable theatrically. Moral content does not automatically make for good drama; it must be shaped into an effective piece of dramatic writing. The Christian director first asks whether the play can command, sustain, and satisfy the interest of an audience. These are the criteria of entertainment. Entertainment occurs when a drama is capable of capturing the attention of an audience and keeping it throughout the performance. The play also should give the audience something worthwhile to think about. Unfortunately, many Christian plays fall short in this area. There is, of course, an appropriate time for slapstick comedy and skits, but they should not be the main diet of a dramatic-arts program. Finally, the director must ask whether his producing organization (cast, facilities, budget) is capable of mounting a successful production of the play. For example, *Hamlet* is certainly worthy of production by Christian schools, but its dramatic scope is beyond the reach of most. A director with a keen appreciation of his limitations in the three areas mentioned above will select dramas which can be produced to the satisfaction of both audience and participants.

These principles of play selection apply also in the other areas of speech communication. The interpreter of poetry or dramatic literature must use them in selecting literature for classroom and public performance. If the literature is to be performed publicly, it must be thoroughly analyzed for content as well as style to ensure that its message is consistent with a Christian world view. Of course, selections studied in the classroom may be used as examples of the world's philosophy for edifying or warning the students. For example, Oscar Wilde's "The Ballad of Reading Gaol" contains no language that a Christian would find offensive, but the philosophy runs contrary to the Biblical viewpoint.

Likewise, the Christian teacher must be guided by Scriptural principles in helping his students choose material for speeches, discussion or debate, or radio or television broadcast. In every discipline the performer must learn to be responsible for the message he communicates, realizing his ultimate accountability is to God.

Practical application in the classroom

The teaching of oral interpretation of literature affords the Christian speech teacher unique opportunities to influence his students for Christ. A good beginning point in the Christian school classroom is oral performance of the Scriptures. There are many passages of Scripture that are dramatic in nature and lend themselves readily to oral presentation. An example is the account of David's slaying of Goliath from I Samuel 17. The passage from the Authorized Version is vivid in description, rich in imagery, and vital in characterization. A student could be assigned to read this passage as a solo performance, or it might easily become a group-interpretation project with students assigned to the different characters of the story.

The poetical books such as Job and Psalms are rich treasuries of poetry to the performer. Of course, the teacher would emphasize the unique elements of Hebrew poetry and encourage the student to trace the historical and Scriptural allusions associated with the individual poem. A performance of Psalm 100, for instance, would emphasize the pastoral beauty of the psalm as well as its comforting spiritual message. Oral performance of Scripture, be it poetry or prose, will enhance the meaning of the passage for the student, make it come alive for the listeners, and help to create a hunger for the Word of God in all who participate.

Interpretation of secular literature, both classic and modern, offers other opportunities to the Christian speech teacher. A dramatic reading of classical works by Sophocles, Homer, Shakespeare, and even Dickens will make great demands on the student's performance skills and help him develop a command of his body and voice that will last a lifetime. Poor posture, diction problems, and weak breathing become glaringly conspicuous when attempting such challenging material. Reading aloud of the more modern works of Robert Frost, O. Henry, and James Thurber, as well as many others, helps the student develop analytical skills and subtlety in his performance. A balance of both the classics and modern literature provides a well-rounded approach to the effective use of the voice and body to communicate an author's ideas.

Exposure to a broad range of the human condition in other cultures and historical settings is also a valuable by-product of this study. Through the insightful observations of the world's great writers, the student comes in contact with God's creation and its history. As the student prepares a dramatic reading from a Charles Dickens novel, such as *Nicholas Nickelby* or *A Tale of Two Cities,* he becomes closely acquainted with a period of history that might elude him otherwise. At the same time, he meets characters from every walk of life and learns to empathize with their struggles. Hence, the student may gain a greater capacity for the godly traits of mercy and compassion.

Of course, interpretation is not confined to solo performances of literature. The use of more than one reader often provides additional insight into the literary experience. A short story such as "The Open Window" by Saki is easily adaptable to group performance and could provide the interpretation class with an excellent opportunity to perform for the whole school or even the general public. Some high schools have developed traveling teams to present Christian literature in local churches. This type of performance gives the student an opportunity to take what he has learned in the classroom and apply it in Christian service.

The Christian teacher of interpersonal communication has a unique opportunity to mold the character and personality of a student in the image of Christ by using the Bible as his text. Scripture is replete with advice and examples to inspire the instruction of such informal speaking as interviewing, group discussion, and conversation. In fact, many of the psychological principles developed in this century have their parallel in Scripture.

The importance of perception could be taught beginning with the principle the Lord asserts in Samuel: "Man looketh on the outward appearance, but the Lord looketh on the heart" (I Sam. 16:7). Indeed, God judges righteously with a perfect knowledge of each individual. But man, with limited perception, must rely on external evidences to evaluate and interact with other men. The importance of self-disclosure (openly revealing personal knowledge) can be seen in the conversation between Christ and Nicodemus. On that occasion the Lord gradually revealed more and more about Himself, until He finally uncovered the fact that He was the Son of God. The importance of conflict resolution can be illustrated throughout the Bible. In Matthew 5:23-24 the Lord teaches the importance of immediate reconciliation of interpersonal conflict with a Christian brother.

As in the other areas of speech, the Lord Jesus Christ is a perfect example of effective interpersonal communication. A study of only one of his many personal confrontations, the interview with the woman at the well, teaches much about effective interviewing. The Lord masterfully used the immediate setting, the well, to find a common experience with the Samaritan woman—the need of water. His rapport with her is seen by the statement "His disciples . . . marvelled that He talked with the woman" (John 4:27). It is evident that, in contrast with Him, they would not have associated with her. He used a probing statement to unveil hidden information when He said "Go, call thy husband, and come hither" (John 4:16). He knew she had no husband. The depth of His knowledge about her personal life disarmed her completely. It is no wonder she "perceived" (John 4:19) that He was a prophet.

Group discussion could be taught from the Council in Jerusalem (Acts 15:6-29). In that meeting a free exchange of ideas eventually led to a satisfactory solution for all concerned. We see demonstrated interpersonal conflict (v. 7), good listening skills (v. 12), paraphrasing the responses of others (v. 14), use of evidence (vv. 15-18), and an effective consensus solution (vv. 20-22).

If one is to choose "a word fitly spoken," Scripture makes plain the need of adapting to each situation as unique. Proverbs 26:4 and 26:5 seem to contradict each other. The former says "Answer not a fool according to his folly," while the latter says "Answer a fool according to his folly." The Christian teacher could lead a class discussion to resolve this paradox. The conclusion must be that sometimes it is unwise to answer a fool in his folly and sometimes an answer is needed to correct his folly. In applying this principle, the Christian teacher can stress the obvious need for God's wisdom to discern what response is appropriate for a particular situation.

One problem encountered by every teacher of public speaking is the student's fear of facing an audience. Several studies seem to indicate that the fear associated with standing in front of an audience and giving a speech is among the foremost fears in America. The Bible provides an excellent resource for dealing with this problem. The Christian teacher needs to direct the student's attention to the enabling power of the Holy Spirit with such verses as Philippians 4:13 and I Corinthians 2:1-3. The teacher should further attempt to focus the student's attention on the message he is to deliver and not on himself. Paul is an excellent example of one who succeeded not from natural ability but because of the power of God upon him and the urgency of the message he was to deliver. Moses had a classic case of stage fright. When God called him at the burning bush, Moses resisted, arguing that he was not "eloquent" but rather "slow of speech, and of a slow tongue" (Exod. 4:10). God then appointed Aaron as a spokesman for Moses. Significantly, however, when Moses allowed himself to be consumed with the message from God, he found he was able to speak. Moses got his eyes off himself and onto the message he had been given.

The Christian teacher of public speaking makes his students aware of the importance of adapting the message to each audience without sacrificing the integrity of the message. Here, again, Paul provides an excellent example. In his sermon to the Greek thinkers on Mars Hill, Paul did not begin with the Old Testament Scriptures, as he frequently did in addressing Jews, but tried to meet them within the context of their own cultural experience. Paul used their altar to an unknown god (Acts 17:22-23) and their own Greek poets (Acts 17:28) to direct their thinking to the gospel of Jesus Christ. The gospel was the same but the approach was adapted to his particular audience.

Good elements of public speaking could be reinforced by examining model speeches from the New Testament. Peter's sermon on the day of Pentecost, Stephen's address to the council, and many sermons by Paul all provide excellent opportunities for analysis in terms of purpose, style, argument, organization, and support material.

The use of electronic media provides new opportunities for the speech teacher. Student use of audio and video recorders has become commonplace in secondary schools and in some elementary schools as well. The Christian teacher stresses the fact that these media can be legitimate and effective tools for advancing the cause of Christ. For example, the videotaping of student performances can be especially valuable in helping students overcome their fear of speaking before a group and in revealing problems with nonverbal communication. On the other hand, the student can use the camera to produce dramatic or documentary videos dealing with issues of particular interest to the Christian community. Finally, the Christian student can learn to discern un-Biblical philosophy and anti-Christian bias by critically analyzing material from network television.

Dramatic-arts programs typically take two forms in the secondary school: informal and formal. Informal dramatics are defined as role-playing exercises which are not intended to culminate in public performances. These are primarily classroom exercises used in the teaching of subjects such as literature, history, or government. For example, after having a class read the play *Julius Caesar,* the teacher might select some key scenes, divide the parts among the class, and conduct a "staged reading" (no actions or settings) of the scenes. To illustrate the judicial process, a teacher of government might stage a mock trial, with the students playing the parts of the judge, lawyers, and jury. Informal dramatics can also be used to teach the value and practice of certain activities, such as soulwinning. Many churches have experimented in their soulwinning training classes with having students act the parts of the lost person and the Christian witness. The many techniques available to the soulwinner can be demonstrated in this way. It is interesting that the prophet Elisha used a type of informal dramatic activity to communicate his message to King Joash in II Kings 13:14-19.

Formal dramatics are defined as a sequence of rehearsals intended to culminate in a public performance. The exercise of formal dramatics is conducted primarily outside of the classroom. Extracurricular drama activities have value both in terms of the product and the process. Performances may be scheduled in an auditorium with admission by ticket, or they may be taken to several locations, as in the case of a traveling drama team. Some schools have successfully combined these two approaches by first presenting the production to their school family and then taking the production "on the road" to nearby churches (in the case of a Christian drama) or schools.

Additional opportunities for speech training outside the classroom occur in forensics competition. Generally, forensics includes debate, public speaking, oral interpretation, and acting events. Competition in these areas allows the student to refine skills developed in the classroom as well as expand his experience into types of speaking not included in the curriculum. It also provides the opportunity to involve students in speech activities who otherwise might not have the time or inclination to take a speech course.

Forensics puts into the learning experience an excitement and enthusiasm that is at best difficult to achieve in the classroom. Debate, for example, puts students into the library doing independent research and then applying their own analysis and reasoning to the data. Reasoning, independent research, analysis, and communication are all goals that are at the top of every taxonomy of educational objectives. When these goals are incorporated into a competitive format, the student works toward them voluntarily and enthusiastically without the pressure of a grade.

Competition against public schools provides an excellent context for helping the student develop his witness for Christ. It puts him into direct contact with unsaved young people with whom he has a common interest and gives him an opportunity to witness. Additionally, the entire forensics squad through its deportment can be a testimony to coaches and contestants of other teams.

While there is much to be gained from competition with public schools, there are also dangers. Since secular students may perform material that is totally unfit for Christian consumption, the Christian teacher must carefully select and monitor the events into which he enters his students. He should also be certain that he is taking only students who have the spiritual maturity to exert a strong positive influence for Christ.

When developing the forensics program, the teacher should keep in mind that its purpose is to supplement and reinforce principles taught in the classroom. The omnipresent danger is that sound educational objectives will be sacrificed to the desire to win. Instead of stretching and expanding the students' skills, the program focuses on a star performer who becomes a vehicle for garnering trophies and acclaim. Rather than being challenged to attempt more difficult material that would be educationally valuable or to attempt innovative approaches, the student is led to perform something that wins. This type of emphasis is not healthy for either the student or the program. A good forensics program encourages broad participation and places a premium on the development of particular goals for each student, so that at the end of competition the student is able to experience a sense of accomplishment and personal achievement, regardless of whether trophies were received. The teacher must guard against allowing pride and ambition to turn healthy competition into obsessive prize-seeking.

Points of conflict with the secular teaching of speech

Aestheticism—The Christian speech teacher rejects the worldly concept of aestheticism, or "art for art's sake." This concept views a work of art as an imaginative representation of life with no objective content or world view. It argues that a play or piece of literature cannot be analyzed for meaning. A Christian teacher selects literature on theological as well as theatrical grounds. He presumes the presence of meaning in a work when he sets out to analyze it. Aestheticism leads to permissivism in the field of speech because it holds that anything is acceptable for the sake of art. It is this belief which stems from and leads to an elevation of art to the level of religion. Such an elevation prompts the artist to deny any amount of objectivity in his creative processes. Certainly art has value as an aesthetic experience—this is rooted in our creation in the image of God—but the aesthetic experience is never isolated from its communicative function.

Communalism—A related danger that is a special problem for the Christian involved in the dramatic arts is the trap of "communalism." The ensemble nature of theatrical activity can quickly degenerate into unhealthy relationships between actors. Because of this necessary closeness, the Christian is very cautious about uniting with unbelievers in a theatrical endeavor. Some students drawn to the dramatic arts program will be sensitive and insecure. The Christian director recognizes the need for Christian fellowship among his students, but he also stresses the need for individual Christians to rely on Christ for hope and encouragement (Ps. 25:1-2; Jer. 17:5).

Mysticism—A current trend in dramatics, public speaking, and interpersonal-communication training is the increased use of self-awareness techniques characteristic of the Near Eastern mystical religions. It is not uncommon for businessmen and professionals to attend seminars in communication that are based on the meditative and highly reflective practices of these religions. These techniques as a whole are inappropriate for Christian speech teaching because they suggest that the solutions to the problems in life (including speech) can be found within man rather than in total reliance on Christ.

The Christian drama teacher combats this trend by utilizing an objective rather than a subjective approach to actor training. He does not deny the role of the imagination and emotions in role-creating; he simply insists that the use of these subjective elements be tempered with reason. The actor is an artist who is in conscious control of his vocal and bodily instruments at all times. He rejects extreme theories of acting which advocate a total submergence of the actor's personality and will to the extent that he "becomes" the character he is portraying. The imagination is to be reined in by the intellect, and both are to be consecrated to Christ for His leading (Rom. 12:1-2; II Cor. 10:5).

Egoism—Public performance of any kind can quickly lead to pride in the performer. The Christian must be taught to acknowledge that his abilities as a performer are from God (James 1:17). The teacher is constantly sensitive to the attitude of his students. He looks for the first hint of a "haughty spirit" and deals with the problem of pride at an early stage. It is healthy for student performers to enjoy the fruits of their successful work, but they must be taught to give the glory for their success to God.

Pragmatism—The Christian speech teacher, especially in the area of public speaking, must constantly be on guard against a results standard for speaking. The secularist may at times conceal, twist, and even falsify data in an effort to achieve his objective. The Christian speaker must be made to realize that his goal is not to substitute effectiveness for truth, but to present the truth effectively.

Relativism—Current communication theories tend to emphasize the relative nature of our world and ignore or denigrate any idea of absolutes. They assert that truth depends upon each person's perception and that the meaning of something is whatever the individual assigns it. They go so far as to insist that, since the world is in a state of constant change, one should avoid state-of-being verbs. The goal for interpersonal communication is the establishment of stable, mutually satisfying relationships with little or no regard for absolutes. It is crucial that the Christian teacher contrast these concepts with Biblical truths. An external objective world created by God exists apart from individual perceptions. While we live in a state of flux, there is that which is permanent and unchanging. God changes not; Jesus Christ is "the same yesterday, and to day, and for ever" (Heb. 13:8); and the Word of God is forever settled in heaven (Ps. 119:89). Meaning ultimately exists in the mind of God, and personal satisfaction and happiness are not God's criteria for determining our behavior. While many of these communication principles contain practical helps, they reflect philosophic positions that are antithetical to the Word of God—positions which must be challenged by the Christian speech teacher.

Conclusion

One of the greatest fears that a Christian young person faces is the fear of speaking before others. Yet public speech is an essential part of his Christian duty. He is commanded to communicate his faith to others: "How shall they hear without a preacher?" (Rom. 10:14).

If Christian education is to train leadership for the future, it must address this basic need of the student. Leadership is by definition a communicative process. Speech communication is the primary means by which most Christian young persons will make their impact on the world. This tool is sharpened and made ready for the Master's use through good speech training in Christian schools.

The Christian Teaching of Music

Definition

Music is that process and product of human creativity which utilizes in varying degrees the elements of melody, harmony, rhythm, and tone color (timbre). Music may be with or without text, vocal or instrumental (or both), sacred or secular in nature. As an academic study, music includes theory and composition, history and literature, pedagogy, aesthetics, and instruction in performance.

Justification

Reflections of God in the subject matter

The study of music can serve the purpose of Christian education—to conform redeemed man to the image of God—because musical elements reflect the character and works of God. First, it is clear that God approves of music. From Genesis through Revelation the Bible is replete with references to music, and music is repeatedly mentioned in the Scriptures as one of man's chief means of praising God.

The creation itself is musical. The basic elements of music—melody, harmony, rhythm, and tone color—are evident throughout nature. The warbling of a bird, the rippling of a brook, the roar of the ocean, the howling of the wind, and the chirping of insects are but a sampling of the multitude of natural *melodies*.

The changing seasons, day and night, the waxing and waning of the moon, the rotation of the earth on its axis, and the revolving of the planets in their orbits are magnificent examples of the *rhythm* of nature. The myriad sounds in nature all represent the possible *tone colors* of the Creator's palette. Together these musical features of creation exhibit a sublime *harmony*.

It is interesting that God uses musical imagery in the Scriptures to describe physical or natural phenomena. For instance, we read that on the occasion of God's laying "the foundations of the earth" and "the corner stone thereof," "the morning stars sang together, and all the sons of God shouted for joy" (Job 38:4-7). Similar references abound, particularly in the poetic and prophetic sections: "then shall the trees of the wood sing out" (I Chron. 16:33); "the fowls . . . which sing among the branches" (Ps. 104:12); "the valleys . . . shout for joy, they also sing" (Ps. 65:13); and "Sing, O ye heavens; for the Lord hath done it: shout, ye lower parts of the earth: break forth into singing, ye mountains, O forest, and every tree therein: for the Lord hath redeemed Jacob, and glorified himself in Israel" (Isa. 44:23). It is difficult not to see in the Scriptural view of creation the importance of music as an expression of the mind of God.

The musical character of creation is especially evident in the creature for whom the world was formed. Music, whether verbal (vocal) or nonverbal (instrumental), is one of man's primary means of communication, both intellectual and emotional and at all age levels. It is often spoken of as "the universal language." As a form of human communication, music can reflect the divine nature; for communication, both verbal and nonverbal, is an attribute of God. When the ideas and feelings of man communicated in his music are controlled by God and used for His praise and in His service, music can be especially reflective of the Creator. But even in the music of non-Christian composers and performers may be seen elements of the divine image implanted in man—when these works adhere to the highest standards of artistic excellence.

Manifestations of godliness in the resultant knowledge, attitudes, and skills

In general Christian character and service—Man's exercise of creative musical gifts, both in performance and in composition, distinguishes him from the lower creation and reveals in him the image of his Maker. The more distinct, logical, truthful, beautiful, and appropriate man's musical utterance, whether in performance or in composition, the more completely it reveals his likeness to God. Music teaches through experience the value of beauty, form, order, balance, contrast, activity, and repose—characteristics that are revealed in God's creation, though flawed now by sin. The more the Christian student applies his knowledge of these attributes to the shaping of his musical utterance and the greater the knowledge of music literature he brings to bear upon his task, the more he improves in his ability to imitate God both in his musical communication and in his musical discrimination and preferences. He becomes increasingly able to express and to favor "things that are excellent" (Phil. 1:10). Good music gives the student the opportunity and develops in him the capacity to think on things that are true, honest, just, pure, lovely, and of good report (Phil. 4:8). To ignore or scorn good music is no sign of spirituality. On the contrary, it shows a different view from that of God, who commands that man's musical creativity be employed in His praise and to His glory (Ps. 149:1).

The development of musical ability and discrimination is therefore a matter not of mere preference and whim but of responsibility to God. It is relevant to the Great Commission. The greater the student's knowledge and understanding of the musical utterance of man throughout history, and the greater his resulting cultural awareness, the more adaptable will be his approach to the lost (I Cor. 9:19-22), particularly to the "cultured lost." The Christian student cannot afford to ignore his musical heritage if he wishes to witness with the strongest impact to the widest possible range of society. Musical training and judgment are, however, especially relevant to the vitality of the Church. God gives music an important place in the spiritual life and exercise of His redeemed people (Pss. 40:1-3; 147:1; I Sam. 16:16-18; I Chron. 23:4-5; II Chron. 5:11-14; Col. 3:16). Music is a divinely appointed part of worship and praise, even in the presence of God Himself (Rev. 14:2-3; 15:2-4).

Since music is of such obvious importance and interest to God, man does well to develop a proper appreciation of music, recognize the musical gifts of others, and exercise to God's glory whatever musical gifts he himself may possess. The perfecting of all the faculties engaged by the study of music—whether in singing or playing an instrument, in creating his own musical compositions or in appreciating and enjoying the enormous legacy of his musical heritage—makes the student more like the One after whose attributes his capacities were fashioned. This process of perfecting also enables the student to reveal his Maker more fully and convincingly to the unbelieving world.

In special vocational service—The study of music and its related disciplines is not only valuable for preparing the student to reflect the character and the work of God in the music which he performs or to which he listens. It is also essential preparation for careers in teaching music, church music, solo and ensemble performance, composition, and research and writing about music. Whatever the occupation, the Christian's testimony is validated and enlarged by thorough preparation in the musical disciplines.

The Christian music teacher capitalizes on every opportunity for developing godly character and conduct in the student. He gives constant attention to the student's musical expression, exerting a continuing effort in the disciplining of the student's mind and talent. He forms the student's musical and aesthetic judgment according to Biblical criteria (Phil. 4:8) so that his discernment and musical preferences will conform to the judgment of God and his musical performance will be to the glory of God. He helps the student improve his ability to comprehend and interpret the music he hears so that he will have continuing and greater access to other musical works that are supportive to his development in the image of God. He orients the student to musical culture from a Christian point of view so that he may be reinforced in his spiritual convictions and strengthened against ungodly influences in his society. He himself seeks to excel in the skills and qualities he teaches (Col. 3:23), upholding by his example a standard of excellence in music appreciation and performance and in godliness of life. The consequence for himself and his students is a more powerful influence for God among men.

Distinctiveness

The Christian teaching of music partakes of the same theoretical and historical information as its secular counterpart. However, the Christian music teacher, while teaching skills and concepts and developing discriminating musicianship in the student, has a higher goal. He seeks to inculcate in the Christian student a desire to conform to the image of God and to lead the student to an understanding and development of his talents and skills for the glory of God. The Christian teaching of music conforms to God's Word in prescribing a Scriptural standard for excellence; a Scriptural philosophy for communication; and a sound, Scriptural attitude toward performance. The Christian teacher accordingly emphasizes the truth that musical composition and performance should be God-centered rather than ego-centered. He stresses the importance of music as communication and the need for the vehicle's being suitable to the message. His purpose as a Christian educator—to help students develop in the image of God—reinforces his conviction that musical training is for all rather than just for the specially gifted (Matt. 25:15). He recognizes the moral value of the discipline required in musical training and points up the relationship between achievement and hard work. He particularly stresses the importance of exercising musical skills in the work of God and undertakes to form the students' tastes in sacred as well as secular music. To this end he is knowledgeable about many types of music, but he chooses judiciously within Scriptural guidelines the music, secular or sacred, that will be most worthy of the students' listening and performance and most suitable to Christian educational aims. He teaches Christian judgment by both precept and example, combating the bad by generous doses of the good (I Thess. 5:22; Rom. 12:9).

Practical application in the classroom

A unit on the music of Johann Sebastian Bach offers the Christian teacher a fine opportunity to impress students with the truth that the Christian use of talent is God-centered, not ego-centered (I Cor. 10:31). Students should be fascinated to learn that one of the greatest composers of all time (if not the greatest) was a devout Christian who both composed and performed solely for the glory of God. Bach, probably the supreme example of humility and God-centered musical talent, insisted that the object of all music should be the glory of God and the recreation of the mind. The unit might divide Bach's life and music into three primary periods: (1) the Weimar period, when Bach was a church organist and the majority of his compositions were for the organ; (2) the Coethen period, when Bach was a court musician and the majority of his compositions were secular; and (3) the Leipzig period, when Bach was a schoolteacher and church music director and the majority of his compositions were sacred choral works. While teaching selected compositions from each of the three categories, the teacher could stress continuities: not only the magnificence of Bach's music and his masterful craft of composition but also the important fact that Bach's faith is everywhere manifest in his music, be it sacred or secular.

The Christian musicianship of Bach could be highlighted by a comparison with the accomplishments of such composers as Richard Wagner and Claude Debussy, both of whom achieved great stature and dramatically altered the course of music and yet were highly egotistical in their attitudes toward art and their own genius. The student, having been taught to dedicate his talent to God and to use his music, under whatever circumstances, for the glory of God alone, now can be brought to understand that all good and great music, whether written by Christians or non-Christians, is a gift of God to mankind (James 1:17) and can be received gratefully by God's people. God, who bestows His gifts both on "the just and on the unjust" (Matt. 5:45), endows believer and unbeliever alike with musical talent, and each is capable of enriching or debasing his cultural environment. Musical talent and perception are not necessary adjuncts to spirituality, though it is natural for artistic taste to improve along with growth in other areas of the believer's life. Correspondingly the artistic value of a musical composition is not determined on the basis of whether the composer was a Christian but on the basis of its intrinsic artistic merit—its fulfillment of the universal aesthetic criteria of beauty, form, order, balance, contrast, activity, and repose. Even unregenerate musicians and composers can make valuable contributions to our cultural lives, and we are able to learn from them. Just as the Christian profits from studying masterpieces of literature, sculpture, and painting, so does he profit from giving his attention to the symphonies, operas, oratorios, songs, chamber music, and so forth that have become an important part of our cultural heritage. Though the Christian musician has a higher motive for musical composition and performance than has the non-Christian, his artistic standards are the same. The Christian listener can legitimately enjoy music, whether sacred or secular, that meets these standards—standards that originate in the character of God.

The comparison of Bach with unbelieving, egotistical composers, or perhaps a comparison of the three periods of his own career, could easily lead into a clarification of the nature and role of sacred music. Sacred music is a special responsibility of the Christian musician. Such music has a sacred text or is of such character and mood as to be in keeping with devotion. It glorifies God by fulfilling its Biblically mandated function as a vehicle for worship and praise; for teaching, uplifting, or admonishing the believer; or for reaching the lost with the message of the gospel (Pss. 40:1-3; 147:1; 150; Col. 3:16).

Sacred music, while often expressive of exuberant Christian joy, is not to be confused with amusement or entertainment. This stricture does not discount the place of entertainment in the Christian life nor the use of music in entertainment. Once again we recall the admonition of the most outstanding Christian musician of history, J. S. Bach, that the object of all music should be the glory of God and the recreation of the mind. Just as a church service is not the place for amusement, it is not the place for musical entertainment. Sacred music, wherever performed, communicates Scriptural truth and brings spiritual joy and blessing to the hearer; but it does not merely entertain him. Thus, applause, while appropriate at secular concerts, is inappropriate in church. Applause indicates approval of man's performance. The church musician seeks not human approbation but renders his music solely for the glory of God. He does not pander to sensual responses by imitating the physical and musical mannerisms that are the tools in trade of the popular singer and instrumentalist. He presents his message with straightforward, heartfelt conviction, avoiding the catalogue of evocative ''pop'' stylings that range from unfettered wailing to deliberately intimate, sensual crooning.

Christian entertainment, while not the subject under primary consideration here, is of great importance and cannot be avoided where music is concerned. There is reading of a primarily recreational variety, suitable to the Christian reader, though not possessing the highest literary quality. There is pictorial art that is harmless, though not of the highest artistic merit. Likewise there is music which is relaxing in nature and purporting to no such high standards as the musical classics. However, there are points beyond which it is not safe for the Christian to go in what he reads, sees, or hears. Legitimate recreational literature and art are not to be confused with the vulgar and pornographic. Legitimate recreational music is not to be confused with offensive popular styles of music, not merely because of their associations with evil but also because of their emphasis on carnal physical effects, their cheap and shallow texts, and their tendencies toward the wild and unrestrained in the extreme.

The *text* of good sacred music is Scripturally sound and recognizes a moral standard. The Apostle Paul instructs, "Let the word of Christ dwell in you richly in all wisdom; teaching and admonishing one another in psalms and hymns and spiritual songs, singing with grace in your hearts to the Lord" (Col. 3:16). The best sacred music is rich in Biblical wisdom and inspiration. Heresy and blasphemy are no more tolerable in sacred music than they are in the pulpit. We must reject all religious music, whether popular or formal, whose texts deny or distort doctrinal truths and profane the holy character of God. Likewise, worldliness is no more acceptable in sacred music than in the lives of those who minister the Word to God's people. The Apostle John commands us, "Love not the world, neither the things that are in the world" (I John 2:15). Although the texts of sacred music need not be of the most profound doctrinal implications or literary merit, they must not—in message or manner—encourage error, carry worldly associations, or partake of the cheap and shallow. Much of the greatest sacred music uses texts directly from the Bible itself or is based firmly upon the Bible. No text for sacred music should in any way contradict Scripture or violate Scriptural principle, either directly or by implication.

The *music* of a sacred selection should fit the mood of the text. For example, the music to "Onward Christian Soldiers" and "Lead On, O King Eternal" is understandably somewhat martial in character. "Holy, Holy, Holy" and "O, For a Thousand Tongues" are sung to tunes that match the texts in majesty. The tune to "Nearer, Still Nearer" matches the devotional mood of the text; and the spirit of joy and thanksgiving are reflected in the music of "Rejoice, Ye Pure in Heart" and "Great Is Thy Faithfulness." "Jesus Saves" expresses, in text and tune, the joyful sound of the good news that is the gospel. Only frivolous and shallow texts should be sung to frivolous and shallow tunes; and since such texts, often filled with vain repetition, are totally unbecoming to God and all that is sacred, they should not be sung in church at all. This is not to suggest, of course, that sacred music be at all times so "classical" in nature that it ministers only to the musically educated and the aesthetically elite. Sacred music can communicate God's message warmly and enthusiastically to people at all levels of aesthetic development without recourse to the cheap and shallow practices of the world.

Sacred music avoids the distraction of worldly associations; for the Christian's music, like his body, must be presented a living sacrifice, holy, acceptable unto God, and must not be conformed to the world (Rom. 12:1-2). Melodies, harmonies, rhythms, tone colors, stylings, or performance practices that are associated clearly with dancing, drugs, drunkenness, or moral looseness have no place in sacred music. Many so-called secular compositions are by their conservative, restrained, and noble nature more appropriate to sacred use than are many so-called sacred compositions which, because of their obvious imitation of popular musical styles, sound much more secular than sacred.

Sacred music should exhibit a thoughtful application of our understanding under the control of the Holy Spirit (I Cor. 14:15). When the Apostle Paul says that he will "sing with the spirit" and will "sing with the understanding also," he is not referring to two experiences, one intellectual and thoughtful and another humanly uncontrolled but guided by the Holy Spirit. Rather he is referring to a Spirit-filled and Spirit-controlled understanding. Good sacred vocal music should be sung, whether by congregation, choir, ensemble, or soloist, both with spiritual understanding of the sacred text that brings glory to God, edification to the believer, and conviction to the lost and with sufficient musical understanding to convey the sacred text appropriately. Instrumental sacred music should be characterized by these same qualities, the primary difference being that no text is sung. Christian congregations should be taught to comprehend the wealth of spiritual meaning in the texts of good sacred music and to recognize the cheap and shallow, whether in text or in music or in both, and to eschew it as they do the unworthy in other areas of their lives.

Points of conflict with the secular philosophy of music education

Distinctively Christian music teaching requires the rejection of certain approaches to its subject matter that derive from the climate of modern thought. Such approaches not only should be avoided by the Christian music teacher but also should be explicitly condemned.

Egoism—The Christian music teacher recognizes and imparts to his students the principles that the application of musical talent is God-centered, not ego-centered ("And what hast thou that thou didst not receive?" [I Cor. 4:7]). The Christian composes and performs to express rather than to impress, and what he desires to express is in keeping with his character as a humble child of God. There is clear and vital communication in the Christian's musical performance, but it is disciplined and directed by God. It does not partake of unfettered self-expression but is marked by order and balance (I Cor. 14:40), whether in communicating the artistic "message" of a secular composition or the Christian message of a sacred composition. The Christian performer does not take unwarranted liberties with a piece for the sake of endearing himself to the audience or flaunting his expertise. This is not to say that the Christian does not put himself into his performance in a vital way. He does. But he regards his abilities as instrumental to the purpose of the work, not the work as instrumental to his abilities. Though he sings or plays "heartily," he does so "as to the Lord, and not unto men" (Col. 3:23).

Permissivism—Though the Christian music teacher desires to expose his students to a wide and representative variety of musical styles and works, he recognizes that not all styles and works are of equal merit or suitability for the classroom. He realizes that the sounds and words of music can interact so as to stimulate wrong desires and seal out spiritual influences. Of course, the knowledgeable Christian teacher recognizes that he cannot simply equate good music with the serious music of Western civilization during the last five centuries. The conventional octave is by no means the only way to divide the scale. What sounds jarring and strange to Western ears may make good sense to oriental ears. He realizes the difficulty of distinguishing legitimate new directions in music from degenerative trends, for music of real integrity has sometimes been temporarily misunderstood and rejected as an affront to good taste. Nevertheless, he knows that there has been in most eras a kind of music that conscientious Christians have felt compelled to condemn for its worldly associations, psychological effects, or philosophical implications. Licentious music may vary in form from age to age and its effects may to some extent vary, but it speaks its message clearly to the debauched or shallow audience of its day, a message often frankly acknowledged by its composers and performers. The Christian teacher understands the enormous and subtle power of music to influence for good or evil the entire personality—both body and mind, emotions and intellect, the physical and the spiritual natures. He knows that music is not morally neutral and that Christian judgment must operate in the musical sphere as well as in other areas of Christian experience.

The Christian teacher of music therefore rejects the secular permissivism that regards all kinds of music as educationally valid. He realizes that judgment in music must proceed by universal aesthetic and moral standards that have their origin in the character of God. He also realizes that his selection of musical materials must reflect Christian rather than secular educational aims. Music such as the ''classics'' that can uplift and ennoble the spirit, stimulate and inspire the mind, and enrich the emotions of the hearer or, on the other hand, less exalted music such as genuine folk music or ''light'' music that can entertain and relax the listener without in any way appealing to his baser instincts—such music is a marvelously effective tool in the hands of the Christian teacher for helping mold his students into the image of God. On the contrary, degenerative types of popular music such as jazz and rock music that appeal primarily to the physical nature rather than to the spiritual, intellectual, and higher emotional capacities are in conflict with the goals of Christian education. Even some types of serious music are potentially destructive. The absurdist world view projected by the aleatoric or ''chance'' music of some existentialist composers and anti-art movements is an expression of modern religious unbelief. Defenders of this music do not take into account that no single sound or musical ''event'' is automatically and irreducibly unique. It has value only as it finds its place in a musical utterance that reflects the universal, God-given criteria of beauty, form, order, balance, contrast, activity, and repose. The informed, conscientious Christian teacher rejects and condemns the objectionable in both popular and serious modern music. The sensualism of the one and the cynicism of the other are expressions of a mind in rebellion against God. Neither emotional nor intellectual lawlessness can be encouraged or condoned in the Christian classroom. Both defile the mind and disable it from accomplishing the will of God.

Aestheticism—Although artistic creativity is one of the noblest of man's capacities and the appreciation of beauty one of man's richest and worthiest enjoyments, the pursuit of beauty cannot preoccupy the Christian so entirely as it does the artists and connoisseurs of the world. The Christian cannot make art, musical or otherwise, his religion. The veneration of art for art's sake is a form of hedonism in which aesthetic pleasure is sought solely as an end in itself. In such veneration, physical manifestations of an attribute of God—beauty—are worshiped rather than God Himself. Aestheticism is therefore a kind of idolatry in which the creation replaces the Creator as an object of worship (Exod. 20:3-4; Rom. 1:25). In aestheticism the realm of music is viewed as morally neutral. The work of music is regarded as properly existing for its own sake rather than for some purpose beyond itself. Its physical and psychological effects upon the hearer are considered irrelevant to evaluation of its merit and beyond the scope of criticism. Aestheticism therefore excludes the moral criteria that Christians must apply in all areas of their experience. It prevents the critic from assessing a work in a Christian way—from attempting to see it as it appears totally in the view of God. Consequently aestheticism, as a critical viewpoint, offers an incomplete and therefore erroneous basis for musical judgment. As a way of life, it is a false religion.

Conclusion

Music is an essential part of a genuinely Christian education. There is perhaps no single, extra-Biblical influence more powerful than music and more responsible for shaping attitude and action in our churches and schools and, indeed, in society at large. Yet, there is no other element in the Christian community in our time that has been more lightly treated, more misunderstood, more misused, and more divorced from Scriptural foundations than music.

Although music is an abstract mode of expression, the Christian music teacher cannot ignore the standards that God's Word delineates for every aspect of the Christian life. His music must glorify God, who is holy. Consequently his music achieves a pleasing balance of the elements that reflect the image of God. He guides his students to an understanding of the mind of God through a study of good music, both secular and sacred, that reflects the divine attributes. He teaches his students to seek that which is best and most beautiful, not as an end in itself but to the end that they may be "throughly furnished unto all good works" (II Tim. 3:17).

The Christian Teaching of Art

Definition

Art is the process of producing a visual image or object using the expressive elements of line, shape, mass, texture, value, and color in accordance with the unifying principles of repetition, harmony, contrast, and balance and proportion, in order to communicate a concept and to give aesthetic pleasure.

Art education guides the child in a gradual development of (1) skill in the use of these elements and application of these principles with art tools and materials and (2) his creative imagination. During art training the teacher helps the student achieve a balanced and disciplined use of his intellectual, emotional, and imaginative capacities for fashioning pictures, designs, and objects. Christian art teaching encourages student artwork that reflects the beauty and order found in God's creation.

Justification

Reflections of God in the subject matter

The study of art can serve the purpose of Christian education—to conform redeemed man to the image of God—because the elements of art reflect the character and works of God. The theoretical considerations, the materials, and the resulting skills of art studies all come from and point to God, the Creator, as He manifests Himself in the handiwork of all His creation.

It is obvious that the divine Creator values beauty. The beauty of nature is evident on every hand. In beauty of form and material, God's creations far surpass even the best of man's. The Lord pointed out some lilies along His path and directed His disciples to look at them (Matt. 6:28-30). There is no material more beautiful than that of which flower petals are made. It is simultaneously firm yet soft, smooth but also textured, matte yet also sparkling like little diamonds. It comes in a breathtaking array of colors that are bright without being harsh or gaudy. The value of flowers to God derives from their reflection of Him. Certainly the most lavish of Solomon's robes could never equal the beauty of the material or variety of design of one of God's simple creations, the lily of the field.

The beauty of God's natural creation is never in conflict with utility. The beauties of the petals and the stamens of a flower, while giving pleasure to the beholder, attract the insects necessary for pollination. Its beauty therefore enables the perpetuation of its species as well as other species by its place in the food chain. But the beauty of God's creation is not limited to utilitarian ends. Nature displays a lavish extravagance in its variety and abundance of beautiful details. From the standpoint of pure utilitarianism, God could have created just a few plants—one tree for strong wood, another for growing food; one animal for use as transportation, another for wool, another for food. With very few forms He could have made a creation that would function. But instead He created a great variety of forms—some duplicating the functions of others, some with no apparent practical function at all. Certainly the beauty of the flowers of the field is in a degree far in excess of what is necessary to their practical function in the system of nature. We know therefore that God intends beauty for pleasure as well as for utility. Since only an infinitesimal fraction of the beauties of the universe are seen by human eyes, God must have provided them for His own enjoyment as well as for man's. Modern telescopes, electron microscopes, and photographic images transmitted from space probes have revealed unsuspected glories—a richness of colors and symmetries pervading vast expanses of creation ordinarily visible only to the Creator Himself. God, speaking to Job, catalogues beauties of His creation of which man can be only remotely aware (Job 38). Man's pleasure in beauty is evidently only an imperfect reflection of God's own.

In the study of God's creation, man finds that all things bear the beauty of His being in the abstract order of their design as well as on the visible surface. The beauty that we see in nature derives not only from surface detail but also from basic abstract principles that underlie natural forms. The lines, shapes, colors, and textures of natural things are organized into interesting and varied groupings by ordering principles such as repetition, harmony, contrast, proportion (of part to part), and balance (of part with part) that are all basic to the beauty that God created in nature. Through the beauty of His creation, both concrete and abstract, God reveals Himself to mankind (Ps. 19:1-6). Man, in fact, is "without excuse," because having seen the character of God in His creation, men know enough to seek God (Rom. 1:20). This knowledge is "manifest in them; for God hath shown it unto them" (Rom. 1:19). Evidently every person, on the peril of his soul, is obligated to respond to the beauty and grandeur of creation and to recognize in that beauty and grandeur the goodness and greatness of God.

It should not be surprising that man, created in the image of God, has a capacity for appreciating and even creating beauty. Man, the image bearer, is also an image maker. It is true that man cannot, like God, create *ex nihilo,* from nothing. He must create "after God." In fact, imitation of God's creation in human art, both representational and nonrepresentational, is virtually inescapable, however blurred and distorted the reflections may be. But the best art is that which conforms most fully to the principles of divine creativity. It exhibits, though in finite degree, the artistry of the observable specific forms. Moreover, it does not violate the character and will of God in its moral tone.

Therefore the proper study of art points inevitably to God, the author of all loveliness and the ultimate source of all that is good in man. The Christian teaching of art turns the attention of the students to God through His handiwork, in nature and in themselves. It also directs them to the products of human artistry as reflections, though flawed, of the creativity of God. The student may learn something of God from His reflection in even the imperfect efforts of man to express the beauty and order of nature or the order man discerns in himself.

Christian art teaching places the products of human genius in a critical perspective that helps clarify for the student his own obligations to God as a moral being and as an artistic creator. In associating beauty with holiness, God has established a twofold standard for the evaluation of man's creations (Ps. 29:2; Gen. 1:31). This standard prescribes excellence in both composition and moral tone. The goal of the Christian artist is to apply this twofold standard to the production of his artwork in order to reveal God to the viewer as God has revealed Himself to man in His creation. Artwork that maintains positive moral tone but is weak compositionally is marred in its image bearing and, in its disorder, expresses godlessness (I Cor. 14:33). Artwork that is beautiful compositionally but negative in moral tone reflects God in its structure but denies His authority over the moral life. Works that are disorderly in structure and morally negative deny God on both accounts. The final evaluation of artwork must therefore include both its formal structure and its moral tone. In condemning lawlessness in both spheres, Christian art teaching respects and reveals the nature of God.

Manifestations of godliness in the resultant knowledge, attitudes, and skills

In general Christian character and service—Not only in the practice of art itself but also in the development of his aesthetic capacity the art student cultivates qualities of character reflective of God and prepares himself for service.

The study and exercise of art in the classroom develops the student's aesthetic capacity in four important ways. First, he learns to understand the visual "language" used by artists in communicating their ideas to the viewer. Second, he develops his own capacity for imaginative response to his surroundings. Third, he develops his aesthetic taste by learning the criteria for evaluating artistic work. Fourth, he gains aesthetic enjoyment both from his own creative efforts and from the artwork of others. These benefits enhance an aspect of the divine image in man—the aesthetic—evidently very important to God. They also promote the emotional stability of the student by helping him to fulfill his visual and kinetic needs.

The study of art encourages the development of good work habits such as following instructions, planning and finishing the job, choosing the correct tools or materials for a task and using them properly, working with a reasonable degree of neatness, and exercising objective self-criticism. Finishing the job involves craftsmanship—the thorough way in which a Christian attends to each detail of the constructing and presenting of his work. In this day of rampant casualness, diligence in detail is an important part of manifesting God-likeness. By the art teacher's example as well as by precept, the student learns to subject his abilities to God's service (Exod. 31:2-6). Practical projects that promote school or church functions can encourage this attitude if they are not allowed to crowd out other meaningful instruction.

In special vocational service—Vocations in art are vital both in the secular business world and in Christian ministries. Every printed object has to be designed by somebody. Churches need to be decorated tastefully; products need to be designed, packaged, and advertised—all jobs done by artists. In a less commercial sense, artists visualize the attitudes and beliefs of a society and influence the values of people by the kinds of objects and images they create. For example, Dutch Protestant artists not only reflected but also reinforced Christian belief in the Bible by painting Biblical events set in scenes and populated by characters that were contemporary. By portraying Mary and Joseph as ordinary people as the Bible does, de Grebber's *Adoration of the Shepherds* (p. 198) brought the incarnation back to its Biblical emphasis. Catholic artists of Italy and Spain, by contrast, had elevated Mary to near godhead by portraying her as an ideal beauty in finery befitting a queen. Such Catholic art drew worshipers to Mary, and thus to the church, rather than to the incarnate Son of God.

Among the vocations available to the gifted, well-prepared student are those of commercial art. Its practitioners include, for example, the advertising artist who works on packaging and selling products; the publication artist who designs magazines or books, jackets for recordings, and other published materials; the illustrator and letter designer who work on specific details of published materials; the industrial designer who designs and builds products ranging from hand appliances to vehicles; video artists who design materials for use on television; and the architect who designs and engineers buildings.

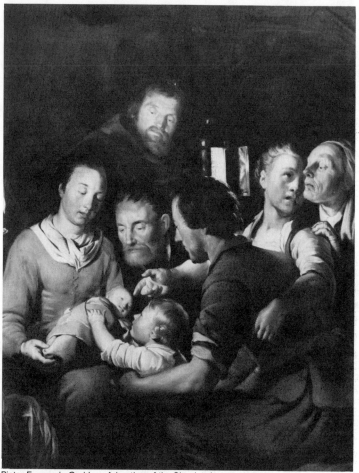

Pieter Fransz de Grebber, *Adoration of the Shepherds,*
Bob Jones University Collection of Sacred Art.

The Christian art student may feel led of God to become a
teacher. All levels from elementary to college require qualified
art teachers. Working with retired people and handicapped people
are two worthwhile extensions of the art-teaching profession.

Last, though not least, is the studio craftsman or painter,
making his living by creating beautiful objects or paintings for
people. Because of the inexpensive objects and printed pictures
available today, this is the most difficult of the three types of
vocations to rely on for self-support. However, given the poor

design and look-alike nature of manufactured goods, there will always be a demand for unique handmade things. The studio artist must simply be willing to work hard to make his living. As compensation he is relatively free to devote his mind and his time almost totally to the activity he enjoys most and does best and to perform it as an expression of his love for God.

Distinctives

A well-rounded art program in the Christian school is similar to a good secular art program in many of its commitments and procedures. Both Christian and secular art teachers recognize the tremendous potential in art studies for developing confidence in the activities of the imagination, skill in the creative organization of elements into a whole, and sense of the dynamics of structural relationships. Both, therefore, insist on the value of art education for the child and adolescent beyond that of learning to draw, color, and model. The Christian teacher knows that there is more to the art session in the elementary or secondary program than the development of a coordination between eye, mind, and hand, as important as this is; for the advantages of art classes at these levels of education extend to the entire mind and personality of the student. Though these benefits may have little to do with the making of an artist, they have much to do with mature, productive leadership in all walks of life.

Therefore, a good art class, whether secular or Christian, encourages the personal involvement of each student in making his own artwork and evaluating it. It structures art projects so that the student makes his own aesthetic decisions and judgments. It avoids the use of preplanned, preprinted art surfaces or manufactured kits, which, while guaranteeing a pleasing result, harm the student by circumventing his own independent participation, lessening his learning experience, and undermining his confidence. A complete art program, Christian or secular, includes instruction in the use of art tools and materials appropriate to the grade level. It introduces the study of basic design principles that underlie nature and art as students are capable of understanding them. Kindergartners begin with color and shape. Older children gradually learn more advanced concepts. Through second and third grades the teacher gently motivates and guides the simple honesty of expression and originality so natural to small children. In the middle grades the child, while still encouraged to use schematic or stylized representations of his own ideas, can benefit from more motivational pressure and guidance. Junior high students will become interested in realism and need help in perspective and shading. They can learn simple balance and composition. High school students are capable of working with all the basic principles and elements. Because of the insecurity of adolescent years, the high school student needs strong and even disciplined encouragement in getting his own ideas and developing his own art projects. The development of his individuality and character must not be curtailed by resorting to preplanned artwork or to mere copying. The alternation of projects designed to teach principles with projects utilizing these principles in creative ways keeps high school classes from becoming ''dried out'' or merely theoretical. For example, a project in which students mix a color wheel from the three primary colors, giving them the theory of color mixing, may be followed by a project in painting in which the students are not allowed to use any color straight from the bottle. Together these projects can give the student an understanding of the nature of color and its use.

A good art program, secular or Christian, provides physical facilities suitable to art activities: flat tables, a sink, storage space, and adequate light. Although the art room may be shared by other classes, it is not cluttered or crowded with equipment or other objects that interfere with its primary use. In addition to the studio activities of the classroom, the program provides short appreciation sessions using carefully selected illustrations from texts, printed reproductions or slides, and occasionally field trips to local museums and historical locations where art usually abounds. The Christian art teacher, like the secular, views his role with great seriousness, all the more so in that its importance is generally unrecognized. He realizes that encouraging and nurturing the creative energy and resourcefulness that God has implanted in man are of primary importance in the complete educational program. He realizes, furthermore, that art class is the best and almost the only means of beginning the development of this great gift of God, a gift that has remained dormant or stunted in so many of His children.

A Christian art program, however, differs in several important ways from secular art programs. The Christian art teacher cultivates an atmosphere in his classroom that promotes the "beauty of holiness" both by precept and example. He requires a reasonable degree of cleanliness during work sessions, for sloppiness does not help the artist work any better and wastes time by disorganizing his work space. The Christian art class is teacher-directed in its activities, establishing solid, well-defined learning goals for each project. The Christian teacher avoids the random, nondirected approach that allows each student to do what he pleases whether it is constructive or not. He realizes, of course, that art classes of necessity will be more casual in their organization than academic classes. Students must be free to move around and get materials during the lesson and may be allowed to talk in low voices. Too rigidly structured a classroom inhibits the freedom of access and of relaxed structure. But purposefulness and discipline are essential. The Christian teacher remains in control, setting goals, standards, and rules and insisting that these be respected.

The Christian art teacher is alert to opportunities for identifying wrong attitudes and for encouraging good attitudes in students as these are expressed in their art. He is well grounded in God's Word so as to be prepared to take advantage of these opportunities to channel his students' feelings in positive spiritual directions. In encouraging objective evaluation by the student of his own and others' work, the teacher promotes a mature attitude in the student toward himself and his work. He also encourages a respect for high standards. As his own work exemplifies these attitudes and standards, he is better able to encourage the same in his students.

The aim and result of art instruction in the Christian classroom are not self-centered expression. They are rather the cultivation of the student's artistic talent and the development of his appreciation for visual balance, order, and overall beauty, as well as a more imaginative and constructive attitude toward all of life's activities. They give the student the opportunity, through the disciplined use of his God-given talent, to produce unique art objects for his own satisfaction and for the glory of God. This artwork will be aesthetically sound and spiritually edifying (Rom. 14:19).

Practical application in the classroom

A study of the tabernacle and the temple in the Old Testament will provide the Christian art teacher with an excellent opportunity to discover God's aesthetic principles and their application in our own age. The tabernacle is revealed in Exodus 25-27 and constructed in Exodus 36-39; the temple is revealed in I Chronicles 28:1-19 and completed in II Chronicles 3-4. In studying them, we can learn much that is important for the Christian study of art. God used the tabernacle and the temple not only for a spiritual object lesson but also for teaching man how properly to use art for His glory. A number of valuable points can be made.

First, art is not an end in itself but a means of glorifying God. God was at work even before the building of the tabernacle giving man instruction concerning the proper use of artistic creativity. In Exodus 20:4-5 He tells the people not to make graven (carved) images for use as gods. That this ban did not exclude art *per se* is apparent since God Himself directed the use of sculpture in the one place we would be least likely to expect it. God directed Moses in Exodus 25:18-20 to have three-dimensional sculptures of cherubim made for the ark of the covenant. The lesson to be learned is that art is not wrong or forbidden but that it is to be used carefully and properly for God's glory.

Second, beauty is found in the materials as well as the form of a work and grows out of their relation to function. In directing the plans of both the tabernacle and the temple, God specified not only the items to be made but also their form, decoration, and materials. God places a high value on beauty—so much so that to express even a tiny fraction of His glory to man, nothing was too expensive to be used.

Third, art may or may not have a practical function. The wedding of beautiful design and function can be seen especially well in the design of the tabernacle. Since it was to be a portable building, the construction had to be planned so that the pieces could be easily disassembled and transported. The design for these parts makes an aesthetic occasion of necessity by providing decorative ways of joining parts (Exod. 36:11-13; 17-18). But other decorative elements were unrelated to practical function: for example, the gold-leafed walls inside the holy place and the embroidered cherubim on the curtains. Some of the most demanding design work was simply "for glory and for beauty" (Exod. 28:40).

Fourth, artwork may or may not be naturalistic. The priests' robes were embroidered with red, purple, and blue pomegranates (28:33). The pomegranates required in this design were, of course, recognizable natural forms. But the use of the color blue can be little else than a purely aesthetic decision unifying the robes with the dominant color scheme. In the temple pomegranates again appear hanging from chains—one hundred pomegranates per chapter (II Chron. 3:15-16). Since pomegranates do not grow from chains, this "abstract" device can be assumed to be purely symbolic and decorative.

Fifth, God uses man's creativity and a variety of human skills to glorify Himself. Though both the tabernacle and the temple were planned in detail by God, He allowed men to use their creative talents in the task of building them. He prepared a talented man, Bezaleel, and his assistant, Aholiab, and filled them with His Spirit to make the objects for the tabernacle and to supervise others (Exod. 31:2-6).

Sixth, genuinely Christian artwork is dedicated to God's glory even though it may find a common use. The focus of the beauties of the tabernacle and the temple was God's glory and enjoyment, not man's pleasure. Once the workmen had finished, the furnishings would be assembled and would never be seen in their entirety again by man. Only those men designated as closest to God would share even temporarily in the beauty that existed inside the house of God, and then much of it would be shrouded in God's shekinah glory. Clearly the beauties there were reserved for God's enjoyment.

As we seek to dedicate to God's glory the creative work that we do, we must then learn to manage the wide variety of materials with which we may glorify God. Even a brief list of the arts and crafts of the tabernacle includes sculpture in the round and relief; embroidered two-dimensional images; cabinetry; gold leafing; jewelry; spinning, weaving, and dyeing of flax for linen; casting of metals; and engraving. The materials include brass, silver, gold, precious stones, linen, natural dyes, wood, and several kinds of leather (Exod. 36-39). For the modern craftsman and artist, many more materials are available.

Aesthetic activities can be of great value in bringing spiritual blessing to others. God's Word contains many poetic passages not only in the Psalms but also in other Old Testament books. The essence of poetry is language used with careful attention to its aesthetic qualities. David's musical and poetic activities may not have been regarded by his contemporaries as his greatest accomplishment; yet they stand today as one of the most greatly favored portions of the Word. It would be presumptuous to say that David's enjoyment of music and poetry was illegitimate or frivolous. The little poetic book of the Song of Solomon is another example of a section of Scripture replete with beautiful visual descriptions that add to the romantic beauty and power of the work.

For the Christian today enjoyment of and participation in creative activities should be part of his "image-bearing" devotion and service to God. First Corinthians 3:21-22 tells us, "For all things are yours; Whether . . . the world [cosmos], or life, or death, or things present, or things to come; all are yours." As Christ has given us all nonsinful things "richly . . . to enjoy" (I Tim. 6:17), we must use all these things for His glory.

As we can learn about God by studying His works (Rom. 1:19-20), we can also learn about man by studying his works. The history of Christendom is visually exemplified through the many works of art and architecture that have been created for the church. Doctrines and church practices both true and false have influenced church art, and the study of the history of sacred art is a beneficial addition to a young person's education, helping him to "refuse the evil, and choose the good" (Isa. 7:15-16).

Since the majority of art teaching involves studio classes in which the students are actually doing artwork, let us consider a sample studio lesson for the high school level.

Educating the eye and the mind of the student, as well as allowing him the actual experience of working with art media, is very important for the successful art program. The student must be aware that he is in a class that has well-defined learning goals and in which he is expected to participate. The discipline and attitude problems sometimes encountered in art classes are overcome by challenging the student with a real task that he can accomplish. Discipline problems in art classes can arise when art is assumed to be a "fun" class that should not have any learning goals. If a student does not experience the promised fun or feels he cannot achieve success because he lacks "talent," he may develop a negative attitude or become a discipline problem. Well-defined learning goals that are on the proper level for the student give him a realistic way of measuring his own performance and also teach him something that helps him better understand art. The successful studio lesson must therefore begin with the teacher's clear-cut idea of the concept he wants to teach.

If, for example, the concept being taught is composition, some time should be given to discussing and illustrating composition by a variety of examples. The specific principle of repetition/harmony/contrast, for example, is a basic tenet of visual design. Repetition is necessary to the establishing of oneness in the design; yet if one element were exactly repeated a number of times, the design would become monotonous. A design therefore needs contrast to add interest. Yet contrast alone (with no repetition) tends to be disunifying. The solution is to include both repetition and contrast in a harmonious design. This principle can be copiously illustrated in nature. Trees have certain characteristics in common, yet each species of tree has a slightly different combination of specific forms. For example, all trees have leaves containing chlorophyll to manufacture food for the tree, and yet leaves vary widely among species.

In artwork the same use of repetition/harmony/contrast can be demonstrated. Piet Mondrian painted canvasses he called "compositions" because he was interested not in showing the specific forms of nature but in showing the composition or structure of his painting. *Composition in White, Black, and Red* (p. 206) shows a severe grid of black lines with two blocks of color in opposite corners. It contains obvious repetition since each of the lines repeats the horizontal or vertical direction and straight character of the other lines and each shape repeats the rectangular theme. But when we begin to examine the painting for contrasts, we may be surprised to note that no two rectangles exactly duplicate any of the others and no two edges of the painting are the same. Furthermore, two blocks of contrasting color have been included to add weight and to contrast with the black and white color scheme. The result is a harmony of contrasting elements held together by subtle repetition.

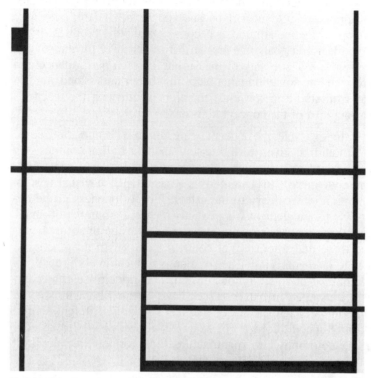

Piet Mondrian, *Composition in White, Black, and Red*, 1936. Oil on canvas, 40 $\frac{1}{4}$ " x 40". Collection, The Museum of Modern Art, New York. Gift of the Advisory Committee.

In a much more traditional way, Philippe de Champaigne (1602-74), used the same devices in his painting *The Christ of Derision* (p. 207). The background of the scene establishes the bare minimum of setting with a predominantly rectangular structure that resembles Mondrian's composition. There is a rectangular theme in which none of the rectangles duplicates any other. The large rectangle on the right contrasts with the smaller shapes on the left, and there is contrast of light with dark. With this abstract composition as his foundation, Champaigne put the figure of Christ against the large blank wall, contrasting the organic and subtly twisting shapes of the human body with the severe rectangular shapes of the setting. He also incorporated a strong raking light to highlight Christ and set Him apart from the shadow all around.

Philippe de Champaigne, *The Christ of Derision,*
Bob Jones University Collection of Sacred Art.

The latter picture of course has something that the Mondrian composition does not have. It has content. The painter uses the

207

abstract organization of his painting to reveal the Biblical story. He moves us up close to the figure and, by making the painting fairly large, encourages us to relate to it in a personal, direct way—as an actual event rather than a picture of a past event. In contrasting the figure of Christ with His background, Champaigne emphasizes the loneliness of His position and also eliminates most of the details that would be distracting. The only important detail included is the single pillar at the left. Since according to tradition Christ was tied to a pillar for flogging, the pillar is symbolic of His suffering (John 19:1).

Having spent some time explaining and illustrating the principle of repetition/harmony/contrast, the teacher will devote the next class period to getting the students started in their own project. A simple way for young people to work with composition is to have them cut out pieces of paper and glue them onto a contrasting background piece. Students are given an idea of how many pieces to cut (usually an odd number from three to seven) and the family of shapes to be used (perhaps rectangles). They then cut out a variety of these shapes and begin arranging them on the paper. When the students feel satisfied that their designs contain both repetition and enough contrast to be interesting, they glue the pieces down. The teacher may give help at any time, but he is wise to let the students individually work out the first stages of the problem.

When the pieces have been arranged and glued on, they may be hung up for general class critique by the teacher and fellow students. The class may be asked to choose the good designs and explain why they are good. Poorer designs can be tactfully used to elicit suggestions from the class for improvement. Emphasis is on positive, encouraging comments. Designs are identified by number rather than name.

Teacher evaluation of the project will emphasize its adherence to the teacher's directions for the project as well as its aesthetic success.

The project just described emphasizes theory. Because the design is nonrepresentational, it focuses the student's attention on the problem of composition. It can be profitably followed by a project in painting still lifes in which the students choose objects and arrange them with the principle of repetition/harmony/contrast in mind. The students then paint the still life, applying their under-standing of the principle to their painting. This project may be preceded by a study of still-life paintings so that students may see how such principles were applied consciously by the artists.

Points of conflict with the secular teaching of art

Distinctively Christian art teaching must confront many philo-sophical ideas and attitudes that have become woven into the fabric of the art and culture of the modern world. Insidious con-ceptions and values can be most subtly involved in the visual arts and, therefore, must be clearly identified by the art teacher and emphatically condemned.

These false conceptions and values have distorted modern concepts of art education. The contextualist view insists that the art-education curriculum should be used to accomplish social goals. Therefore, it maintains, the curriculum should vary accord-ing to the social status and educational background of the stu-dents. This view regards art as a tool to accomplish its question-able goals rather than as a subject with intrinsic worth. In the experiential view, propounded by John Dewey, art should be taught as a unique experience that helps the young person enrich his life. It is the height of feeling to which art elevates him that gives art its importance. This special experience should not be made to serve other ends. The idea that aesthetic feeling exists only to enrich life experience is, however, contrary to Scriptural example. It restricts the aesthetic value of art to subjective ex-perience and precludes objective evaluation of the art object, since it is the experience rather than the object that is said to matter. This view also tends to promote a laissez-faire spirit of classroom organization. In the essentialist view, art has its own values and context and should be taught for what it can contribute that other subjects cannot. It should not become a means to any other end. This view is correct except in its insistence (with the experiential view) that art cannot be used for any purpose external to itself. Art can be and has been used to inspire civic pride and awe; to convey religious meaning; to elicit worshipful devotion, sympa-thy, and humor; and to provide general aesthetic enjoyment. These other purposes, far from diminishing and degrading the importance of art, have enhanced it. Such misconceptions of the role of art studies in elementary and secondary education are indebted in various ways and degrees to the following fundamental errors.

Aestheticism—The "Ivory Tower" attitude that puts self-gratification and aesthetic purity above all else ignores the legitimate use of art for various nonaesthetic purposes. This attitude tends to look down on commercial art, for example, as less expressive and therefore less valuable or less aesthetic than painting. But art can be of value in beautifying offices, homes, and churches, if used carefully and tastefully. Art can glorify God by embodying His forms, colors, and principles of design. The artist can give visual form to positive values. Furthermore, art performs a vital service to Christian publications and other visual ministries. Aestheticism not only excludes important functions of art but also produces an uninvolved moral neutrality in the production and evaluation of artwork.

Modernism—The communication of a chaotic, destructive, or violent spirit by deliberately working in haphazard ways and avoiding (or deliberately destroying) harmonious relationships and resemblances to actual objects is in conflict with the Biblical view of the world. Modern artists' statements reveal their search for a "spiritual inner reality" which they believe can be found by shattering external likenesses. To the artistic modernist, work which is harmonious and orderly is too peaceful, lacks tension, and therefore falsifies life. On the contrary, it is the modernist world view, denying divine order and purposiveness in the universe, that misrepresents reality.

Existentialism—The existentialist philosophy has had a profound and pernicious influence on contemporary art. First, because of its view of life as absurd, it has tended to encourage random, haphazard work with a minimum of control by the artist over his product. This "chance" effect mirrors the existentialist concept of "reality." Second, its view of personal rebellion as a way of authenticating oneself pits the creative soul against all the "deadening" influences of society. The conflict thus established may involve moral or political rebellion as well as aesthetic rebellion. Third, the existentialist view of man as hopelessly flawed and abandoned in his despair has produced a tendency to treat the image of man in a negative, destructive way.

Self-expressionism—The artist who uses concrete means to vent negative feelings is substituting catharsis for art. Such activity is random, pointless, and unlikely to give a positive aesthetic response to the viewer. To the person who holds this view, the value of painting is in the doing of it rather than in the object produced or in the communication. Self-expressionism manifests itself in the classroom in the experiential view of art education. It ignores the fact that true artistic expression is the giving of visible form to ideas and feelings evoked by visual experience or memory and formed by the materials with which the artist is working.

The artist sage—Renaissance humanist philosophers invented a concept of beauty as the force which can elevate man toward the "divine." The artist then became not just a skilled craftsman but a sage with great ideas to communicate. He was regarded as being before his time. It survives today in the notion of autonomous self-expression. Critics may evaluate the form of the work, but its content and moral nature are regarded as arising from the profound insight of the artist sage and are above question. (This idea also exists in the value that the art establishment puts on cultural activities as being spiritually elevating.) The anti-art spirit of pop art, happenings, environments, and conceptual art is a reaction against this idea.

Indiscriminate exposure of the human figure—The Christian teaching of art excludes all methods and subject matter that conflict with its educational aim of developing the student in the image of Christ. While recognizing that artists historically have painted and sculpted the unclothed human figure in a generalized way without erotic implications and that nakedness in itself is not evil, the Christian teacher is careful not to jeopardize the spiritual health and growth of his students by the use of materials that immodestly reveal the human form. It is true that college courses in the history of art, even of sacred art, must illustrate Western artistic traditions with examples chosen from the best and most representative works of all periods and types. In such courses the Christian teacher would need to show the practice of the classical Greeks, who used the nude figure to display the beauty of human anatomical symmetry and to show the dignity of man and the intellectual strength that conquers passions. He would want to show, in contrast, the practice of Michelangelo, who used nudes almost exclusively to express his view of man made in the image of God—fallen, suffering, yet redeemable. Nevertheless, even for mature students specializing in the study of art on the college level, such illustrations are chosen with care and presented in a Christian pedagogical perspective that qualifies their use. On the elementary and secondary levels, such examples are needless and are eschewed.

The use of nude models in art classes and studio work is indefensible by Christian moral criteria and, furthermore, is professionally unnecessary. The serious student of art can gain the needed mastery of human anatomical form from careful study and reproduction of modest two- and three-dimensional anatomical studies and from studio drawing of clothed live models. In the Christian study and practice of art, moral and spiritual concerns override all other considerations.

Conclusion

Few things influence young persons more powerfully than visual stimuli, especially in the form of pictures. Since the source of contemporary pictures is usually secular publications, movies, and television, even Christian students are being educated visually by the world. The study of good art and the creative production of artwork need to be a part of Christian education to give students an alternative to the secular imagery that is all around them.

Training in basic art skills and the development of creative imagination is vital not only for those whom the Lord calls into art professionally but also for those entering any other area of service. Art meets basic human needs and develops human capacities that have been implanted by God in man and reflect His nature. Finally, aside from considerations of human needs and possibilities, it seems beyond question that students should be taught to care about things of importance to God.

PRACTICAL
STUDIES

The Christian Teaching of Physical Education

Definition

Physical education is an integral part of the education process. Its primary concern is the physical development (basic motor development, physical fitness, and sport-skill development) of all the students. It promotes this development through the use of well-planned physical and classroom activities. Elementary physical education programs incorporate activities designed to facilitate and enhance the basic physical development of the child. As the student becomes able to perform more complicated and intricate activities, he is taught sport skills that further the development of these capacities. Sport skills are instrumental to physical development rather than physical development instrumental to sport skills. Extracurricular sport activities—whether intramural or interscholastic—are kept within the same educational framework. The nature and extent of these activities are governed by considerations of the student's physical readiness and growth needs. To ensure proper physical development, the program provides diagnostic fitness testing at frequent intervals as well as instruction in health.

Justification

The teaching of physical education in the Christian school has a strong Biblical foundation. God is interested in the body as well as the soul. He Himself indwelt a human body in order to reveal Himself to and redeem mankind (Phil. 2:5-8; Heb. 2:14-16). The Son of God, after His crucifixion and resurrection, offered Thomas the evidence of His wounded body, sacrificed for man's sin (John 20:27). He requires of believers an offering in response to His own: the presentation of their bodies as "a living sacrifice, holy, acceptable unto God" (Rom. 12:1). The body of the believer, furthermore, is "the temple of the Holy Ghost," and he must glorify God in his body and in his spirit, both of which "are God's" (I Cor. 6:19-20). The Christian teacher of physical education takes Biblical injunctions such as these as a mandate for physical development as well as spiritual. It is to the end that God may be glorified through his body that the Christian student is physically educated. His growth in godliness requires taking seriously the needs and appearance of his body—the physical vehicle of his testimony and service. He must maintain himself both spiritually and physically as "a vessel unto honour, sanctified, and meet for the Master's use, and prepared unto every good work" (II Tim. 2:21).

Reflections of God in what is taught

It might seem strange to insist on reflections of God in the content of physical education. Must God maintain physical fitness? Does God engage in sport competition? Obviously, no. And yet the Christian teacher of physical education, health, and recreational skills is not trifling with the sacred when he finds in the revealed character and work of God a pattern for the habits, attitudes, and values he teaches. God works and rests (Gen. 2:2). God battles (Jer. 21:5; Zech. 14:3; Rev. 2:16), resists (James 4:6), endures (Amos 2:13; Matt. 17:17; I Cor. 13:4), subdues (I Chron. 17:10; Ps. 47:2-3; I Cor. 15:24-28), and makes peace (Ps. 85:8; Zech. 9:10; Eph. 2:14-15). His activity is planned, controlled, patiently purposeful (Isa. 46:9-10; II Pet. 3:9). He binds Himself by covenants and agreements (Gen. 9:9-17; Acts 2:30; Heb. 6:16-18) and does not swerve from them (Mal. 3:6). He sets boundaries and respects them (Exod. 19:12-13, 21-24; Jer. 5:22-24; Acts 17:26). He arbitrates and mediates (Job 42:7-8; Luke 22:24-30). In judgment He is discerning, impartial, and fair (Gen. 18:25; Acts 10:34-35). He hates pride and dishonesty (Prov. 6:16-17; I Pet. 5:5; Isa. 5:20; Zech. 8:16-17; 9:9). God values human friendship (John 15:12-15) and fellowship (Prov. 8:30-31), tests those He loves

(Gen. 22:1-18), and continually seeks the good of others (Jer. 29:10-11).

These characteristics of the nature and work of God are able to be emulated by the Christian student of physical education inasmuch as physical discipline is training for life and inasmuch as sport competition is a microcosm of life. Qualities of character display themselves readily when a person is under stress—even the artificially induced stress of physical conditioning or sport competition—and especially when he finds himself gratified or frustrated by the results of his efforts. Irritability, impatience, arrogance, deception, unprincipled opportunism—these and other expressions of self-centeredness or moral immaturity come quickly to light in spirited competition or in a demanding regimen of physical fitness. The Christian physical education teacher has an almost unparalleled opportunity to show the student a mirror of his character in his conduct in class, in the gymnasium, or on the playing field, and then to point him to the divine example—the character and work of God revealed in the Scriptures.

Manifestations of godliness in the resultant knowledge, attitudes, and skills

Since the habits, skills, and attitudes taught in physical education can reflect the character and work of God, the Christian teaching of physical education can enhance the student's development in the image of God.

In general Christian character and service—Through a carefully planned and supervised program of physical education, the Christian student can grow in godliness. He can become more like God in his moral and spiritual character and more useful to God as a result of improved physical habits and skills. Regardless of his physical abilities, he can learn to excel in stewardship, sportsmanship, friendship, and leadership—qualities that reflect the character of God and enhance the service of God.

1. *Stewardship.* The Biblical command to "mortify therefore your members which are upon the earth" (Col. 3:5) requires daily crucifixion of inordinate physical desires—sexual licentiousness, covetousness, and other "deeds of the body" (Rom. 8:13). In response to this injunction some monastic sects have practiced a ritualistic affliction and privation of the body, tormenting the body and denying it necessary food and rest. Even some Bible-believing

Christians take satisfaction in driving themselves to the point of exhaustion and scorning normal nourishment and rest. The assumption is that to weaken the body is to strengthen the soul. Physical asceticism is not, however, commended in Scripture but condemned as contributing to spiritual pride—as exalting rather than humbling the fleshly nature (Col. 2:20-23). In fact, Paul's description of the Church as a body whose head is Christ makes clear that to satisfy the needs of the body is natural and right. Husbands should show a tender regard toward their wives as to their own bodies. "For no man ever yet hated his own flesh; but nourisheth and cherisheth it, even as the Lord the church" (Eph. 5:29). To teach the proper nourishing and cherishing of the body is therefore a legitimate concern of Christian physical education. Indeed growth in godliness requires a Biblical attitude toward the body—as an outward expression of inner goodness, as a vehicle of service, and as a gift of God to be valued and maintained.

The nourishing and cherishing of the body consists of providing it with the proper food, rest, and exercise; attending to its medical needs; and avoiding harmful substances such as alcohol, nicotine, and other drugs. Obviously the preservation of health can be carried to un-Scriptural extremes. Hypochondria and health mania indicate an unspiritual, excessive anxiety for the state of the body and sometimes even a fear of death. The Corinthian Christians, when invited to dinner, were to eat what was set before them, asking no questions (I Cor. 10:25-27). Paul was willing to "spend and be spent" for these same Corinthians, taxing himself physically as well as in other ways (II Cor. 12:15). The excessive pampering or hyperdevelopment of the body indicates unspiritual values as well as physical pride. "Favour is deceitful, and beauty is vain," we are warned in Proverbs (31:30). "He that glorieth, let him glory in the Lord," enjoins Paul (II Cor. 10:17). Overindulgence in physical exercise and recreational pleasures indicates a confusion of means for ends and a subordination of eternal values to temporal (I Tim. 4:8). Nevertheless, a respect for the needs of the body is a respect for its Creator and for the purposes the body was designed to serve. Though it is true that bodily exercise profits only for "a little" time—for the duration of this earthly life—it is this "little" time that is our present opportunity of service. Like Christ we must work "while it is day," for "the night cometh, when no man can work" (John 9:4). A properly trained and maintained body can increase the Christian's capacity for work and preserve his active ministry for as long as it should last.

The care of the body also benefits the mind. Proper rest and diet encourage a sense of total physical, mental, and emotional well-being and a positive attitude toward oneself as a redeemed child of God. Regular vigorous physical exercise assists in the handling of stress and is a proven therapy for some emotional disorders. The wise teacher of children will not try to control restless students by depriving them of recess. Nor do wise adults regard periods of physical recreation as a waste of time. Times of play, whether physically relaxing or taxing, restore both body and mind. A habit of regular physical exercise, formed early, can help the believer maintain physical fitness, combat emotional stress, and keep his mind keen and alert for the service of God.

Therefore, stewardship of the body is as much a Christian's responsibility as stewardship of money, talent, and time. The body is a basic part of the resources granted to the Christian for the service of God. If he gives it the proper care, it will function acceptably for the duration of the ministry he has been assigned by God and will be a pleasing expression of his redeemed personality and of the person of the Redeemer Himself. Even the least skilled and the least physically attractive individual possesses a marvelous instrument exquisitely designed by God. To be careless of the body is no more indicative of spirituality than to make the body the major focus of one's attention and time. In teaching this stewardship, Christian physical education develops in the student godly habits and attitudes that will help form him in the image of God and prepare him for the service of God.

2. *Sportsmanship.* Christian sportsmanship combines qualities that may seem contradictory. On the one hand, the Christian competitor, imitating the divine example, shows humility and good will. He submits readily to the rules and to the decisions of the officials. He does not seek an unlawful advantage or challenge authority. In team competition his behavior is not self-serving but supportive of the success of the team. He cheerfully accepts an inconspicuous role if it is assigned him rather than insisting on a position of leadership or greater crowd visibility. He shows graciousness in victory or defeat. He can yield the benefit of the doubt in a difficult call and can acknowledge a superior performance by

his opponent. In sport competition as in other areas of life he takes seriously the divine injunction: "Let nothing be done through strife or vainglory; but in lowliness of mind let each esteem other better than themselves" (Phil. 2:3). He is solicitous of an opponent's interests as well as of his own, in keeping with the commandment, "Look not every man on his own things, but every man also on the things of others" (Phil. 2:4).

On the other hand, while striving lawfully in keeping with the rules and in consideration of his opponent's needs and interests, he does indeed strive (see II Tim. 2:5). He understands that he owes his opponent as well as himself and his God the best he can do to win. The Christian competitor does not quit when he is hopelessly behind or when he is unhappy with a decision. He does not become apathetic and sullen when frustrated with himself and with the game. He realizes that in sport competition, as in other things, it is no sin to fail but it is a sin to do less than one's best (Eccles. 9:10; Col. 3:23). Though emotionally controlled, he is emotionally intense. Though self-effacing and courteous, he is enthusiastic and determined. Christian sportsmanship thus includes aggressiveness in the best sense of the word though excludes it in the sense of hostility and intimidation. The Christian competitor cares about a contest because he cares about his testimony and about his opponent. Christian sportsmanship is a paradox to the worldly minded because it reflects apparent contradictions in the character of God (Rom. 11:22).

3. *Friendship.* Closely related to sportsmanship as a cause and effect—as a motive and an outgrowth—is friendship. The basis of all truly Christian behavior is love of God and a godly love of one's neighbor (Matt. 22:35-40). It follows that a Christian motive in competition cannot be pride or envy or any other emotion in conflict with love. The Christian competitor has a purpose beyond subduing an opponent for the mere sake of self-esteem and vainglory. It is to communicate and foster love, whether in fellowship with a Christian brother or for a witness to the unsaved. He does not regard a tennis match or a game of basketball or chess as a moral parenthesis in which he may indulge carnal attitudes condemned by society or by the Word of God. The Christian competitor does not consider himself freed by the artificial nature of sport to take up for an hour or two "all malice, and all guile, and hypocrisies, and envies, and all evil speakings" that he has been

commanded by God to lay aside (I Pet. 2:1). Out of the same mouth may not proceed blessing and cursing, any more than from the same fountain can come sweet water and bitter (James 3:10-11). The motive of competition between Christians therefore is not the glorification of self and the humiliation of an opponent but fellowship and mutual encouragement in the will of God. The model is the example of Christ, who tested those He loved but also strengthened them (Matt. 15:22-28; Mark 6:45-50). The motive of competition between the Christian and the unsaved is to communicate the love of Christ and bear witness to His goodness. Obviously a show of anger, irritability, contempt for an opponent or team member, or even self-contempt does not reflect the character of God. Nor does a contempt for rules and decisions of officials or an attitude of unprincipled opportunism reflect the work of God. Of the early Christians it was said by pagan observes, "Behold, how they love one another." Conscientious Christians do not permit themselves a mode of behavior in sport competition that they would heartily condemn in other areas of life. Christian competition does not give occasion to the unsaved to exclaim, as they might of themselves, "Behold, how they hate one another." Even the hard-fought contests of sport, to the Christian, are opportunities to show the love and goodness of God.

4. *Leadership.* The Christian teaching of physical education provides opportunities for moral and spiritual growth in various areas of the student's personality. One of these is leadership. The wise teacher understands that the best leaders are not always those most eager to lead. Accordingly he undertakes to develop the potentiality for leadership in *every* student. In the early years he distributes opportunities for class direction among the students rather than limiting them to the most forward. He provides that students take turns at being captain or squad leader. At the high school level he requires students to earn positions of leadership, stressing Christian maturity and responsibility. He recognizes that Biblical qualifications for leadership are moral and spiritual as well as personal (I Tim. 3:2-12) and that the moral and spiritual qualities must be developed before the personal can come fully into play.

In the Christian physical education program the student is taught a Biblical idea of leadership. True leadership, he discovers, is motivated by an unselfish desire to serve rather than by an obsession to rule and be served (Matt. 20:25-28). It requires self-denial rather than selfish ambition. It demands submission—to others' good—rather than self-will. Conscientiousness is more important than charisma. Leadership may make painful demands upon a person's time, strength, and freedom, narrowing the scope of his activities and limiting his enjoyments. It tends to increase rather than lighten his burdens. Furthermore, it makes him liable to greater condemnation by man and by God (Matt. 7:1-2; 24:45-51; James 3:1) as well as capable of greater commendation and reward (I Tim. 3:13; 5:17-18). He learns that authority is relative to responsibility and that responsibility includes both the success of the cause and the good of those he commands. He becomes aware that the exercise of authority is predicated upon subordination to a higher authority—that it is presumptuous and self-deluding to expect a higher degree of obedience from those beneath than one is willing to show to those above (Matt. 8:9). He comes to understand that self-control precedes control of others and becomes able to show, as the situation requires, severity as well as love (Rom. 11:22; Jude 22-23).

With a Biblical attitude toward leadership, the student is able to acquire through guided experience the purposefulness, resourcefulness, decisiveness, concentration, perseverance, and poise that characterize strong leadership and that reflect the example of Christ. He learns to grasp quickly the realities of a situation, react intelligently, and motivate others to follow. Meanwhile those gifted with unusual insight, initiative, and ability to inspire will come to the fore, imbued with the moral and spiritual qualities that will make their leadership Christ-like, worthy of loyalty and trust.

In special vocational service—The Christian teaching of physical education not only contributes importantly to the Christian growth of all the students but also provides special additional training for certain ministries. These ministries include teaching physical education in a Christian school, coaching in a Christian school, directing church recreational programs and camp activities, and conducting adult physical-fitness programs. The well-taught Christian physical education specialist has the spiritual maturity and professional knowledge to serve the Lord effectively in these and other fields.

The Christian physical educator draws the student's attention to these reflections of God. He identifies the intricate workmanship of the body and conveys to the student the importance of physical fitness to the functioning and efficient operation of the body. He points to the fact that the body's physical processes are regulated by godly laws and that we are to fulfill these laws in order to have our physiological processes in concert. He encourages the student to develop a lifestyle that provides him the necessary time to maintain his body at optimum efficiency for the Lord's service. He purposefully identifies godly attributes inherent within assigned activities and molds the student's behavior to conform to these attributes. To sum up, the physical educator awakens and sharpens the student's interest in the growth, development, and maintenance of his physical body so that he may be more fully conformed to the image of God.

Distinctiveness

Christian physical education, like secular, recognizes the importance of the body and serves its growth, its health, and its efficiency. It recognizes the connection between bodily health and the health of the mind. It gives due attention to both physiological and recreational functions of physical education, fostering physical fitness and developing sport skills instrumental to physical fitness and emotional health. The Christian physical education teacher prescribes activities so as to accomplish program objectives rather than just to gratify his own or the students' recreational preferences. He diagnoses student needs by means of a regular and systematic health and physical-fitness testing program, consulting with medical authorities as necessary. He correlates sport-skill training with physical maturity and helps students acquire sport proficiencies that will make their physical recreation more enjoyable and encourage a habit of regular physical exercise. The well-prepared Christian teacher of physical education therefore takes his role just as seriously as does the diligent secular teacher and draws on similar professional knowledge and experience while pursuing his objectives. Behind his objectives, however, is an entirely different educational purpose and rationale. The secularist with his man-centered philosophy of physical education desires a fully developed and trained body for his own gratification and well-being. The Christian desires the same so that he can better glorify and serve the Lord.

Specifically, the secularist believes that physical education should gear its program to meet human needs that grow out of increasing urbanization. He feels a responsibility to deal with sedentarianism as an aspect of life brought about by modern technology. Physical education, he thinks, should teach fundamental skills so that all labor will be more efficient and less fatiguing. The greater ease and productivity will benefit both the individual and society. He finds other potential benefits in the greater freedom from injury and disease, increased enjoyment of life, enhanced physical appearance and self-esteem, and improved self-discipline. The Christian, while not denying these benefits, considers their purpose. To him these benefits are means to an end rather than mere ends in themselves. He reasons as follows. When the body is not disciplined to expend energy and accomplish work, its capacity to achieve difficult tasks for the Lord is impaired. In addition, its appearance, marred by fat cells and flabby musculature, is not reflective of the discipline and stewardship that distinguish Christian character. Society has grown accustomed to deformity of this kind because it is commonplace, but Christians recognize it as a defacing of God's property through overindulgence and neglect. Physical fitness enables the Christian to persevere and endure in whatever the Lord has called him to do and to look and act his best while he is doing it. The Christian physical educator endeavors to help each student achieve his total potential as a child of God, an integral part of which is his physical development. He desires for his students what was said of the child Jesus: that He "increased in wisdom and stature, and in favour with God and man" (Luke 2:52).

Practical application in the classroom

The conscientious Christian physical educator is careful to explain to his students the Biblical bases for the skills and attitudes he desires to teach. A lecture on physical fitness might take as its starting point the high death rate from heart attacks today— among Christians as well as non-Christians—and the resulting loss to the work of God. It would go on to argue that the body must be respected and maintained as an expression of the character of God and as a vehicle of His service. The teacher would point out that the human body, as much as the soul, is part of the creation of God which He pronounced good (Gen. 1:31). The psalmist marveled at its intricacy of design and development and found evidence there of infinite wisdom, power, and goodness (Ps. 139:14-16). The body is created as a servant of the spiritual nature and an instrument of its purposes. It is honored in use rather than in disuse or abuse. The present earthly body is meant to endure only so long as its service is required by the soul and therefore need not be spared the most exhausting labor or even death when necessary in the will of God. Physical maintenance is therefore not an end in itself, and the care of the body should not take precedence over the interest of the soul (I Tim. 4:8).

However, although the body is expendable in the service of God, it possesses dignity as a creation of God and, in its resurrected form, as a permanent part of the human personality. The believer's present body, though temporary and perishable, is likened by Paul to a temple in which God delights to dwell and desires to express His nature and purposes to the world (I Cor. 6:19-20; John 2:18-22). This earthly "tabernacle" will eventually be replaced with a "house not made with hands, eternal in the heavens" (II Cor. 5:1). We may not therefore allow less dignity to the physical body than God Himself has bestowed upon it. We may not take less seriously our stewardship of the body than did the builders of the Old Testament tabernacle and temple the instructions according to which the earthly house of God was to be built and maintained. Though a servant, it is an honored servant (Eph. 5:28-29). As a temple it must be clean and attractive as well as serviceable for the worship of God.

The ideas of beauty and utility unite in the Biblical ideas of the body as a "living sacrifice." Christians are admonished to offer their bodies as "a living sacrifice, holy, acceptable unto God" (Rom. 12:1). The Mosaic law required that animals presented for sacrifice be physically attractive and healthy—without blemish (Lev. 22:20-22). Though the symbolism of the sacrifice refers to moral rather than physical character, the implication is clear that God cares about the vehicle as well as about what it conveys. To neglect or abuse the body and permit an unnecessary deformity is to impair its usefulness and mar its beauty as a living sacrifice. What the believer is willing to offer God physically is an indication of what he has given of himself spiritually. Man draws conclusions from the outward appearance alone. God looks on both the outward appearance and the heart (I Sam. 16:7; Matt. 23:27). True ambassadors for Christ, like their political counterparts, desire nothing to be amiss in their physical appearance in order that nothing distract from the message to be communicated or detract from the desired impression.

The body is kept at maximum efficiency and attractiveness by obedience to God and imitation of the divine example. Even before man's fall into sin, God ordained work and sanctified rest. He created the world in six days, rested the seventh, and placed Adam in the Garden of Eden "to dress it and keep it" (Gen. 2:2-3, 15). After the fall, God ordained strenuous work under conditions resistant to success. The ground would bring forth thorns and thistles. Man would labor to supply his needs "in the sweat of [his] face" (Gen. 3:17-19). This work was ordained for man's punishment but also for his good. A routine of taxing effort has proved necessary to his physical and emotional health. Without regular physical exertion—the kind that produces perspiration and an elevated heart rate—the body deteriorates and even the mind may become disordered. From infancy human beings show a basic need for movement. The small child needs no urging to move. Running, skipping, and playing are natural activities. Even the developing embryo is continually moving. During sleep, movement is necessary to aid circulation. But as the child grows older, habits of inactivity are established until, with adulthood, his lifestyle often includes little or no meaningful exercise. Even when the adult becomes aware of his need, his efforts to incorporate exercise into his life may be ineffective because of his ignorance of physiological principles. The first concern of physical education is to educate the student in effective movement—movement that will contribute to a more efficient, healthy, and attractive body.

A well-structured physical education program based on sound physiological principles incorporates (from kindergarten through the twelfth grade) a collection of activities designed to provide for necessary development in all areas of physical conditioning. These areas include cardiovascular fitness, abdominal strength, upper-arm and shoulder strength, as well as general muscular endurance and flexibility. The Christian physical educator assesses and prescribes, on a developmental continuum, optimal target levels for students in each of these fitness areas and evaluates their progress at periodic intervals. Meanwhile the students are challenged Biblically in their need to work for proper conditioning and warned that not to work will result in deterioration of their physical being. They are encouraged to establish a habit of regular vigorous activity that they can continue into later life as a part of their total personal discipline. The Christian instructor inculcates a sense of this responsibility by both Biblical precept and personal example.

In his efforts to teach physical fitness the Christian instructor has an ally in the natural human enjoyment of play. Children typically demonstrate a willingness to play, and it is upon this human trait that rests much of the fitness skills taught in physical education. The purposeful structuring of a child's playfulness is the major methodology for equipping the child with necessary skills. These skills are refined to the point that the student will eagerly enter the world of sport activity and enjoy a relative degree of success. His pleasure in success will in turn motivate him to maintain his personal optimal level of physical fitness. As the student grows and matures, the selection of games and sport activities parallels his needs, providing him the opportunity to develop the various physiological systems necessary for an efficient body. Activities developing fundamental motor skills are introduced early in the program. Activities requiring greater physical maturity are added at the proper times, culminating in organized sport activities that further develop the physiological systems. Thus game selection is predicated upon the physical-conditioning needs of the students and not simply on the predispositions of the teacher or the students. While much of the conditioning efforts can and should be fun, the Christian student must accept the fact that they require a diligent and dedicated spirit, much akin to that required for daily personal Bible reading. The teacher must understand that games in which only a few are selected or in which many are eventually eliminated should be avoided since they do not meet the activity needs of each student.

In teaching the importance of both work and rest for physical fitness, the Christian teacher will find the first harder to teach convincingly than the second. Human beings have a natural aversion to difficult work. However, some Christians, who rightfully regard work as a moral duty and are able even to take pleasure in it, may need to be persuaded that rest is equally legitimate and necessary. The amount of sleep needed daily varies among individuals. To take more than one needs is a form of dissipation condemned in the Scriptures (Prov. 6:9-11; 13:4; 21:25-26). Habitually to take less than one needs for no better reason than watching a later program on television or reading for pleasure is an equally serious and perhaps far more prevalent form of dissipation today. Research has shown that rest returns the body to a normal functioning level and that the rested body is more able to handle stress. God's resting on the seventh day of creation was a divine precedent for Israel's keeping of the Sabbath. Whatever one's convictions about Sabbath-keeping, it can hardly be disputed that one day out of seven devoted to relief from weekly toil is legitimate and desirable. An even rhythm of work and rest, weekly as well as daily, promotes physical fitness and health.

More controversial than daily and weekly rest is the importance of leisure: a time reserved for doing something that one finds relaxing and enjoyable. Pleasure is not as worthy a motive as duty. Does pleasure have a place in the consecrated life at all? It is interesting that God associated His worship and praise with periods of physical rest and enjoyment rather than of strenuous labor. These periods, moreover, were annual as well as weekly and required travel. The Jewish feasts were times when pleasure was not only tolerated but also commanded (Zech. 8:19). It is likely that the annual feast of the Passover was, for Joseph and Mary, an anticipated social as well as religious occasion; for they evidently became so preoccupied by the fellowship of friends and kindred that they left Jerusalem without their son (Luke 2:41-45). The Lord regularly observed these national feasts with His disciples. He also provided them with special times of relaxation after periods of fatiguing exertion. After the disciples had returned from their preaching mission, Jesus drew them apart for a time of rest. "And he said unto them, Come ye yourselves apart into a desert place, and rest a while: for there were many coming and going, and they had no leisure so much as to eat" (Mark 6:31). The fact that their leisure was soon interrupted by the multitude does not make it any less legitimate.

Clearly the physical demands of the disciples' mission justified a time of rest. However, work that entails mental and emotional fatigue rather than physical exhaustion may necessitate another type of relaxation. Research has shown that for many individuals vigorous physical activity is better physiologically than is sedentary rest. That such activity may take the nature of play does not seem to be excluded by the Scriptures. It is interesting that the return of divine blessing to Israel is described by the prophet as a time when "the streets of the city shall be full of boys and girls playing in the streets thereof" (Zech. 8:5). The frequent references to sport activities in the Scriptures would seem strange if we were meant to regard them as wholly frivolous for adults also. Of course, recreation may take as many forms as there are differences among individuals. One man's recreation may be another man's work or may even be a function related to a person's work that he particularly enjoys. It seems likely that David found personal pleasure as well as utility in his music, Jonathan in his archery, and Paul in his craft of tentmaking—all skills that require mental concentration and frequent practice. The Christian student therefore may learn through Scriptural examples that he needs frequent times of restful activity or inactivity and that duty and pleasure can converge in purposeful leisure.

For most persons in today's sedentary society, the most necessary recreation is physical. Intense, vigorous bodily exercise regenerates the physiological systems. In doing so it also combats the degenerative effects of stress. Often, when one thinks of stress, he pictures an emotional stirring, a psychological trauma. Stress can be promoted emotionally, but it also can be physically induced. We cannot and should not avoid stress; rather we must learn to deal with it. It is therefore necessary for the Christian student to grasp the significance of the relationship between sound physiological functioning and stress management. Much premature physiological deterioration is directly related to the body's inability to adapt to various stressors. The syndrome of just being sick has been directly linked to this same inability. Since a well-conditioned, healthy individual is more able to withstand life's stressors, the Christian physical educator has the duty to provide within the physical education program a curriculum that promotes sound principles of stress management and provides the skills necessary to make physical recreation useful and enjoyable. Necessary recreation for many Christians can be obtained through a wise selection of sport activities such as basketball, soccer, tennis, racquetball, and handball, as well as jogging, swimming, rope skipping, and bicycle riding. Though it is possible to engage in each of these activities at such a low intensity level as to gain little benefit, the well-skilled, motivated individual will likely gain more than adequate physiological stimulation. The Christian teaching of physical education equips each student with the requisite skills and knowledge for as many of these activities as time and facilities allow so as to help him gain the greatest physiological and psychological benefit from his recreational time.

A prime motivator of physical fitness efforts is the love of competition. Though competition is important in all areas of human interaction, physical and nonphysical, the physical education class is the obvious place to teach students a Christian view of competition. Here they will learn that the desire to compete is a natural impulse, implanted by the Creator, important to growth in youth and to success in later life (Gen. 25:21-26). It helps the young discover their aptitudes and chart their progress towards goals. It reveals to the individual his moral and emotional maturity and gives him a view not only of what sort of a person he is but also of what he may expect of himself in future years. A student's behavior in competition reveals deeply rooted attitudes toward himself and toward life and signals to himself and to his teacher his needs for growth and correction. The Christian physical educator seizes his opportunities to cultivate in his students a wholesome pleasure in competition and to use competition to prompt their growth in necessary areas—physical, moral, and spiritual. He helps his students form attitudes and habits of competition that will make their competitiveness a benefit to themselves and to others rather than a curse. He prepares them in these necessary ways for the time when their field of struggle will expand from the dimensions of a ball field or gymnasium to the grand arena of life.

The commercialization of sport and the philosophy of expediency that permeates worldly athletic competition—in recruiting, training, and game tactics—have discredited sport competition in the eyes of some observers. Competition can bring out the worst in human character as well as the best. Some professional sports encourage in spectators as well as participants an almost criminal mentality—an appetite for the violence and fraud that must be condemned and punished in society. When winning is all that matters, life is dismal indeed for the inevitable loser—for the nine of ten teams that fail to reach the top, their coaches, and their coaches' families; for the thousands who finish second or worse in the Boston Marathon; for all but the very best in any line of athletic endeavor. The compulsion to win at any cost entails an attitude of unprincipled opportunism and—since more must lose than win—a depressing view of life. And yet it is interesting that the New Testament writers repeatedly drew upon their knowledge of the Roman games for images of the successful Christian life. Christians, like dedicated athletes, commit themselves to winning (I Cor. 9:26), shed hindrances (Heb. 12:1), discipline themselves rigorously (I Cor. 9:25, 27), box purposefully (I Cor. 9:26), wrestle tirelessly (Eph. 6:12), and "run with patience" and endurance the race that is "set before" (Heb. 12:1). They "strive for masteries" and are crowned if they have striven "lawfully" (II Tim. 2:5). Evidently something very much like an athlete's zeal to win is essential to the success of the child of God in a world whose powers are mustered to defeat him. He needs more than a "want to" or a vague "hope." He must have the same burning desire to win that motivates an athlete to prepare himself carefully, discipline himself constantly, and bring all his powers and resources effectively into play in the heat of the contest. It is this winning attitude that so often in life as in sport competition amounts to the margin of victory.

What complicates the matter for the Christian is that on the other side of the court may be another Christian competitor to whom winning is equally important. What is the Christian competitor's relationship to his Christian (or potentially Christian) opponent, and what obligations does this relationship entail? The Lord summed up the duties of man toward man in the command of Leviticus 19:18: "Thou shalt love thy neighbor as thyself." (See also Matt. 22:39.) The Christian competitor desires for his opponent what he desires for himself: a fair, hard-fought contest that will help him measure his progress in skill development and physical conditioning and provide him the physiological and emotional benefits essential to health. His opponent is therefore not an enemy but a friend, or potential friend, to whom he owes his best effort. It follows that Christian competition is conducted in a spirit of friendship and mutual encouragement. The Christian competitor does not blame others for his failures or make excuses when beaten. Retaliation and threats are not part of his competitive motive or manner. He takes seriously the Biblical injunction of "preferring one another" (Rom. 12:10), showing humility and deference in difficult calls. He is able to ascribe worth to his opponent and to his opponent's effort because he is confident of his own worth in the eyes of God.

In competition the Christian shows a concern for his testimony. He can be gracious in either victory or defeat. He avoids the extremes of self-exaltation and self-degradation that reveal moral immaturity. He avoids the displays of temper, sullen apathy, and dishonesty that so often mar worldly sport competition. He plays within the spirit as well as the letter of the rules, avoiding deliberate fouls that threaten injury or rule-bending for an unfair advantage. He rejects a policy of expediency, desiring the approval of God as well as the respect of men. He recognizes that in recreational competition as in the Christian life the competitor must "strive lawfully" if he is to deserve the prize (II Tim. 2:5). The desire to win, though admirable and necessary, does not for him take precedence over honesty and principled action.

Through these and similar admonitions the Christian physical educator or coach instills into the students a godly consideration for their opponents, their testimonies, and the rules of the contest, without blunting their desire to excel. He points out that unless one cares about winning he cannot appreciate the victory of Christ. He also points out that unless one strives lawfully he cannot share in that victory. Through purposeful game and team selection the teacher ensures meaningfulness of competition and provides that even the least skilled of the students may enjoy frequently the experience of winning. Through purposeful supervision of competition he ensures that the necessary values and character traits are learned. He takes pleasure in the spiritual as well as physical progress of his students as he endeavors to mold them into the image of Christ.

Points of conflict with the secular teaching of physical education

Distinctively Christian physical education teaching requires the rejection of certain approaches and emphases that derive from the climate of modern thought. These approaches and emphases not only are avoided by the Christian physical educator but also are explicitly condemned.

Egoism—Secular advice on sport competition often gives the impression that a "healthy ego" with brimming self-confidence is necessary to success in a strenuous contest. Belligerent self-assertiveness is condoned and even applauded as an evidence of proper earnestness and intensity. The alternative to a fierce, egotistical drive, we are told, is defeatism and lassitude. Both experience and the Word of God indicate otherwise. Moses, Peter, and Paul all had to be cured of their volatile impetuousness before they were ready for the trials of leading God's people. Moses became the meekest of men (Num. 12:3). Peter, as he matured, grew in both boldness and patience (Matt. 26:69-74; Acts 4:13; 11:1-4). Paul was more conscious of his weaknesses than of his strengths (I Cor. 2:3-5; II Cor. 12:9-10). In motivating intelligent, sustained effort, arrogant self-assurance is a poor substitute for humble confidence in God.

Pragmatism—The willingness to use any tactics necessary to win is an attitude of expediency that Christians must condemn in sport activities as in other areas of life. The world of professional sport often sets a poor example for Christian young people in recruiting practices, game tactics, and playing of the injured. Considerations of moral principles and of the athlete's well-being are overridden by the need to win. A Christian regard for moral principle and for the good of others requires that participants abide by established regulations, play honestly by the rules, and submit to decisions of the appointed judges, even when it may not appear to be in their immediate best interests to do so. Christian coaches do not condone in their players an attitude of moral expediency that conflicts with basic Christian beliefs. In fact, fairness and evenness of competition, which the rules are designed to protect, is desired rather than circumvented by the Christian competitor. Respect for the rules that define the game is necessary to the growth and fellowship that are the end purposes of Christian competition.

Coeducationalism—Christian physical education acknowledges the social values of sport participation and training. (A Christian program of sport competition may include coeducation opportunities in lifetime sports—for example, badminton, racquetball, tennis, volleyball, and the like.) It does not permit contact sports between the sexes. Neither does it include dance in the curriculum or rock music in rhythm training or exercise programs.

The Christian school cannot encourage students to pursue the "youthful lusts" the Bible commands them to flee (II Tim. 2:22).

Athleticism—In a time when amateur as well as professional sport competition has become big business, the Christian school does not permit interscholastic competition to become an end in itself. All too easily education can become instrumental to sport competition rather than sport competition instrumental to education. Such competition must remain *functional*—with regard to both physical and spiritual objectives. To impoverish a school to provide expensive equipment for competition in which only a few participate or to allow sport practice and competition to crowd out other studies would be to violate the priorities of Christian education and of the Christian life. To encourage physically talented students to prepare for careers in professional athletics and to enroll for this purpose in secular rather than Christian colleges and universities would be to gravely misdirect them and to teach to all the students a set of values that is worldly and carnal. Christian interscholastic sport competition is kept within an educational framework and is firmly controlled by Christian educational objectives.

Conclusion

The Christian physical educator finds abundant support in Scripture for the attitudes, habits, knowledge, and skills he desires to impart to his students. Whether in physical-fitness training, health instruction, or sport competition, his goal is to help his students conform more fully to the image of God in Christ. Since the body is instrumental to the soul and to the God who desires to indwell it, physical exercise can support Christian service. Since competitive attitudes and habits carry over into life, to teach godliness in sport competition is to teach godly character for life. The Christian physical educator approaches his teaching with great seriousness, realizing the importance of his part in the producing of vessels "sanctified, and meet for the master's use, and prepared unto every good work" (II Tim. 2:21).

The Christian Teaching of Home Economics

Definition

Home-economics studies consist of the practical knowledge and skills that strengthen individual and family life. As an art, home economics teaches certain intangible traditions and qualities, such as beauty, taste, and values, that enhance personal and family living. As a science, home economics applies knowledge that has been arrived at through experimental research. As a set of skills, home economics includes not only manual, routine operations of household life but also habits of mental discipline necessary to implement these activities in line with predetermined goals. Home-economics education takes the form of instruction in personal and home management; consumer economics; housing, equipment, and home furnishing; clothing selection, care, and construction; nutrition; food selection and preparation; home entertaining; textiles; family relations; and child care and development. Home economics, as a curricular area, includes not only courses focusing on specific homemaking competencies but also courses in family living designed for all the students.

Justification

The Christian teaching of home economics is especially crucial in a society increasingly disdainful of traditional family roles. Because the home is the primary environment for the development of godly character, it is imperative that home economics be taught so that students can grow in Christ-likeness in their present homes and learn to establish thoroughly Christian homes of their own in the future.

The focal point of home-economics teaching is the family—its roles and relationships, its purposes and functions. The Bible makes clear that the family is an institution which is ordained of God and which remains of paramount importance to God. It also shows that the family has been a prime target of Satan from the beginning. To strengthen the family in the will of God is therefore to further the purposes of God in the world and to thwart those of Satan. Even the practical skills of home management can heighten the quality of life of a Christian family and increase its spiritual impact on the community. Home-economics teaching is important because the family is important—to the spiritual life of its members and to their revealing of God to the world.

Reflections of God in what is taught

The Christian home-economics teacher has frequent opportunities to point to reflections of God in the course content. God, having established the family, used family relationships to reveal His character and His relationship with His people. The Bible explains the relationship of Christ and the Church as that of bridegroom and bride, husband and wife (Eph. 5:23). It illustrates the enduring love of God for His people by the permanence of the marriage covenant (Mal. 2:14; Matt. 19:6). Believers pray to God as to a father (Deut. 32:6; Hos. 11:1-4; Matt. 7:11). God provides for and corrects them as a parent would a child (Prov. 3:11-12). He pities as a father (Ps. 103:13), loves and comforts as a mother (Isa. 49:15; 66:13). Christ is to the redeemed the firstborn, an elder brother (Rom. 8:17). On earth He was both Son of God and Son of Man (Matt. 16:16; Luke 19:10). Christ comforted His disciples with the assurance that He would be leaving them in order to "prepare a place" for them in His Father's house (John 14:2). Family roles are thus sanctified by divine example as well as by precept. So too are the diligence (Prov. 27:23-27; John 9:4), perceptivity (Luke 8:46; 19:5; John 2:24-25), resourcefulness (Matt. 14:16-19; Mark 4:1), efficiency (Mark 6:39-40), thrift (John 6:12), graciousness (Luke 4:22), and hospitality (John 1:39; 21:9) necessary to the functioning of the well-ordered household and to its ministry to the family and the community.

Manifestations of godliness in the resultant knowledge, attitudes, and skills

The study of home economics can help the student grow in godliness by revealing to him these reflections of God and by inspiring him to imitate God in his family relationships and responsibilities and in his service of God outside the home.

In general Christian character and service—Christian instruction in home economics is valuable preparation for life for all the students, not only for future wives and mothers. A study of God's plan for the family and principles of family living encourages the student to develop qualities essential to success in his personal life, family life, and service for God.

Instruction in the discipline of home management confronts students with their need to be good managers in all areas of their lives. They learn the importance of leadership at all levels of the family hierarchy. Parents must be good examples of wise, dedicated leadership—setting priorities and goals, working patiently and purposefully to bring plans to fruition. Children must accept responsibility for certain chores and regulate their time and resources to accomplish them. Both parents and older children must give constant attention to priorities, to definition of goals, to identification of problems, to allocation of time and resources, and to coordination of operations if the family order is to be preserved and its purposes are to be accomplished.

Students learn the importance of cooperation. They are taught not only the Biblical scheme of authority in the home, requiring the submission of the wife to the husband and of the children to the parents, but also the unselfish submission of each to the good of the others that is the foundation of Christian courtesy and the spirit of Christian service. Obviously the husband cannot leave home management and child rearing entirely to the wife if her efforts as a homemaker are to succeed. Likewise, the wife cannot make family routine inviolable—so rigid that it becomes an end in itself—if the husband is to provide for the family and perform his vocational ministry in any adequate way. While bearing his own burden, each must bear the burden of the other (Gal. 6:2, 5). Their strengths must unite in such a way as to compensate for one another's inadequacies. Students are given the example of the selflessness of Christ, who ''came not to be ministered unto, but to minister, and to give his life a ransom for many'' (Matt. 20:28). This Christ-likeness appears in their present conduct as child, sibling, and friend as it will in their future conduct as spouse, parent, neighbor, citizen, host or hostess, and guest.

Students learn also the importance of diligent stewardship. Successful home management requires thrift and efficiency. Both wife and husband must practice economy of time, energy, money, and other resources if family needs are to be met and the Lord's work is to receive proper attention. The means provided by God are not to be squandered or misdirected. Students learn that there is an art to effective labor and that there is satisfaction to be gained from the accomplishing of work with a minimum cost in time, effort, and materials. They learn that failure to conserve family health by proper nutrition, hygiene, rest and relaxation, and medical attention can defeat stewardship efforts in other areas. Especially they learn the importance of spiritual life of the family by inhibiting worldly influences and providing for daily individual and family devotions.

But leadership, cooperation, and stewardship are not the only contribution of home-economics studies to the personal and family lives of the students. The family is not only an organization but also an organism, a living whole greater than the sum of its systems and functions. Accordingly, home-economics studies include not only management skills but also the intangibles that grace family life and beautify all human relationships. Social proprieties are important to the Christian who, like Paul, would ''give none offence,'' who would ''please all men in all things . . . that they may be saved'' (I Cor. 10:32-33). A sense of decorum—on the part of a host or hostess, a guest, a dating or married couple, or even a committee chairman conducting a meeting—conveys kindness and humility; for the basis of etiquette is an unselfish desire to serve others and not to offend. Good taste in dress and grooming expresses a godly care for beauty and modesty and a desire to please others. Tasteful furnishings, chosen for both practical and aesthetic reasons, give the home a pleasing ''personality'' and contribute to an atmosphere of Christian warmth. Even the crafts of homemaking—cooking, sewing, and decorating—can be expressions of love when time is given to the extra touches that please. Graciousness, like charity, begins at home. Genuine hospitality and social grace emanate from a home atmosphere of mutual love and supportiveness. Christian social attitudes and skills, like management efficiencies, depend upon qualities that originate in the character of God.

In special vocational service—The study of home economics is also important preparation for employment—part-time or full-time, permanent or temporary—outside the home. A Christian well prepared in home economics can serve Christ in education, homemaking, extension, food-service, dietetics, human development, interior design, family resource management, clothing construction and design, business, or journalism. Christians in home-economics-related occupations have many opportunities to teach and exemplify God's plan for individual and family life.

Distinctiveness

Both Christian and secular home-economics classes teach management principles and skills, selection of clothing and home furnishings, family relationships, child rearing, and the other standard subject matter. The instruction draws from much the same body of information and develops for the most part identical skills. The difference consists in the purposes of their study and the value systems that underlie it. The Christian home-economics teacher measures the success of his teaching by the extent to which his students develop godliness of character and acquire attitudes and competencies essential to their life service to God.

Christian home-economics students learn to conserve time, energy, money, and other physical resources in order to accomplish more for God. Work simplification, energy conservation, and money management can enable family needs to be met sooner and more easily. The result is more time for personal and family devotions, church participation, and special opportunities of Christian service, and more money for the support of Christian work. Christian students learn to set financial goals appropriate to their life service for Christ and to show godliness of character in their stewardship of resources. Students in a secular classroom may study management principles primarily as a means of having more money for luxuries and more time and energy for activities they enjoy. Or they may be led to believe that family problems can be significantly reduced through financial freedom, purchasing power, and plentiful leisure. The difference between the Christian and the secular approaches is the difference between spiritual and material values, between needs and wants, and between self-denial and self-gratification.

Christian home-economics teaching, like secular, inculcates aesthetic and practical values in home decoration, clothing selection, and personal grooming. But the Christian desires a comfortable, attractive, orderly home and a pleasing physical appearance for the glory of God, not only for personal satisfaction. He adheres to permanent Biblical standards of cleanliness, neatness, and beauty and of modesty, moderation, and utility rather than slavishly imitating the extremes of the fashion industry. Christian teachers take a balanced approach to wardrobe planning, giving precedence to inward over outward beauty. They may cite the example of the virtuous woman of Proverbs 31, beautifully dressed outwardly in silk and purple while adorned inwardly with "strength and honor." They stress that "a meek and quiet spirit" is far more important to the Lord than fashionable outward ornament (I Pet. 3:3-4) but also that the outward appearance must not be neglected. Clothing and grooming must be taken seriously by the Christian who desires both inwardly and outwardly to reflect the image of God in Christ.

Christian students learn to regard their bodies as temples of the Holy Spirit (I Cor. 6:19-20). For this reason they provide proper diet, rest, and exercise for their bodies and do not abuse them by overeating or by using alcohol or other harmful drugs. They learn that good nutrition, proper rest, and exercise not only build resistance to infection and stress in the present but also have cumulative benefits for later life. They learn that health maintenance yields energy necessary for their God-given tasks.

Christian home-economics teaching prepares students for Christian parenthood. They learn to foster not only the physical, mental, and social growth of their children but also the moral and spiritual. They learn that God has ordained the procreation of children for the continuation of His work on earth and gives children to parents as both a blessing (Ps. 127:3) and a responsibility (Prov. 23:13-14; Eph. 6:4). They are taught that parenting responsibilities include demanding obedience, administering discipline, and displaying genuine love (Prov. 3:11-12; 23:13). They come to understand that true family unity depends upon the obedience of all to the will of God and that parental authority is an expression of the authority of God in the home. They are taught that once the right vertical relationship (between the individual and God) is established, the right horizontal relationships (between the individual and others) become possible. Though secular insights are not neglected—concerning, for example, the importance of family communication and interaction—family unity is taught as primarily an outgrowth of obedience to God and conformity to His plan for the home. The Bible, not secular theory and advice, is recognized as the basic source of family standards and rules and as the guide to family happiness.

Practical application in the classroom

Christian home-economics teaching centers on the Biblical concept of the family. A unit on the family might begin with a discussion of Satan's attack on the home. As modern society drifts farther from God, the family suffers. Secularists question its necessity, suggest alternatives to the traditional family structure, and emphasize the rights of the individual family member above the need for subordination and discipline. Women's rights and children's rights challenge the rule of the husband and father. Courts undercut parental authority, regarding children as wards of the state and denying parents the right to determine their sons' and daughters' education. Within the individual family, Satan is at work, weakening the loyalty of husband to wife and of wife to husband, of child to parent and of parent to child. Fathers refuse to lead; wives and children, to follow. Love dwindles. Obviously the traditional family, formed on the Biblical pattern, is under siege. It obstructs the natural social evolution, envisioned by humanists, toward an absolute classless society in which parental influence has been displaced by governmental control. Even Christians may fail to recognize this threat or, while recognizing and resisting it, fail to comprehend all that the Bible has to teach about the family. Other lessons might go on to make the following points.

The Christian home is not only a place but also a set of relationships rooted in Biblical convictions and attitudes. It is the most visible fulfillment of the petition, "Thy will be done in earth, as it is in heaven" (Matt. 6:10). The Biblical family order is a hierarchy that reflects the government of God (I Cor. 11:3). At the top, immediately accountable to God for the family, is the father, who is to be obeyed and reverenced by the wife (Eph.

5:22-24, 33; Titus 2:5; I Pet. 3:1-6) as well as by the children (Mal. 1:6; Heb. 12:9-10). Second in authority (or first, if the husband is deceased or absent) is the wife. She has her special dignity in the home as the beloved choice of the husband and his cherished possession. In honoring her husband she honors herself also, for she shares in, as well as submits to, his headship. Her subjection is no more demeaning than that of the believer to Christ, who accepts His rule but also throughout eternity will reign with Him (II Tim. 2:12; Rev. 3:21) and participate in His glory (John 17:22; II Cor. 3:18). Children must obey and honor their parents (Eph. 6:1-3). Obedience to parents must continue throughout dependency; honor, throughout life. Obedience to husband and parents is conditioned neither on the wisdom of the leadership nor on reciprocity (the husband's fulfilling his obligations or the parents' theirs). It is limited only by the higher obligation to God. As the husband's authority is above the wife's, God's is above both; and obedience to husband and parents, as to all human authority, must be "in the Lord" (Eph. 6:1; Col. 3:18).

The husband has a corresponding duty to the wife, as do both parents to the children, to love and provide. This duty is even more challenging than the duty of wife and children to obey and is likewise unconditional. Husbands must love their wives and not be bitter toward them (Col. 3:19). They must live with their wives "according to knowledge," allowing for their special weaknesses (I Pet. 3:7). The Old Testament law is considerate of the needs of the woman, both physical (Lev. 12:1-5) and emotional (Deut. 24:5). The New Testament warns of the ways in which marriage inevitably and quite properly complicates the priorities of the young man or woman, even in matters of service to God (I Cor. 7:32-35). Husbands may not disregard the needs of their wives, or parents of their children, any more justifiably than children may ignore the needs of their aged parents, even for the noblest of reasons (Mark 7:9-13). This obligation of the stronger to love and care for the weaker rests principally upon the husband and father. A neglect on his part to show kindness and consideration toward wife or children incurs the extreme displeasure of God (I Tim. 5:8; I Pet. 3:7).

These responsibilities are clarified and reinforced in Scripture by the analogy of God as a father, husband, and bridegroom, and of His people as children, wife, and bride. God rules unselfishly and purposefully through both severity and love (Rom. 11:22; Heb. 12:5-11). Fathers likewise must correct their children conscientiously, not capriciously (Eph. 6:4). Husbands must love their wives "as Christ also loved the church, and gave himself for it" (Eph. 5:25). Conversely, "as the church is subject unto Christ," so must "the wives be to their own husbands in every thing" (Eph. 5:24), "for the husband is the head of the wife, even as Christ is the head of the church" (Eph. 5:23). Husbands and fathers, like Christ, are first in love and sacrifice as well as in authority. Like Christ, they lead in self-denying service, demanding more of themselves than of their followers. The wife serves the husband, and the children the parents, so as to be better served by husband and parents. Loyalty, like love, runs in both directions—from the top down as well as from the bottom up. Happiness results as each member learns to subject himself to the will of God and to the good of the others.

The Christian young man must understand that when he marries, and especially when children are born into the family, his responsibilities widen. He receives authority from God commensurate with his responsibility and is answerable to God for the exercise of that authority. He must put a higher value on time than ever before and must discipline himself to put duty above pleasure. A decision to enter Christian vocational service especially tests the strength of his leadership in the family. His credentials for spiritual leadership outside the home include effective leadership within the home (I Tim. 3:2-5, 12). Since Christian work sometimes does not enable the father alone to meet the full financial needs of a family, his decision may put pressure on the wife and children, requiring a willingness on the part of everyone to have a share in the support of the family and to subsist materially with less.

The Christian young woman must understand that marriage will require of her subjection to the rule of her husband and to his needs and the needs of the children. It is a joyous subjection, however, that raises rather than lowers her. The family will become her chief responsibility and the focal point of her interests, energy, and time. It need not—indeed, should not—occupy her exclusively, but other interests and concerns must give way when in irreconcilable conflict with those of the home. A decision by the husband to enter vocational Christian service tests her priorities and makes special demands upon her management skills and self-discipline. She and the children will almost inevitably become participants in the ministry, and special discretion and cooperation will be necessary if neither family nor ministry is to suffer by overcommitment in one area or the other or in both. Family and ministry can be mutually supportive rather than destructively competitive when parents and children cooperate eagerly in the service of God. The wife must seek divine strength and guidance in assisting her husband and in mediating between the needs of husband and children, family and ministry.

Children must learn to accept their subordinate rule in the family as ordained of God for their good. What a child perceives as an unusually restrictive home environment may later turn out to be a benefit when he is older and more competent to judge. Even the imperfections of parents or of family circumstances may be a means of prompting spiritual growth in him and of enriching future service. Children of parents who have dedicated themselves to vocational Christian service should not chafe under the burdens and restrictions of the ministry. They should instead respond cheerfully to their parents' godly initiatives, sharing willingly as a privilege whatever sacrifices that ministry entails. Wise parents in turn will provide frequent enjoyable family activities so that Christian service does not appear a matter of grim duty to be stoically endured.

A discussion of family structure and responsibilities leads naturally to a discussion of self in relation to others. The fragmentation of the modern family through divorce, delinquency, and careerism has weakened the sense of security and identity among persons of all ages, especially the young. Even Christians need to be reminded that they are worth more than how they look, how much they own or can earn, or what they can do. There is a proper as well as an improper self-esteem. The child of God is "not to think of himself more highly than he ought to think" but rather to rejoice in his function in the body of Christ (Rom. 12:3-8). Members of the household of faith serve their Master eagerly and diligently, confident of their own worth while "in honour preferring one another" (Rom. 12:10-11). Even the child without loving parents can experience the blessings denied him by taking his place in the family of God. The Lord stands ready to supply the lack of anyone who, whether from circumstances of birth or from loyalty to the gospel, has missed the blessings of a loving, unified home (Ps. 27:10; Mark 10:29-30).

For the Christian student with a low self-concept there is rebuke and comfort in the Word of God. Does he despair of conquering his sins? He can confess them and live in the victory of Christ (I John 1:9; Rom. 6:1-14). Does he resent the way he is made? He must not despise the work of God. Self-rejection, like self-murder, shows contempt for the image of God in man, distrust in the purpose and power of God, and rebellion against the will of God. The Bible appeals to believers on the basis of their self-respect as well as of their regard of God. They should not sin against their bodies by fornication (I Cor. 6:18). Men should not shame themselves by wearing long hair (I Cor. 11:14). Israel should not debase herself by stooping before idols of wood and stone (Jer. 10:3-16). We dishonor God and ourselves when we do not respect "his workmanship" (Eph. 2:10).

Low self-regard is often signaled by a contempt for physical cleanliness and adornment. Is a student neglectful of his appearance and scornful of attractive dress and grooming? He should realize that God is interested in physical as well as spiritual beauty. The Creator "hath made everything beautiful in his time" (Eccles. 3:11), sparing no pains to clothe gorgeously the "lilies of the field" though their term of life is brief (Matt. 6:28-29). Of course the believer should not set his heart on that which fades (Prov. 31:30; Matt. 6:19). But neither should he disparage the beauty, though transient, that God has dispersed so richly throughout His creation. Physical beauty is not unimportant because some have more than others or because it is less important than spiritual beauty. It is not ungodly for a woman to beautify herself for her husband or for a husband to adorn his wife to show his love for her. "Can a maid forget her ornaments or a bride her attire?" asks Israel's rejected God (Jer. 2:32). Ought the virtuous woman of Proverbs 31 to have clothed herself in less costly material (31:22)? Biblical examples abound of godly concern for adornment that extends beyond considerations of mere utility. Abraham's servant placed beautiful and costly bracelets and earrings on Rebekah (Gen. 24:22). God commanded that Aaron and his sons be clothed in garments "for glory and for beauty" (Exod. 28:40). Good grooming and attractive dress therefore need not signify self-love or mistaken values. They may indicate instead a desire to enhance the image of God and to express the goodness and beauty of His person. Likewise, physically to adorn another or to beautify a home for another may be a quite natural and godly expression of selfless love (Ezek. 16:10-14; John 14:2; Rev. 21:2, 10-21).

Not only the examples of Scripture but also the specific concerns of home economics can help to foster a proper self-esteem. A regard for cleanliness, neatness, good posture, and hair and skin care enhances the testimony for Christ while reinforcing a positive self-concept. Good nutrition aids weight control and increases energy, improving bodily appearance and vitality and thereby raising the self-concept. A strong Christian family life and careful selection of friends can fortify a weak sense of personal worth. A knowledge of etiquette gives confidence and poise in formal social situations. In these and other matters the Christian must judge himself not by comparison with others (II Cor. 10:12) but in relation to what he has done with what God has given him (Matt. 25:14-30). He must remember that everything about himself over which he has no control—his natural appearance, abilities, and circumstances—has been perfectly planned by God.

Points of conflict with the secular teaching of home economics

Christian home-economics teaching requires the rejection of certain approaches to its subject matter that derive from the climate of modern thought. These approaches not only are avoided by the Christian home-economics teacher but also are explicitly condemned.

Feminism—The modern drive for equality, though in some cases politically defensible, challenges God's plan for the home. The Bible does not deny independence to self-supporting unmarried women. Most of the instruction to women in the Scriptures assumes a family relationship, since in Biblical times respectable unmarried women (with the exception of wealthy widows) remained with their families. The Bible does not encourage the subjugation of women prevalent in cultures unaffected by the gospel. On the contrary, it implies that the wife should be given the management of the household (Prov. 31:14-27; I Tim. 5:14) and gives examples of influential women who assisted the work of God (II Kings 4:8-10; Acts 16:14-15). Titus 2:5 instructs wives to be "keepers at home" (i.e., good housekeepers and home managers); it does not require them to stay at home. The Bible does not deny the woman equal worth with the man. Husbands and wives are spiritual equals as "heirs together of the grace of life" (I Pet. 3:7). The sexes are mutually dependent: "Neither is the man without the woman, neither the woman without the man, in the Lord. For as the woman is of the man, even so is the man also by the woman; but all things of God" (I Cor. 11:11-12). But concerning the authority structure of the family, the Bible is emphatic and its teaching unmistakable. Paul concisely delineates the hierarchy for the Corinthians: "I would have you know, that the head of every man is Christ; and the head of the woman is the man; and the head of Christ is God" (I Cor. 11:3). Paul is equally clear concerning the woman's subordinate role in the church (I Tim. 2:11-12).

The Biblical hierarchy of authority in the home is obnoxious to women who desire more freedom and to men who desire less responsibility. Selfishness makes family members competitors rather than colaborers and family organization a balance of powers and interests rather than a theocracy. Biblical discussions of marriage insist on the responsibilities of family roles, rather than just the privileges, and give the heaviest burden to the man. Biblical leadership is self-denying rather than self-gratifying, and those who understand what it entails accept it as a duty rather than as an opportunity for self-advancement. Neither the wife's nor the husband's role in the Biblical family brings the freedom sought by feminists, for neither wife nor husband exploits his position for selfish gain.

Androgyny—Some feminists disclaim any intention to minimize the differences between the sexes. Others frankly advocate sexual sameness, explaining that society's exaltation of masculine traits causes negative self-concepts in females. Progressivists recommend a balance or mixture of masculine and feminine traits as the norm for both men and women. Secular publications suppress gender role distinctions. Designers promote unisex fashions in dress and hair styles. Psychologists urge feminine sensitivities in men and masculine assertiveness in women. Mannish women and effeminate men flaunt androgynous lifestyles while crusading for women's rights.

This revolutionary viewpoint and program for reform militates against Biblical teaching concerning sexual differentiation in dress (Deut. 22:5) and the division of responsibility in the family (I Tim. 5:8, 14). By weakening sexual identity, it encourages homosexual behavior, which corrupts society and brings the judgment of God. Sexual sameness is an enemy of the sexual complementarity taught in the Scriptures. It destroys the Biblical family hierarchy and with it the symbolism of the marriage relationship as the union of Christ and the Church. It is altogether to be abhorred, shunned, and condemned by the child of God.

Careerism—Both feminism and its offshoot, androgyny, encourage women to pursue public careers, especially those traditionally dominated by men. Women compete fiercely with men in the job market, demanding equality of opportunity and (understandably) equal pay for equal work. Many working women, divorced or abandoned by their husbands, have become career-minded by necessity. Some prefer the single life. Others insist on continuing a single lifestyle within marriage. These last naturally advocate a reordering of family priorities so as to accommodate their career ambitions. Their guiding assumption is irresponsibly selfish: that the home exists for the sake of the mother—as a means of her self-fulfillment—rather than the mother for the sake of the home. The effect is disastrous to family unity and stability and to the personality development of the children.

The Bible assumes that marriage is normal for the woman and defines her marriage role as one of service to her husband and to the children. Her reward is their honor and praise (Prov. 31:28-31) and the satisfaction of seeing God's purposes fulfilled in their lives. To regard another mode of life as more honorable and praiseworthy for the woman than marriage is a departure from Biblical values. To make the wife the breadwinner and the husband the homemaker is an un-Scriptural reversal of roles (I Tim. 5:8, 14). To give selfish desires precedence over family duties commanded and sanctified by God violates the two great commandments (Matt. 22:25-40). The Christian woman entering marriage, like the man, assents to a Biblically defined role of unselfish service. The unmarried woman is free to serve God in another way.

In denouncing selfish careerism on the part of married women, Biblical Christians do not condemn all activity by wives and mothers outside the home. To say that the married woman's first concern should be her family is not to say that it need be her only concern. We must avoid the error of those who demean the role of homemaker so that a woman who makes homemaking her "career" feels inferior and guilty. We must also avoid the opposite error of extolling homemaking in such a way that women who are not exclusively occupied with their roles as wives and mothers feel inferior and guilty. The body of Christ would be much poorer without the accomplishments of gifted and dedicated women who served God in more ways than one without neglecting their families. God gives special talents to women as well as to men, and married women are responsible to God for the exercise of these talents within the limits of their Biblical priorities as wives and mothers. Paul commended married as well as single women for their labors in the gospel (Rom. 16:1-15). Furthermore, family interests may take a woman outside the home. Special expenses may require the help of all members of the family if the family is to meet its financial obligations. The employment of the wife or child or both may be a sacrifice the family must accept to provide the children an education in a Christian school. Some jobs enable women to remain accessible to their younger children. Some women are capable of more than others. Thus, conservative opposition to careerism can be unreasonably and un-Biblically restrictive. Restricting the woman to the home and her role to vassalage within the home violates both common sense and Biblical example. Nevertheless, there is no question that split allegiances between family and career on the part of married women have brought grief to many families and are in conflict with the teaching of the Word of God.

Christian home-economics teaching influences students to seek God's will in vocational decisions. It encourages the woman student to get as much education and employment experience as possible before marriage in order to be prepared to help in the support of the family, if necessary, and to be better equipped to serve God inside or outside the home. It encourages her to engage in her vocational service to the extent that it is in agreement with the family role she assumes. When she marries, she and her husband will analyze her employment status with regard to God's will for their life together. When children are born into the family, the couple will evaluate her employment status in relation to her family's needs and her ability to fulfill her responsibilities in the home. In these decisions, career satisfaction will be subordinate to family obligations, material priorities to spiritual. Christian vocational decisions, of both men and women, are controlled by Biblical rather than selfish priorities.

Alternatives to the traditional family—Christian home-economics teaching recognizes (1) the nuclear family, established and regulated by marriage and consisting of a father and mother and their children, and (2) the extended family, a larger unit including other relatives (such as a grandparent living with his daughter's family). It sanctions single-parent households and childless marriages as unavoidable necessities, not as preferences. Modern society, on the other hand, allows some living arrangements that are not options for the Christian. It permits unmarried cohabitation and parenthood, condemned by God as illicit (I Cor. 6:18; I Thess. 4:3-7), and even homosexual marriages, though homosexuality is strictly forbidden in the Scriptures (Lev. 20:13; I Cor. 6:9-10). It looks favorably on multiple living arrangements, such as group marriages and communes, as being more complex structures that are able to perform more functions than the nuclear family. Such arrangements show contempt for the family order established by God. Polygamy, though practiced in the age of the Old Testament patriarchs and kings, led to heartache and ruin and was not an option for the New Testament believer (I Tim. 3:2). The communal sharing of wives and husbands is adulterous and comes under the judgment of God for all sexual immorality (I Cor. 6:9-10). The only form of sexual cohabitation acceptable to the Christian is monogamy, the marriage of one man to one woman.

Divorce—In the secular view, permanence in marriage is dependent upon the relationship's continuing to meet the needs of the partners. Some secular theorists take a positive view of the high rate of marital failure, predicting that the quality of married life will rise as unsatisfactory marriages are terminated and replaced by better ones. They do not consider the low quality of postmarried life: the suffering undergone by rejected partners and by children from broken homes. They also do not consider the commandments of Scripture. God has established solemn obligations of the marriage partners to each other (Matt. 5:31-32; 19:3-9; I Cor. 7:10-11). These obligations have nothing to do with mutual gratification or fulfillment of expectation. Biblical marriage is a permanent, exclusive relationship (Mark 10:9). Its vows are binding until the death of one of the partners (Rom. 7:2-3). Malachi warns apostate Israel, ''The Lord hath been witness between thee and the wife of thy youth, against whom thou hast dealt treacherously: yet is she thy companion, and the wife of thy covenant. . . . Therefore take heed to your spirit, and let none deal treacherously against the wife of his youth. For the Lord, the God of Israel, saith that he hateth putting away'' (Mal. 2:14-16). To initiate divorce for reasons other than fornication is an act of cruelty, perfidy, and brazen defiance of God's law. The person who divorces in order to remarry is an adulterer and shares responsibility for an adulterous remarriage entered into by his rejected spouse (Matt. 5:32). In no social issue—with the exception of legalized abortion—does God's law contrast more sharply with the mores of modern society than in the practice of easy-entrance, easy-exit marriage.

Servility to fashion—Christian responsiveness to fashion trends is limited by obedience to Biblical principles of modesty, stewardship, and decorum. While desiring to be up-to-date, the Christian avoids immodest and grotesque extremes of style that mar or obscure his spiritual testimony or require the annual replacement of his wardrobe. In selection of clothing, grooming aids, and home furnishings, the Christian student steers a middle course, seeking attractiveness, appropriateness, and durability within budget limitations, while continually attending to the impression created for Christ.

Conclusion

In Christian home-economics teaching, spiritual concerns imbue, activate, and give meaning to the practical. When Jesus was in Bethany at the home of Mary, Martha, and Lazarus, He admonished Martha not to be ''cumbered about much serving'' (Luke 10:40) but to follow Mary's example of emphasizing spiritual things. Encumbered service in the home may be a result of ignorance or of improper values and goals. The Christian teaching of home economics strives to reduce these hindrances. Proper management of resources makes the achievement of spiritual goals possible. The virtuous woman of Proverbs 31 is a good steward of her resources, though not, as the rich man of Luke 12, merely in order to heap up wealth. Her activities are unselfish and show her fear of the Lord. With similar purpose, Christian home-economics teaching prepares the young man and woman for a ministry to a family and, through a family, to a needy world.

The Christian Teaching of Business

Definition

To understand business means that one has some degree of knowledge of the movement of goods and services within society. This involves a pattern of complex activities in the lives of its people concerning all those functions which govern the production, distribution, and sale of goods and services. The simplified circular flow of business activity illustrated on the next page shows how individuals exchange their labor skills for income, which in turn is either saved, taxed away by various governments, or used to purchase goods and services. Constructing a circular flow model that accurately describes all economies in detail would be difficult, if not impossible. Some of the world's economies have strong private sectors with limited government involvement, and others have governments which own much of the economy's resources, including production plants and financial institutions. In addition, individuals possess various degrees of freedom to exchange their labor skills as they choose. But regardless of the relationship among these business entities, their existence appears to be universal; every economy has a government which somehow taxes the earnings individuals receive from employers. And although economies vary considerably, each has some system of financial institutions which exerts a degree of control over the making and flow of its currency. The business life of any society centers on the complex working of these various exchange markets for goods and services.

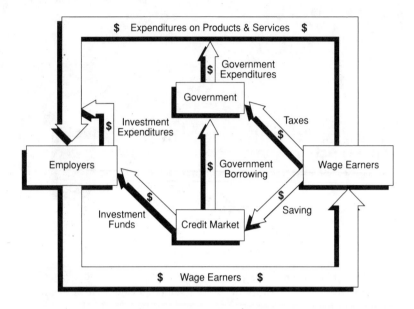

The foundation of business education is laid at home and is built upon as a student progresses through primary, secondary, and postsecondary schools. An elementary school student learns that his parents work and earn money to provide for the family's needs. Junior high school students are taught the basics of different economic systems. Secondary students learn about governmental functions relating to business and certain economic laws, such as supply and demand. Some secondary students also enroll in business courses in which they learn the basics of bookkeeping, accounting, keyboarding, office skills and procedures, and the various organizational structures of business firms.

College business education provides a general knowledge of economics, accounting, finance, marketing, production, and the management of people, information, materials, money, and time. Students learn that business relies heavily on the communication of information which must be gathered, stored, analyzed, and retrieved. Some will assume management positions while others will provide administrative support such as document preparation, data entry, bookkeeping, and records management.

Justification

The Christian teaching of business prepares the student to conduct his business affairs in a distinctively Christian manner and thereby bring glory to God. It points the student to reflections of God in the subject matter and teaches him to imitate God in his character and service.

Reflections of God in the subject matter

A Christian view of business recognizes God as the exemplary administrator, provider, and servant. The Christian teacher can point to God's authoritative management of His creation as an illustration of the administrator's duties of direction, leadership, and protection. God wisely directs the affairs of the universe, bringing the seasons in their appointed times, keeping the oceans in bounds, ordering and preserving the balance of nature, and even setting up and bringing down rulers (Ps. 104; Dan. 2:21a). As an administrator of His creatures, God is gentle and compassionate and "doth not afflict willingly nor grieve the children of men" (Lam. 3:32-33; Ps. 86:15). God is a faithful leader, guiding, protecting, and fulfilling His promises to His people (I Kings 8:56; Ps. 78:52-53). God, like human managers, supplies the resources to carry out His will (Phil. 4:13; Gen. 28:15; II Cor. 9:8). As an administrator, God delegates authority to man, giving him responsibility for directing his family, for cultivating the land, for taming animals, and, in general, for being a good steward of His provisions of time, talents, and treasures (Deut. 6:6-7; Gen. 1:26; 2:15; Eph. 5:16; Matt. 25:14-30).

Christ, as God in human form, exemplified in His earthly authority the divine pattern of administration. Christ was compassionate even to death when, as the good shepherd, He laid down His life for the sheep (John 10:11). Christ was just and impartial, consistently cleansing, forgiving, and granting rest to all who came to Him in simple faith, consistently condemning all forms of hypocrisy (I John 1:9; John 3:15-16; Matt. 11:28; 23:23-28). He was frugal, commanding the gathering of the fragments left after the feeding of the five thousand (Matt. 14:20). Christ faithfully guided, protected, and fulfilled His promises to His people. When He sent His twelve disciples to preach to the Jews,

He did not merely command them to go; He furnished them with instruction and guidance before their departure (Matt. 10:5-42). Christ not only guided His disciples but also protected them when He calmed the raging waves of the Sea of Galilee (Matt. 8:26) and when He reached out His hand of protection to Peter, whose faith waned as he walked toward Jesus on the water (Matt. 14:31). In addition to guiding and protecting, Christ also fulfilled His promises. On various occasions he promised that after His departure He would send the Comforter to the disciples, and He fulfilled that promise at Pentecost (John 16:7; Acts 2:1-4).

God provided for the physical and spiritual needs of His chosen people in their wilderness wanderings (Deut. 2:7). He provided food to satisfy Elijah's hunger in time of famine, water to quench the thirst of Israel's army as they faced Moab, and oil to supply sustenance for the widow (I Kings 17:2-6, 16; II Kings 3:17-20; 4:1-7). God's provision for His own was also demonstrated by Christ in His earthly ministry. In one instance Christ provided His disciples with a profitable catch of fish following a night of fruitless labor. With His own hands He provided a meal to fill their hungry stomachs, and with His words He provided spiritual encouragement to fill their hungry hearts (John 21:5-14). Even on the cross Christ continued to provide for the needs of those in His care, when He provided a home for His mother with His disciple John (John 19:26-27).

God's provision includes benefits even toward His enemies. He "maketh his sun to rise on the evil and on the good, and sendeth rain on the just and on the unjust" (Matt. 5:45). In the Sermon on the Mount, Christ admonished His disciples, "Give to him that asketh thee, and from him that would borrow of thee turn not thou away. . . . Love your enemies, bless them that curse you, do good to them that hate you" (Matt. 5:42, 44). Christ exemplified this love on Calvary when He provided His enemies a means of salvation from eternal punishment.

Christ's earthly ministry also supplies the student with examples of the divine ideal of the employee or servant. Christ was intent on working the works of the Father, who is His authority (John 9:4). This service to God was more important to Him than were His own personal desires (John 6:38). When the disciples on one occasion asked Christ to eat, His answer evidenced His devotion to the work He was called to fulfill: "My meat is to do the will of him that sent me, and to finish his work" (John 4:34). Christ submitted to human authority, as long as that authority did not conflict with that of His Father (Luke 2:49-51; Matt. 17:24-27; 22:15-21). He exemplified what He taught His disciples when He declared, "He that is faithful in that which is least is faithful also in much: and he that is unjust in the least is unjust also in much. . . . And if ye have not been faithful in that which is another man's, who shall give you that which is your own?" (Luke 16:10, 12).

Manifestations of godliness in the resultant knowledge, attitudes, and skills

In general Christian character and service—The study of business concepts contributes to the student's understanding of the authority of both God and man in his life. Through this study the student develops a proper view of men as creations of God Almighty (Ps. 139:14) and exhibits godliness by maintaining a respect for those he directs and serves (Job 31:13-14). In learning to motivate and direct personnel, the student comes to understand godly leadership.

The Christian teaching of stewardship leads the student to a Scriptural understanding of financial management. A Christian student understands that money is a means to an end, not an end in itself, and his life reflects God's view of possessions (Luke 12:16-34).

From God's love of justice and His fairness (Prov. 16:11) the student learns the importance of high standards of quality, hard work, honesty, and equitable rewards (I Pet. 2:12; II Cor. 8:21). These godly qualities will lend credibility to his testimony and will glorify his Creator as his character is displayed before others (Matt. 5:16).

The Christian student reveals godly character in working diligently (Prov. 13:4; 22:29). His diligence reveals to others the character of God, who is honored by his enthusiasm for his work (Col. 3:23-24).

In special vocational service—Business studies equip the Christian student to show these godly characteristics in a variety of occupations. God may call graduates to fulfill the administrative, financial, or secretarial needs of churches or Christian schools. God may, instead, lead them to positions in other business-related fields such as corporate management, secretarial and office administration, small-business management, management consulting, production management, industrial accounting, government service, investment analysis, public accounting, corporate finance, public relations, labor relations, wholesaling, real estate, retailing, auditing, banking, or sales.

Distinctiveness

The Christian and secular teaching of business may appear to have much in common. Indeed, both Christian and secular teachers of business mathematics, bookkeeping, typing, computer applications, and other skills teach the mechanical aspects of their subject areas in virtually the same manner. However, these similarities overlay fundamental differences. Motivating the Christian teaching of all business concepts is the teacher's desire to be used by the Holy Spirit to mold each student into the image of Jesus Christ. This fundamental attitude produces a business education that differs from the secular in several specific ways.

Secular business teaching encourages the belief that personal success in business is the criterion for all ethical choices. Christian business teaching, however, emphasizes that true success is defined by God. Whereas the world views success as the achievement of personal wealth and prestige, God defines it as obedience to His Word (Josh. 1:8). The Christian teacher instructs his students in a way that attunes them to view all things from God's perspective. He prepares them to respond in a godly way to the multitude of ethical choices they will face over the course of a lifetime. For example, if an employer requires his bookkeepers to falsify records in order to improve the financial image of the company, the well-taught Christian will know that the only correct choice is to be truthful. He does not inordinately value his position of employment but realizes that if his "ways please the Lord, [God] maketh even his enemies to be at peace with him" (Prov. 16:7). Though the decision has the potential of costing the bookkeeper his job, the loss would be insignificant compared to the eternal gain from doing right (Col. 3:24).

The Christian teacher stresses the value of strong interpersonal relationships for effective leadership. The teacher emphasizes the strength of these relationships as a realistic measure of the success of the manager. The teacher shows that the scope of this success expands when Christian principles are applied. For example, the Christian businessman desires the success of his employees, not only because he knows their success will help his business but more importantly because he wants them to be successful in God's sight. Realizing he is commanded to give those under his authority "that which is just and equal" (Col. 4:1), the Christian employer does not treat his employees in a demeaning manner (Eph. 6:9). Although the secular view of leadership also emphasizes strong interpersonal relationships, the motivation is for personal gain. The Christian businessman (employer or employee) derives his motivation from Philippians 2:3: "Let nothing be done through strife or vainglory; but in lowliness of mind let each esteem other better than themselves." This concern transcends personal gain and profit and reaches to the needs of others.

The secular teaching of business tends to slight the employee's obligation to his employer, emphasizing instead the employee's duty to himself. The Christian teacher stresses the employee's responsibility to please God (Col. 3:22-25; I Pet. 2:18-19). By being obedient, diligent, and trustworthy, the employee becomes an asset to his employer. These characteristics in the Christian employee may open doors of opportunity for witnessing to the employer and fellow workers (Prov. 11:30b). He, of course, will not steal time from his employer by witnessing when he should be working.

Practical application in the classroom

The Christian teacher presents business concepts in the light of God's Word:

Responsible investing—The Christian teacher could discuss the distinction between responsible investing and gambling. As a steward of material possessions, the Christian is commended for investing wisely and bringing forth an increase (Matt. 25:20-21). This wise investment should not be confused with reckless risk-taking or gambling. Although there is inherent risk in almost all investment opportunities, responsible investing minimizes the risk of loss while seeking to maximize the potential for gain. Gambling, on the other hand, is the deliberate or compulsive expenditure of material possessions in hopes of realizing substantial returns through chance. In addition to determining prudent investments, the Christian must avoid ungodly associations as when one invests in enterprises whose activities are condemned in Scripture.

Equitable labor-management relations—A Christian teacher might lecture on labor-management relations, presenting factors which determine the appropriate wages to be paid to a labor force. These factors include the availability of labor, experience and competency of the labor force, and the cost of living in a particular area. The Christian employer must determine whether the wages paid are suitable for the employment rendered. God will judge the man who will not pay his employees adequate wages (Jer. 22:13; Job 31:13-14; James 5:4). Christians who desire to be in full-time Christian work many times are willing to make financial sacrifices. Christian organizations should not take advantage of this sacrificial attitude but should seek to compensate the employees according to the service performed. It is incumbent upon Christian employers in both secular and full-time Christian work to set an example to the unsaved by paying a fair wage to their employees (Col. 4:1; I Tim. 5:18). Employers are to consider not only the job which the employee performs but also the general well-being of the worker (Lev. 25:43).

Respect for contractual obligations—Because of the wickedness of the heart of man and his tendency to make and later to break obligations as it suits the situation, civil government has sought to protect its citizens through the creation of contract laws which bind men to their promises. An attitude has therefore arisen whereby men feel that if they are not bound by the law to keep their promises, they are not bound. Scripture, however, demands that an individual fulfill his legitimate promises, whether or not performance is demanded by civil government. An example is personal bankruptcy. Where the law states that a legally bankrupt individual is no longer bound to pay those to whom he has obligated himself, he may therefore feel that he is absolved from his obligation. Scripture clearly points out that to what one agrees, one must perform (Ps. 15:1-4).

Honesty—Personal honesty and integrity are much broader in scope than the concept of contracts. First, honesty in business includes truthfulness to consumers by providing full value (Lev. 19:35-36; Prov. 20:10). Second, it includes fairness toward employees in the matter of paying wages in a timely manner

(Lev. 19:13). Third, it includes honesty toward employers. Employees are commanded to abstain from stealing from their employers in failing to provide the quality and quantity of work for which they are being paid or in using their employer's property without authorization (Titus 2:9-10).

Obedience to higher authorities—The world's philosophy of obedience to higher authorities is as relativistic as its philosophy of adherence to contractual obligations. The world's philosophy dictates that if one is not constrained to obey, one need not do so. This idea has governed the actions of individuals in situations ranging from infringement of copyright laws when photocopying to selective obedience to the laws of taxation. Scripture admonishes the Christian to obey authorities (Rom. 13:1-7) and also to display a submissive attitude (I Pet. 2:13-14). Obedience to civil government is demanded by God in order to put unsaved scoffers to silence (I Pet. 2:15-16) and to prevent those of the kingdom of God from mistakenly undermining the kingdom of men. Scripture allows disobedience to civil authorities only when their laws or directives come into a direct and unavoidable conflict with the higher law of God (Acts 5:29). Scripture also dictates that if one is placed in a position where disobedience to governmental authority is necessary, he is to submit with patience to the punishment meted out (I Pet. 2:18-21).

Diligence in labor—It has long been a practice of sinful man to perform the minimum amount of labor required, even if it may at times produce mediocre results. While economizing in the use of labor is an admirable goal, Scripture admonishes us to be diligent in labor (Prov. 13:4). The Bible points out that work is a part of God's plan for mankind. Its importance is shown by God's declaration to Adam in the Garden of Eden that "in the sweat of thy face shalt thou eat bread" (Gen. 3:19), by God's law (Exod. 20:9), and by the energetic self-support of God's servant Paul (Acts 20:34-35). In addition, Scripture demands that labor be performed with an attitude of respect for the employer, as in the example of Joseph, who under even adverse circumstances worked diligently for Potiphar (Gen. 39:1-6).

Benevolence—Whereas the world's philosophy dictates relative benevolence—that is, that the individual or business firm perform benevolent acts in order to gain added positive exposure to potential customers—Scripture admonishes the

Christian to perform benevolent acts with the fundamental motive of pleasing God (Matt. 25:34-40) and not man (Matt. 6:1-4). Scripture also dictates the hierarchy of our benevolence. One is, first of all, to meet the needs of his own family (I Tim. 5:8), second the needs of his Christian brothers (Gal. 6:10b; I John 3:17), and finally the needs of poor individuals outside of the family of God (Gal. 6:10a).

Points of conflict with the secular teaching of business

It should be recognized that Biblically based instruction will come into conflict with the world's philosophy as a matter of course. The root cause of the conflict is that the Christian teaching of business concepts is God-centered, with the primary object being the glorification of God through students who have been transformed into the image of Christ. The world's philosophy rejects such a primary goal and places a host of secondary goals in its place (e.g., personal profitability, social responsibility, maximization of shareholder wealth). Consequently, the Christian teacher must be knowledgeable about the primary points of philosophical conflict and be ready to address them.

Materialism—Contrary to popular misconception, the sin of materialism is committed not when one acquires material goods but when one ascribes to material possessions a place of preeminence (Job 31:24-25, 28; Prov. 22:4). The implication of the definition is significant. Materialism is not an action of the rich but rather an attitude which may be possessed by both rich (the rich fool, Luke 12:15-21) and poor (Achan, Josh. 7). The Christian's attitudes toward the possession of wealth, therefore, should be in line with Scripture.

First, the mere possession of material wealth is not sinful in and of itself. Indeed, Scripture provides numerous examples of godly men and women who possessed great wealth as a result of God's blessing, as in the case of Abraham (Gen. 12:2; 13:2), Job (Job 1:1-3, 10), and Solomon (I Kings 3:12-13). Scripture, however, emphasizes the fact that greed, the desire to accumulate wealth for its own sake, is a temporal distraction produced by Satan, both to preoccupy the carnal man so that he will ignore his lost condition (Rev. 3:17) and to redirect the Christian's energies into spiritually unproductive enterprises (I Tim. 6:9-10; Matt. 6:19-21, 24).

Second, regarding personal business matters, the Christian is a steward of all the wealth the Lord has placed in his care and is to glorify God through wise use of his money. This wise use of resources includes proper spending and investment (Luke 19:13-23), support of the Lord's work (I Cor. 16:1-2; II Cor. 9:6-8), and benevolence to those in need (II Cor. 8:13-15).

Relativism—The study of business concepts within a secular context leads the student to the conclusion that there exist few, if any, absolute standards. The Christian, using the Scriptures as his reference, recognizes the dangers of relativism. The unsaved individual, lacking a Biblical anchor, is left to base his business decisions on standards which may vary from one moment to the next. For example, fourteenth-century European business decisions were made on the basis of profitability to the king and the Roman Catholic church. Between the sixteenth and the eighteenth centuries, this focus shifted to one of increasing the nation's holdings of silver and gold. The twentieth century has produced a confusing diversity of economic ideals and standards. Socialists put forth the goal of the "common good." Capitalists espouse the singular objective of maximization of personal wealth. Environmentalists place prime importance upon ecological preservation and enhancement.

Scripture provides the corrective to the competing philosophies of the world. It dictates through both precept and principle the role of the Christian with regard to social well-being (Ps. 41:1; Prov. 14:21) and personal profitability (Prov. 23:4).

The unsaved man, lacking an absolute standard, is pulled between these various concepts and must look to his own wisdom to decide which goals should be followed and to what degree. This wisdom is influenced by pressure groups, government, expediency, and the decision-maker's personality, and is subject to constant flux.

The Christian realizes that such "a double minded man is unstable in all his ways" (James 1:8) and that the Scriptures present anchoring principles for personal and corporate business decisions (II Tim. 3:16-17). The Christian seizes the standards of the Scriptures and holds to them regardless of the ideological fads of the day.

Desire for power—The vast majority of schools, when teaching business concepts, instruct students to believe that the desire for power is, if not a noble motive, one which is practical. Power, the world believes, should be consolidated and channeled into meeting both individual and organizational goals. Scripture in no uncertain terms condemns this carnal viewpoint and denies the legitimacy of the power motive in the life of the Christian. The desire for power is a manifestation of both pride and dissatisfaction with the position of service within which one finds himself. It is this attitude which prompted a lecture by Christ to His disciples (Mark 9:34-37), a disciplinary action by God upon a king (Dan. 4:25-37), and eternal damnation to a heavenly being (Isa. 14:12-15).

Contrary to the world's philosophy, the Scriptures emphasize that the child of God is to be content in the place of service the Lord has provided (I Tim. 6:6; I Cor. 12:14-18) and "not to think of himself more highly than he ought" (Rom. 12:3). Such contentment should not be translated as complacency in service. The Christian is to "stir up the gift of God" which he possesses (II Tim. 1:6) and to discipline himself for greater service (I Cor. 9:24-27).

Reliance upon worldly systems—In studying the environment of business, students at several points in their curriculum are introduced to comparative economic systems. While there exist various economic systems, including communism, Stalinism, European social democracy, classical liberalism, and radical libertarianism, these tend to be subsets of the two competing ideologies of socialism and capitalism. Those systems which tend to be relatively capitalistic stress the necessity of individual freedom of ownership of one's own property, labor, and financial capital, and the ability to direct such resources freely into those enterprises which will yield maximum personal profit. Those systems which stress socialistic ideals and methods tend to put collective well-being above the profit of the individual. To secure this end, socialistic systems advocate to various degrees the collectivization of property, labor, and financial capital and the centralization of economic decision making.

The world's philosophy is one of reliance upon that system which appears to produce desired results. The socialist looks to his government to correct perceived social, political, and economic inequities, while the capitalist no less fervently looks to his free market to produce his personal financial prosperity. The Christian, however, is instructed to place no confidence in any worldly system or leader (Ps. 146:3; Jer. 17:5); rather he is to place his trust in God (Ps. 144:1-2; Jer. 17:7) and to rely upon Him to meet his every need (Prov. 3:5-6; Matt. 6:31-34).

While the Christian is instructed not to rely on any worldly system, such nonreliance should not be construed as indifference. Indeed, the believer is told to identify that which is good and to be supportive of it (I Thess. 5:21). While one cannot accept all of its ramifications, capitalism, as opposed to socialism, more often supports those values put forth in the Word of God. Where capitalism stresses the importance of private property as a means to personal prosperity, Scripture advocates private property as an essential prerequisite to personal stewardship; after all, one cannot exercise stewardship over that which he does not possess (Prov. 3:9). Capitalism falls short of the Scriptural ideal, however, in that it emphasizes personal satisfaction as opposed to Biblical stewardship. The Christian's desire should be to please the Lord with his substance (II Cor. 9:7).

Socialistic systems, on the other hand, while posing as just and compassionate, actually hold to ideals opposed to principles in the Word of God. Socialism is dependent upon expropriation of property, which is condemned in Scripture both in principle— "Thou shalt not remove thy neighbour's landmark" (Deut. 19:14)—and by example—such as when Ahab was condemned for covetousness toward Naboth's vineyard and for the murder which made it possible for him to gain its possession (I Kings 21:17-19). Socialism also propagates the error that economic leveling is the greatest of all justices, whereas Scripture indicates that in many cases God Himself is the author of economic disparity (I Sam. 2:7-8) to the end that the individual may be tested (Job 1:10-12, 21-22), blessed (Prov. 3:9, 10), or punished (Prov. 10:4; 21:12-17).

Conclusion

The Christian teacher of business has the privilege of preparing his students for the ministry of business. In his teaching, he finds the challenge of taking God's Word and applying it to the world of commerce and industry. This is in sharp contrast to his secular counterpart, whose vision is limited to preparing his students to perform well in the business world, attain a position of power and prestige, and acquire large sums of material wealth as a sign of success. The Christian business teacher knows that his students will enter professions in which most of their peers are unsaved. He, therefore, takes seriously his ministry of "equipping the saints" to help fulfill the Great Commission and thus bring glory to God.

Conclusion

The foregoing account of Christian education addresses a general audience, not only those engaged in the ministry of Christian education. It explains Christian education to the uninformed and the ill-informed. Let us now turn to some deep implications of this discussion for Christian educators themselves.

The sum of these implications is the need for both spiritual and academic integrity. Obviously spiritual integrity is basic. Without genuine spiritual character and purpose, a school can be Christian in name only. As a wheel without its hub, Christian education without spiritual integrity is totally disabled and, if it continues to represent itself as Christian, is an absolute fraud. It deserves the judgment of God and the mockery of the world. But academic integrity is also very important. Without academic strength a Christian school cannot perform its full educational ministry. As a wheel without some of its spokes, its function is seriously weakened. Academic standards commend a Christian school to the world. They are necessary to its testimony. Both spiritual and academic standards commend a Christian school to God. Genuine spiritual zeal produces high standards in every area of a Christian ministry.

Spiritual integrity

The Christian school exists to produce servants of Jesus Christ. It must therefore have a board, an administration, a faculty, and a student body that are truly Christian. It must have high spiritual and moral standards backed by rules that are consistently enforced by the teachers and administrators and also upheld by their personal examples. No standard can be bent or rule ignored to retain the child of a teacher, administrator, or board member that deserves expulsion. No extremity can justify employing a teacher whose spiritual character is not above reproach. The great majority of the student body must be Christian, for the Christian school's task is primarily educational, not missionary. Intensive, continuing efforts must be made to bring the remaining students to Christ and to suppress their negative influence on the spiritual growth of the Christian majority. Spiritual rather than worldly vocational pursuits must be held up as ideals for the students, so that the intellectual, financial, political, aesthetic, and, notably, athletic achievements sought by the world seem mere vanities by contrast. An unremitting spiritual zeal must appear in the teaching, administration, and policy deliberations if the Christian school is to maintain its spiritual identity.

Academic integrity

Academic integrity in a Christian educational institution must not be confused with stuffy intellectualism. An exclusive emphasis on scholastic achievement can impair even the academic ministry of a Christian school, producing frustration in the less-gifted students and lopsidedness in those who are able to excel. A preoccupation in the classroom with profound and novel truths slights basic learning and encourages in the students an intellectual arrogance and awe that hinder their growth in Christ. Intellectualism is a sinful attitude begotten of insecurity and pride and justified by the mistaken notion that Christian belief and practice must appear respectable in the eyes of the educated world. It accompanies both spiritual and intellectual immaturity and manifests itself in iconoclastic criticism of common notions. There is, on the other hand, a very proper and necessary concern with academic standards and achievement. Christian schools endeavoring to please God academically must strive toward the twin goals of excellence and balance in education.

Excellence—With more highly motivated students and teachers, assisted by the Holy Spirit, Christian schools can be expected to surpass other schools in achieving substantial learning. Many do in fact produce results superior to those of most public schools according to standards generally recognized in secular education. Not all do, however; and some that do excel could accomplish even more. Academic standards must be taken seriously. Cutting corners or merely going through the motions of an educational program is sinful negligence toward the student and a disgrace to the cause of Christian education. Christian schools must ensure that their students are taught by professionally qualified teachers, that these teachers instruct them thoroughly in necessary knowledge and skills, and that student achievement is honestly measured. Insofar as this knowledge and these skills are concerns also of secular education, Christian schools can gauge their academic success by the standardized tests in general use, keeping in mind that academic achievement is only part of the mission of the Christian school. No Christian educational institution should be satisfied with anything less than the most valuable academic program it can offer the student and than the best work of which a student is capable. The Christian student deserves thorough, supportive, inspirational teaching in worthy subject matter and an honest evaluation of his performance and progress.

Balance—The pursuit of academic excellence must not be at the expense of educational balance, for then the result would not be genuine excellence. Whereas excellence implies a reaching of external standards, balance is a preserving of internal proportions and priorities—giving everything its proper place. First things must go first. But putting first things first does not excuse neglecting second or fourth or seventh things, which are also necessary and are commanded of God (Matt. 23:23). Emphasizing training in preaching and personal evangelism does not excuse neglecting the improvement of the students' aesthetic judgment and preferences. A concern for the spiritual qualifications of teachers does not justify ignoring their professional qualifications. An emphasis on scholastic achievement cannot compensate for disregarding the social graces necessary to the students' growth in Christ and testimony to the world. No natural capacity can be neglected if the student is to develop fully in the image of God. The child Jesus "increased in wisdom and stature, and in favour with God and man" (Luke 2:52).

Educational balance implies not only attention to all the students' needs but also attention to all the students. Christian educators must not restrict their educational ministry to only the gifted few in the interests of preserving a reputation for scholastic excellence. Christian education is for all, and those schools that serve all educable students, regardless of their academic abilities or vocational desires, carry out most fully the mandate of Christian education. Teachers should set reasonable goals for all students and assist each student to perform according to his capacity. They should help each student understand that he has been uniquely endowed by God to take advantage of the particular opportunities of service for which he is being prepared and that his gifts and his future service are just as important to God as those of the students more obviously gifted. Christian education inspires every student to be a faithful steward of the abilities and opportunities entrusted to him.

Educational balance in Christian education requires a firm rectitude amidst the troubled seas of the contemporary religious scene. There must be a zealous commitment to separation from ungodliness, both doctrinal and moral. Christian education is threatened by the same compromise that has blighted evangelical Christianity in the later twentieth century. This rectitude includes the ability to distinguish between what is essential and what is nonessential in the issues that separate God's people from the world and from one another, and the avoidance of theological hobbies, quirks, and divisive emphases that waste Christian energy and resources and cause needless strife.

Educational balance also depends upon a sense of equilibrium amidst the crosscurrents of modern educational theory and practice. Christian educators rightly condemn the false premises of secular-humanistic education and the foolish, harmful strategies and approaches they frequently produce. However, there can develop a corresponding quirkishness in Christian education when Christian educators vie with one another in the vehemence of their reactions to secular methods with which they disagree. There can develop a mentality that old is good and new is bad, resulting in an effort to chart the course of Christian education by secular reference points—that is, by simple opposition to all concepts and practices of secular education—rather than by the sure guide of the Scriptures. The result is the creation of another distortion. There is no substitute for predicating a Christian position directly on the premises and example of the Scriptures. The answer to the needs of a Christian young person is not traditional education, which has most certainly been affected by humanistic thought, but a truly Biblical education that endeavors to develop him fully in the image of Christ.

In the ministry of Christian education, as in the design of a wheel, balance is necessary to fulfillment of purpose. When Christian education is improperly centered or when some of its functions, like spokes, are weak or missing, it cannot maintain an even course. The wheel wobbles, if it functions at all. Adopting a sound Biblical basis and methodology is only the first step toward a remedy. These must undergird and control every function of a school's educational ministry. Practice must be brought into line with principle rather than principle adjusted to practice. Certainly it is high time for Christian education to set its house in order. If it cannot justify its existence to God, it may be hard put to justify its existence, legally or otherwise, to the world as outside pressures mount in the coming years.